HAM STREET
WOODS

CHEL
WO

TARNAM'S
COPSE

MIDDLE
WOOD

WOO

CHALKNEY
WOOD

BIRKWOOD

HOPE
VALLEY

NORTHERAMS

COCKAYNE
HATLEY
WOOD

COTTERSTOCK
WOOD

ASHAM
WOOD

ASHRIDGE
WOOD

JESMOND
DENE

WORMLEY
WOOD

WESTONBIRT
ARBORETUM

ROTHIEMURCHUS

PITCHER OAK
WOOD

CAINHOEPARK
WOOD

GIPTON
WOOD

AMAT

FOREST OF
DEAN

OXLEAS WOOD

LITTLE LINFORD
WOOD

WARESLEY
WOOD

QUEEN
WOOD

GREAT
WOOD

BASSETT
WOOD

HATFIELD
FOREST

CROFT
CASTLE

GUISACHAN

WITNESSES
WOOD

CLARKES
CARR

HAZEL
WOOD

THE HAWTH

GLENFESHIE

COOK'S
WOOD

FINESHADE
WOOD

GLEN
CANNICH

WINDSOR
GREAT PARK

HORNSHURST
WO

COLDFALL
WOOD

GONE
GOOD AS GONE
DEPLETED
ARGELY INTACT

A
TALE
OF
TREES

A
TALE
OF
TREES

*The Battle to Save Britain's
Ancient Woodland*

DEREK
NIEMANN

Published in 2016 by
Short Books, Unit 316, ScreenWorks, 22 Highbury Grove,
London, N5 2ER

10 9 8 7 6 5 4 3 2 1

A CIP catalogue record for this book
is available from the British Library.

ISBN: 978-1-78072-275-7

Cover design by Nathan Burton

Printed at CPI Group (UK) Ltd, Croydon, CR0 4YY

Contents

PROLOGUE

Late in the summer of 1940, a German air crew flew far above the dogfighting Spitfires and Messerschmitts, high up in skies of cloudless serenity. As they passed over the land, one man prepared to shoot. He crouched down at an open hatch in the bottom of the fuselage, a place from which other planes would deliver their parcel of bombs. He manhandled into position a metal box the size of a microwave oven, then he reached over and began taking pictures.

That Luftwaffe reconnaissance aircraft, and many others like it, captured moments in time that have become timeless records of British landscapes. These aerial photographs show towns and cities on which bombs would rain down that autumn. They also reveal a countryside on the verge of harvest time, a land of straw-coloured wheat fields, meadows filled with wild flowers, and moors and heaths with purple heather.

Over the Highlands of Scotland, the photographers could make out lone pine trees that had been young when Bonnie Prince Charlie fled Culloden. They could spot the sinuous ghylls and cloughs of northern England, the oak woods on Welsh hillsides that rang in spring with the song of wood warblers, and the verdant dingles, copses, shaws and hangers that had bloomed primrose yellow, wood anemone white and bluebell blue.

At a height of 5,000 metres or more, those airmen could not appreciate the human intimacies of our ancient woods; the historical, cultural and social ties between woods and their settlements. These were written in the trees, the banks, ditches, and the ponds for thirsty cattle, and in the names themselves – Harry's Wood, Spring Wood, Hollybank Wood, Long Leake Coppice, Bishop's Wood, Earlstrees, Birkwood (the 'wood of birches').

Of course, the Germans never invaded, the land never became theirs, and the Luftwaffe crews would never come to walk in any of these special woods.

And nor can we. Not one of the aforementioned woods exists today. They were simply bulldozed out of existence, along with so many others. Thousands more had their oak, ash, birch and hornbeam trees cut down to make way for conifer plantations. In place of bluebells, we had Sitka spruce. In place of wood anemones, we had Sitka spruce. In place of primroses, we had Sitka spruce.

All of this happened at a frightening speed. It was said that, after the war, Britain lost more ancient woodland in 40 years than in the previous 400. Conservationists of the time estimated that, by 1985, more than a third of our ancient woodland had been destroyed. In 1983, a respected university academic had predicted that, unless the decline was halted, there would be no ancient woodland left outside nature reserves by 2020.

How on earth could we have let this happen? We are Britain, a nation full of self-confessed tree-huggers. We love our trees and our woods. We fill whole volumes with sylvan poetry and prose. When the coalition government of 2011 proposed selling off the public forests, it prompted the biggest blast of opposition so far this century. Half a million people signed a petition in a matter of weeks, costumed badgers prepared to march on Downing Street, dormice wrote their angry placards. The government hastily backed down, a minister resigned.

For 30 years, this question has gnawed away at me, and for a personal reason. My local wood – just west of Cambridge – is listed in the Domesday Book of 1086. For 30 years, I have walked Waresley Wood's paths in all seasons, ended up wet and muddy, and shared with others the life-affirming first flush of colour in spring, baby badgers bolting through the undergrowth on a summer's night, the tumble of falling leaves, the stillness of a bare-branched tree in snow. On the day I was born, it was three times the size it is today. And for 30 years, I have wondered how it could have been so easy for so much of it to simply disappear. It happened to this wood; it happened all over Britain. Why?

There were catastrophic losses in the second half of the 20th century because woods were neither valued nor understood as we understand them now, and because a whole series of factors came together to bring about their destruction. The statistics paint a partial picture. They tell us a certain wood was once x hectares and now it is y hectares, but they do not get inside people's heads. They do not talk to the farmer who ploughed out a wood, the forester who cut down old trees, the nature lovers who failed to see what was happening before their eyes. Nor do they talk to the few who understood, fought the ravaging of our woodland heritage and saved what was left for our todays and tomorrows. This book is a tale of trees, but it is also a story about those tales, a story about people.

THE FIRST FEW THOUSAND YEARS

Britain's most ancient woods of all are still with us. Their bare roots poke out like bony black fingers from the sheer side of a newly cut ditch in a highland strath. Waves curl round tree stumps a mile east of Rhyl promenade, molars in gums of sand. Bleached hazelnuts surface in the flotsam on a Llŷn beach, thousands of years after prehistoric winds shook them loose. And farmers' ploughs churn through the dark soils of former fenland, encountering great gnarled branches and even whole trunks. Tractors haul them out into piles at the side of the field. They call this winter harvest 'bog oak'.

These are the ghosts of the wildwood, primeval forest that covered much of Britain after the last Ice Age. It was followed by a wetter phase when it rained and rained, and whole forests were drowned. Scientists call the remnants we find today sub-fossils, but they are still, over 5,000 years later, recognisably wood. Hard as tropical hardwoods, they can be chiselled into sculptures, burned on a fire, or dropped into a fish tank as decorative shapes, oozing tea stain tannins into the water. And if they had remained in the ground for a hundred million years longer, they might have been crushed and transformed into coal.

In the absence of any written records, there are tantalising clues as to what this primeval forest actually looked like. About 3,000 years ago, our Bronze Age ancestors cleared a path through a forest at Thorne Moor in South Yorkshire and surfaced it with a trackway of parallel logs – effectively an early boardwalk – through what was becoming increasingly boggy ground. Under the bark of those timbers, modern archaeologists discovered a tiny, wood-boring species of beetle called *Prostomis mandibularis*. Not just one beetle, but whole generations. You could say this was their family tree.

It was a beetle that was anything but boring, for its habitat requirements were staggeringly exact. It needed to find a particular kind of oak tree; one that was living out in the open, unshaded by other trees, and at least 150 years old. At about that age, spaces begin to open up between earlier growth rings in an oak tree's heartwood, allowing a certain kind of fungus to colonise the gaps. The fussy *Prostomis* burrowed through the outer bark and lived in these narrow corridors, eating the fungal wallpaper.

Long-held notions of a dense, impenetrable forest extending all the way from Land's End to John O' Groats are undermined by both the living and the dead. The *Prostomis* beetle, which required isolated trees, is now extinct, but in prehistoric times it was both common and widespread throughout Britain. Furthermore, nearly three-quarters of our native plants grow in open habitats and only about a sixth flower in woodland.

Everything points to much of Britain resembling parts of today's New Forest in character, with plentiful wide, grassy clearings between well-spaced trees. How could natural processes create such a mixed habitat? Were wild boar, deer and now extinct cow-like aurochs the earliest woodland managers? The evidence is still inconclusive.

One thing we can be certain about is that there is

virtually nothing left today of that pristine wildwood in the whole of Britain. 'Virtually', because it is possible that some of the tiny hazel woods on the Atlantic coast and islands of Scotland and the hazel-dominated rainforest ravines of North Wales are the last untouched fragments.

Early farmers cleared a considerable amount of woodland throughout Britain. In Scotland, by the time the Romans built the Antonine Wall between the Firths of Forth and Clyde, there was very little woodland left to the south of it, and not all that much to the north either. Neolithic farmers and their livestock had stripped much of southern Scotland, while the natural processes of a tough climate had turned parts of the north into peaty sponges, drowning the forests.

Over much of the country, Scots burned peat, not wood, in their fires, and, by medieval times, when the demand for timber for buildings had increased, it was easier and cheaper to import much of what was needed from northern Europe via east-coast ports. There was, therefore, little incentive for humans to preserve woodland. In Europe, only Ireland and Iceland had less tree cover than Scotland by 1750. Much of what remained was remote from settlements and only its inaccessibility kept it from the axe.

The Welsh laws of the early thirteenth century made reference to *coed cadw*, the protected woodlands, one of the indications that Wales was then still a well-forested country, especially in the uplands, where the woods were predominantly of oak. Contemporary writer and historian Giraldus Cambrensis observed that the Welsh 'neither inhabit towns, villages or castles, but live a solitary life in the woods'.

In the next couple of centuries, the Welsh forests were depleted by forces of the occupying Norman kings of England, who cleared vast tracts along major routes to thwart stealth attacks by forest guerrillas. The monks of the country's numerous Cistercian abbeys were assiduous wood removers too. Giraldus said of the monks of one estate: 'They changed an oak wood into a wheat field.' The demands of a growing population also ate away at Wales's tree cover. By 1600, less than a fifth of the country was still wooded.

Over much of Britain, and particularly in the lowlands of England, woods were harnessed by humans to suit a way of living that would last for many hundreds of years. We know from archaeological evidence that our Bronze Age ancestors had discovered the ultimate in sustainability. They found that most broadleaved (deciduous) trees could be cut down and that, far from killing them, this would stimulate dormant buds at the cut base to sprout new growth. The technique, called 'coppicing', could be repeated, not once, but – in the case of hazel especially – every few years, ad infinitum, extending the lives of these trees well beyond their natural lifespan. A single lime tree in Westonbirt Arboretum is thought to be at least 2,000 years old; it was sending forth new shoots about the time when Julius Caesar crossed the Channel.

Every year, the base of the coppiced tree – the stool – would grow a little in circumference, while the coppiced stems could be used for all-important firewood, or for making tools, barrels, clogs, bowls, spoons, thatching spars, bows and arrows. Wood was the go-to product.

Certain trees in the wood, for example oak and ash, would be left to grow to full height as 'standards' and then felled for timber to build houses, barns, town halls, cattle sheds, furniture, boats and ships. Nothing was wasted. Even oak bark was stripped and taken to tanneries for softening leather, the essential material for tough footwear and durable clothes.

When the first significant written records were made in the Domesday Book of 1086, coppicing was practised in all the parts of England and the border counties of Wales covered by the survey. Every village had its smithy, reliant on charcoal from coppiced trees. Even the humblest hovel needed firewood and coppicing provided it. Early industries, such as iron, tin and lead smelting, demanded a supply of charcoal, and operated in areas where those metals were dug from the ground, such as the southern Lake District, Cornwall, Yorkshire, the Forest of Dean and the Weald of southeast England. Woods may have been on the steeper or boggier land that was less suitable for farming, but they were nevertheless the factories of our ancestors.

There were winners and losers in these tree factories. The multifarious insects, fungi and lichens that had thrived in the dead wood of fallen trees and branches, and the decaying heartwood of ancient living trees, suffered under a system whereby every branch and twig was gathered for use, and mature trees were never left to grow much beyond their hundredth birthday, unless they were boundary markers. However, the thick bushy growth of coppiced trees suited nesting dormice and warblers such as nightingales, the periodic explosions of light after blocks of coppice were cut boosted flowers, and the wider paths, called rides, became sunny glades for butterflies such as fritillaries, and meadow flowers such as orchids.

An unknown number of these coppiced woods were modified descendants of the wildwood, containing the same trees, plants, animals and fungi. Their wild inhabitants had evolved and adapted to live in these exacting habitats, becoming accustomed to the ways that humans had first altered the woods, and then managed them for very long periods of time.

Today, we have a name for these woods that have been with us for so long. We call them 'ancient woodland'. But what exactly is an 'ancient woodland'? A wood with ancient trees? An old wood, so old it's, like, ancient?

Woodland historians established a clear definition for this particular habitat: ancient woods are identified as those which appear on the oldest reliable maps (1600 in England and Wales, 1750 in Scotland, where the first maps were made on the orders of General Roy after the Jacobite revolt) and are still there today. There is no written evidence that woods were planted before 1600, so we can be reasonably confident that those shown on these early maps date back to medieval times or before.

Within the woods and forests that we call 'ancient', the continuity has ensured that there is wildlife of astonishing complexity and variety, unmatched in any other habitat.

There are dwarf woodlands of hazel on the Hebridean islands of Skye and Raasay that grew up from hazelnuts that floated across the Irish Sea after the Ice Age glaciers had melted. On their thin trunks are 'hazel gloves', a fungus that looks like an exploded walnut and is restricted to ancient woodland. In the Wyre Forest, there is a species of ant called the slavemaker that captures the workers of other species and orders them to do its bidding. In the Scots pine forests of the Highlands, a single pine needle can host up to 50 types of fungi; while in aspen woodland there is a type of hoverfly that lives solely on the sap of aspens, and only on those trees that have fallen recently. The purple emperor butterflies of southern England choose oaks to feed on, but seek sallow bushes for their eggs. They lay them on broad, shiny leaves and will not land on leaves of any other shape or texture. Herb paris is a rare plant that grows in the depths of the oldest woods. It is thought that it was propagated by wild boar – its black seeds getting caught up in their coarse hair.

There is another kind of ancient woodland, less trumpeted, but nevertheless very important. Today, it's called 'wood pasture'. It was listed in the Domesday Book as *silva pastalis*, and there was probably more of it in 1066 than of the tree-packed areas we call woodland today. Broadly speaking, wood pasture existed or developed as wooded commons, parks or forests.

The most common of these three types is, appropriately enough, the commons! These were open land with scattered trees, where villagers had 'common' rights. Peasants might have had the right to graze their cows or collect firewood, for example. The name lingers in a thousand locations.

The original 'parks' were the product of a fashion among the Norman nobility for keeping deer – the native red deer or the fallow deer they had brought with them from France. Most of these parks were effectively deer farms, enclosed by a wall or a fence of oak palings (hence animals outside were said to be 'beyond the pale'). There were more than 3,000 deer parks in Britain by 1300.

Despite the name, 'forests' were not necessarily wooded; they were large tracts of demarcated land over which the king or a noble exercised certain legal rights, such as the exclusive right to hunt deer, or to fell mature trees for timber.

Wood pasture had a dual purpose; sheep, cattle or deer grazed the ground below the trees, while, at the same time, trees were preserved by having their tops cut off above the reach of browsing sheep, cattle or deer, which would otherwise nibble fresh, young leaves. It was a kind of high-level coppicing known as pollarding (from the word 'poll' meaning head – hence poll tax, for example).

The vigorous leafy growth from the poll would be cut in

late summer and saved as animal fodder or 'tree hay'.Or it would be left for longer to produce useable poles. Nothing was wasted. With regular haircuts, the trees expanded to attain huge girths and lived to great ages – gnarly veterans often lived for six or seven hundred years.

The ancient trees of wood pasture developed features that came to harbour an extraordinary diversity of wild-life. Barbastelle bats slept out the day under loose quilts of bark. In the hollow interiors, grass snakes laid their eggs and hibernated, and great crested newts slumbered. Woodpeckers hunted for grubs by hammering out holes in the trunks, then nested in the cavities they had excavated. Mosses, liverworts and lichens formed grey, green and yellow mats, splashes and rosettes on every twig, branch and trunk. And up to 2,000 species of invertebrate ate their way through decaying wood, digging labyrinthine tunnels under the bark. Some species of bark-boring beetle were not great at dispersing from their natal tree to set up new colonies elsewhere – but why bother when your family can live on a single tree for more than 600 generations?

In economic terms, woods were at their most productive around the time of Queen Victoria's coronation. But as the Industrial Revolution took full effect, they began to lose their usefulness. By the time Victoria died in 1901, they were in steep decline.

One by one, woodland products were supplanted. The oak saplings of the post-Napoleonic wars that were destined to be harvested to make the battleships of Britain's navy grew into obsolescence, as ironclad ships became the norm. The coming of the railways meant that coal could be carried all around the country, dispensing with the need to keep fires burning with less fuel-efficient wood. Coal consigned the charcoal burners to history too. And as the new century progressed, other inventions accelerated the decline. Wooden horse-drawn carts and carriages began to give way to metal motor cars. In 1921, the first injection moulding machine was designed and a life-changing product went into mass production. If was as if a broom were sweeping through Britain's woods. The innovation was plastic and it came in different colours. Hairbrushes, clothes pegs, soup ladles, baskets, tables, chairs – this material was light, cheap, washable, modern. Heavy, slow-growing wood was seen as old-fashioned and redundant.

The year 1945 would be a watershed. Britain's ancient woods were still our richest wildlife habitats, but how much was a bluebell worth? The years that followed were to provide an unhappy answer.

THE WOOD THAT NEARLY DIED

Early one winter's morning in 1973, a commuter on his way to work stopped his car beside a farm field. The driver was a keen amateur cricketer, a beer aficionado and a recorder player. He also happened to be one of the finest professional botanists of his generation.

Luton-born Terry Wells worked for the government's Nature Conservancy as a soil scientist. His area of research was plants of dry grassland, and though his office was at Monks Wood Experimental Station, a few miles south of Peterborough, much of his working life was spent out in the field. In February that year, Wells was preparing for the growing season ahead, making preliminary journeys to the chalk downland of the Chiltern hills, where he was carrying out long-term studies into the effects of mowing and sheep grazing on grassland flowers.

That day, Wells left his home in the Fens as usual, but instead of swinging west towards the A1, as he always did, he took a diversion, threading his way through the villages due south. It's certain that he was acting on a tip-off. He knew this area perhaps more intimately than anyone: as plant recorder for the then county of Huntingdonshire, this bear of a man, jovial, soft-spoken, always bursting with infectious enthusiasm for his subject, was adept at gaining permission from landowners to walk where no one else was allowed. He scrutinised every meadow, every river bank, every copse. The signs said: *Keep Out. Trespassers will be prosecuted*. Wells had a passion for plants and a licence to roam.

Wells drove into a gently rolling landscape, dotted with villages and hamlets – Abbots*ley*, Grave*ley*, Eltis*ley*, Grans*den*, Evers*den* – each name ending with the Saxon-derived indication of a clearing in the wood. Wells stopped his car within sight of the church spire of Waresley. He was familiar with the great wood on the edge of the village, having been there three times within the previous five years to carry out plant surveys. Each of them had taken up the best part of a day.

I have known Waresley Wood for 30 years, and have been there so often that I know it better than any other. Government scientists recognised its value a long time ago – it had been given an official wildlife stamp of accreditation as far back as 1954. In the post-war rush to flag up the country's most important wildlife sites, Waresley had been designated as a Site of Special Scientific Interest (SSSI), and described in words that would excite a dedicated naturalist (but possibly no one else): 'a woodland of ancient origin of the ash-maple community type which has a national distribution restricted to lowland England'.

By 1973, the wood formed an island in an East Anglian landscape where nine-tenths of the hedges were being ripped out, and flower-filled meadows were ploughed and sprayed into sterile, hedge-less prairies. Terry Wells and his fellow botanist wife Sheila were filling every weekend and summer evening recording wildlife that was disappearing even as they counted.

They knew the old woods sheltered rare gems of flowers along their dappled rides and in their clearings. Terry Wells had explored Waresley Wood's paths, exclaiming in delight every time he came upon orchids – his favourite plants. He had found banks of early purple orchids, true to their name, the first in spring to show their brilliance. There were common spotted orchids in great profusion along the main rides, delicate white greater butterfly orchids forming discrete bunches, and mysterious bird's nest orchids, with no need of sunlight, tucked away in shady places. He had witnessed the spring washes of colour in bluebells, violets and primroses. And best of all, at least in botanical importance, the wood was blessed with oxlips, plants with nodding yellow flowers of exquisite beauty, like cowslips with their eyes open, which blossomed here at the westernmost edge of their range in Europe.

On that grey February morning, he looked out over the bare farm fields at a scene that confirmed the report he had received. What he saw filled him with dismay. Where there had been trees, there was a raw churned mass of cold, sticky clay. A great swathe of the wood had been bulldozed, the very area that had contained the greatest concentration of oxlips. There would be no spectacular show there that spring, or in any spring to come. Wells returned to the site some weeks later to find gangs of women collecting stumps, roots and branches, as if they were on a battlefield picking over the corpses for loot. One of Wells's colleagues went there too, a man called George, who dug his spade into the morass to rescue a handful of oxlips and replant them in his garden, a symbolic yet futile gesture.

Could what remained of the wood be saved? There was just a third of the wood still standing when Terry Wells rang a friend. The Bedfordshire and Huntingdonshire Naturalists' Trust was not, on the face of it, a promising prospect for a rescue operation. Only thirteen years old, it was typical of wildlife trusts at that time, surviving on a shoestring. It had a staff of two, the overworked, part-time conservation officer doubling up as administrator. But she was an exceptionally resourceful individual and made the shoestrings go a long way.

Dr Nancy Dawson, who had done her PhD at Cambridge on the beetles in Wicken Fen, was the plain-speaking daughter of pioneering crystallographer Dame Kathleen Lonsdale. She had inherited her mother's genius for innovation and invention. Nancy was used to answering the phone to hear the caller pour forth a woeful litany of natural obituaries. 'People would ring me up and say "this meadow has been ploughed up" or "that wood has been cut down". But this time we had a chance to do something.' Nancy was determined that the Trust would buy the wood and save it, even though it had no money to do so.

In the meantime, Terry Wells pursued official channels. He alerted the regional officer of the government's conservation body, the Nature Conservancy, who met up with the farmer who owned the wood. The farmer told him it was his intention to carry on clearing the wood, but leave a 20-acre block intact. However, the Conservancy officer felt there was room for negotiation. He wrote in hope to a colleague:

> I believe him when he says that he would like to safeguard the major portion of this interesting site and he was receptive to the idea that the Trust be associated with the future management of this remaining portion (extending to 50/60 acres).

It was time for the cash-poor trust to call in a long-standing favour from an organisation based just down the road. Twelve years before, the London-based RSPB had been looking to expand from its cramped headquarters, and had found a Victorian country house going cheap in Sandy, Bedfordshire. The RSPB feared that the sellers would raise the price if they knew it was bidding for the Lodge, and so a well-connected volunteer from the trust acted as a stalking horse, conducting negotiations on the RSPB's behalf, ostensibly as a private individual, guiding it towards the purchase of a sizeable property and a 68-acre nature reserve for just £25,000.

A dozen years later, conversations between the trust and the RSPB now centred on the proposal that the two bodies should buy Waresley Wood jointly. Initial discussions were encouraging, since senior staff at the wealthier partner liked the idea of a local purchase, and two of them had a strong personal connection. Land agent John Day lived in Waresley village itself and counted lapwings nesting in the farmer's fields, though he had never entered the wood. Living a little further away, RSPB director Peter Conder knew and loved Hayley Wood, a nearby site of a similar character, which was owned by the neighbouring trust, the quaintly-named Cambridgeshire and Isle of Ely Naturalists' Trust. On summer nights, when the mood took him, Conder would leave the family home armed with a poncho and sleep out under the trees of Hayley Wood.

The RSPB staff drew up a recommendation to buy and submitted it to the charity's governing council. In those days before the RSPB sold itself under an all-nature banner, a site's importance for birds had to be demonstrably paramount. The wood was pitched to the RSPB council primarily in terms of potential:

Nightingales used to breed and the reintroduction of coppice techniques and other management could well attract both this species and wood warbler, both of which occur on passage. Sparrowhawks breed in a woodland area nearby.

The mention of sparrowhawks in close proximity might have caught the council members' imagination, for it was an extremely uncommon bird then, barely recovering after its numbers had plummeted as a result of DDT poisoning. And then there was the possibility of the wood being used as a kind of overspill education centre: 'The wood will be capable of use by school parties and so help to relieve visitor pressure at the Lodge.'

The sales pitch was to no avail. Minutes of the meeting recorded: 'Council considered the proposal and agreed: that the purchase of Waresley Wood, Huntingdonshire be not proceeded with.' In the memory of those staff present, it was the only time the RSPB council had rejected the recommendation of its own experts. Various reasons have been suggested; one of the most plausible was its timing.

The proposal had come at the tail end of five years of discussion between the RSPB and the trust's parent body about a possible merger of the two organisations. Idealistic aims had given way to rancour and mutual suspicion, as dissenters on both sides stood firm against the proposal and eventually scuppered it. Perhaps the idea of another joint initiative at this juncture was just too much.

Terry Wells was given permission by the farmer who owned Waresley Wood to do a full survey of the wood that November, walking down rides that, over time, had become reduced to narrow tracks blocked with fallen trees, the ride-side ditches choked with vegetation. Many of the elm trees were succumbing to Dutch elm disease, some were already dead and shedding sheets of bark. But there was a scattering of fair-sized ash and oak trees and, at the very end of autumn, this gifted botanist was able to identify 38 species of plant from withered leaves and seedheads.

The trust did eventually manage to buy Waresley Wood, albeit in piecemeal fashion over a period of six years, buoyed along by a mixture of grants, sponsored walks and plant sales. An elderly member bought a sizeable chunk and leased it to the trust for £1 a year. The farmer, meanwhile, who had promised to sell the wood to the trust, was true to his word and remained patient throughout. One of the woodland rides was named after him as a mark of gratitude.

A year after the final purchase was complete, conservationists from all over Britain began assembling evidence to build the case for the most comprehensive piece of wildlife legislation ever enacted in parliament. The proponents of the Wildlife and Countryside Act began by setting out the case as to exactly why existing laws were inadequate to safeguard Britain's wildlife. In their evidence, they cited Waresley Wood, where two-thirds of a supposedly protected site, a wood designated as an SSSI in 1954, one of the nation's finest, had been razed to the ground.

* * *

A generation before, the man who had owned Waresley Wood was running a dairy farm in Cheshire. George Mear, like many food producers across Britain, had a very prosperous war. While the common people suffered the privations of rationing, those who could afford it beat a muddy path to the farmer's back door, where they collected regular supplies of milk, butter and beef. George was well rewarded with fistfuls of cash for providing life's little comforts.

The authorities never caught up with George; after all, the chiefs of police in Manchester were among his best customers. Even so, he never put his illicit earnings in the bank, just in case he was asked where all that money had come from. He stuffed pound notes and ten-shilling notes into a milk churn, until one day he discovered a mouse had made its nest there and shredded all the paper. After that, he took to secreting his stash in more secure hiding places.

George's son, Stephen, detested life on the dairy farm. All through his childhood, he had risen before dawn to hand-milk the cows, and then he had had to set off on the daily eight-mile walk to school. He loathed what he called the cows' 'mucky tails round my ears', spending freezing hours with – as he might have put it – his head up a cow's arse, being spattered with shit from swishing tails, desperately trying to clean it out of his hair afterwards, then heading to school still reeking of cow dung.

When the war was over, rationing continued and George's small fortune carried on building. Stephen was now married and the growing family was beginning to look for a better life away from the little Congleton farm where, as tenants, they had an uncertain future.

The winter of 1947, when deep snow blanketed the ground for two months, might have helped persuade them that there could be an easier, long-term living to be made elsewhere. They decided to follow a post-war trend – like many northern farmers, they gave up their cows and headed south to grow corn and bask in the warmth of a milder climate.

Exactly how much George Mear knew about Wood

Farm, Waresley, when he signed the document in a Cheshire solicitor's office to complete his purchase is open to question. In practical terms, Mear bought 480 acres (195 hectares) of land, together with its horses, pigs and sheep, and he inherited a workforce of 40.

The locals told George Mear he wouldn't last a year. Four farmers before him had gone bankrupt within little more than a decade. When he ploughed the heavy clay fields for the first time in November 1948, he saw water streaming down the furrows. George acquired an ex-army heavy vehicle. It got stuck up to its axles. Villagers derided the place – they called it 'Sludder Farm' after the liquefied mud from the fields that oozed over the farmyard.

At harvest time in those first tough years, dozens of workers were employed to gather the crop by hand, binding and stacking it to dry out in 'stooks', just as farm labourers had done for centuries. A time traveller from the Middle Ages would have recognised much of what was going on. George declared ruefully that he was a dog-and-stick kind of farmer, managing his land with little more than the basics.

Half of the crop was given over to feeding the strongest workers, giant Suffolk horses that provided the farm's horse-power, but at a heavy cost in hay. A fair proportion of the rest fed the wild rabbits, for the fields were overrun. There would be great barren patches where the crops had been nibbled bare. The workers would put up nets and chase hundreds of rabbits at a time into them.

And then there was the wood. At 172 acres, Waresley Wood made up more than a third of the farmer's land. It had been offered for sale in 1932 as part of a much bigger estate as:

Lot 17
About
172 a. 2 r. 21 p.*
of Valuable Woodland
well-known as Waresley Wood
Situated just East of the Village, well and clean rided,
containing a large amount of commercial timber,
including large quantities of oak and elm, etc,
ready for cutting.

*Measured in acres, roods and perches

The wood's prospects had changed for the worse since that sale. During the war, the government had requisitioned and felled all of the useable timber, and the trunks had been dragged up to the farmyard sawmill. Now it was, in the family's own words, 'very poor scrubland, very wet and boggy. You couldn't even walk in it'.

A local woman remembered cycling as a little girl with her sister to pick pretty flowers from the wood in the spring-time. 'We didn't know we were doing anything wrong,' confessed Jan Rodgers half a century later, and nor did most people in that age of superabundance. What was wrong with picking wild flowers when they were as common as blackberries? The farmer wouldn't have cared anyway. When village women came formally to ask if it would be possible to gather bluebells, primroses and violets to deco-rate the church for Easter, as generations of churchwardens had done before them, he readily acquiesced.

The Cambridgeshire hunt might or might not have had the courtesy to request permission for the hounds to cross the farmer's land and run through the wood after foxes. It was of no material consequence to George, and he was happy to keep in with his landed neighbours. Now and then, a thatcher would be allowed into the wood to cut pegs, but that only earned the farmer pennies. The only practical use the Mear family made of such a large part of their land was to raise pheasants for shooting. In later years, they turned their pigs out into the boggy heart of the wood, where they roamed freely all year round, except during farrowing time, when the sows were brought back under shelter.

Born in the year the family came to Wood Farm, George Mear's grandson, John, lived through a transformation in both its management and its fortunes, a process that was complete by the time he reached adulthood. He remembered the arrival of the first combine harvester, towed by a tractor. The next generation of machines would be too large for the small hedged fields. Government grants paid for them to take the hedges out. Mechanisation shrank the workforce. Where there had been 40 labourers, there were just four by the 1960s, and two of those were the farmer and his son. The Suffolk carthorses went. Myxomatosis did for most of the rabbits.

Once a month, a friendly face appeared on the scene. He was the well-spoken man from the ministry and he was there to help. An official from the National Agricultural Advisory Service, armed with the latest advice on improving the farm, he had but one goal. 'He was very keen on you maximising everything. They just wanted food, food, food,' said John.

Yields from the farm's wheat doubled in a decade as new varieties were grown and pesticides and herbicides were applied. The government official guided them through the process of draining their sodden, sticky fields, and obtaining grants which paid two-thirds of the cost. The drier fields warmed up more quickly in early spring, and the crops grew sooner, sending down stronger roots. The wheat and barley, modified descendants of grasses that had grown naturally in arid lands, thrived in such conditions.

By 1962, the farm had passed into the possession of George Mear's son, Stephen, and he had enough money in hand to consider doing something useful with his 'marginal' land. The government advisor had his eye on Waresley Wood and told him he should apply to the Ministry of Agriculture for a grant to 'reclaim for agricultural purposes' the western part of the wood. Government approval came through without question.

That winter, Stephen Mear embarked on the task of 'cutting back' the wood. It would take the best part of six years to clear a full third of the wood, and it was eventually grubbed out as far as an existing broad ride, which now formed the new western boundary. The operations were always carried out in winter, when the bare branches looked as dead as the trees would soon be, when there were no birds' nests in use to fall out, no pretty blooms to be crushed underfoot. The farmer used sticks of dynamite to blast the tree stumps to bits and a tractor on tracks (a 'crawler') rolled back and forth to drag out shattered roots and branches.

Five years after the job was complete, Britain was in the Common Market. The fields that had been covered in commercially unproductive scrub were now growing wheat, which was selling for more than £100 an acre, the farm's prosperity underpinned by European subsidies. John Mear commented that people loved the farmers for growing them food. It was, as he said, 'bonanza time'. There was every incentive to produce more. His father looked again at the woodland, applied successfully for a government grant, and the heavy machinery rolled in once more. A bulldozer began driving into the southern end of the wood.

The first winter of grubbing-out had finished when news

reached the family that a conservation organisation wanted to buy the wood. The farmer and his son were divided. Stephen Mear wanted to clear the whole wood. His son John disagreed. Somehow, the younger man's view prevailed. But the family kept the shooting rights and today, among the trees, there are still the huts and fences of pheasant release pens.

*   *   *

When I asked to meet the Mear family, I did not expect a welcome. I did not expect 'Yeah, sure, when?' from Charles Mear, the fourth-generation farmer. I was unprepared for warmth from all of the family, as we sat around the kitchen table, the hub of any farm, three times in all, drinking coffee while toddlers and a small hairy dog weaved around the chair legs. After all, I had come to talk to them about the wood they cut down.

Charles is a gentle man, and his soft-voiced earnestness has puppy-dog appeal. I warmed to his passion, as he showed me around Wood Farm.

He grows crops, and keeps sheep and chickens. Lots of chickens. He takes me into one of his giant, airy coops, lit by sunshine, a feathery emporium full of curious birds. Happy hens. At least, welfare organisations think so, for these free-range egg-layers are RSPCA-approved, strutting around on grassy fields the size of football pitches.

Charles walks me around the rest of the farm, leading me down the hedges he planted to replace ones his grandfather had been paid to take out. He tells me he maintains them at his own expense. Five thousand a year. That sounds a lot. He speaks of sustainability, points with pride to solar panels on barn roofs, and the place where he plans to install a giant bio-composter.

He takes me down to stand before the spot where his grandfather took out most of Waresley Wood before he was born. 'The family still call it "woodland field",' he tells me wistfully. 'I'd like to plant trees and grow another wood here.' And at this point, I can barely conceal a great welling-up of sadness: that this sincere, well-meaning man should be contemplating making up for the loss of something older and more intricate than the Bayeux Tapestry with the equivalent of a few balls of wool. A wise forester told me that a wood is more than a collection of trees. What was done in the past cannot be undone that easily. But I cannot bring myself to tell him this, for Charles Mear is the present and the future.

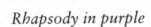

Rhapsody in purple

The textbooks tell us that Britain is home to up to half of the world's bluebells, an island nation with a just-so climate that allows them to bloom here as nowhere else. We are, in effect, a carpet showroom. And it feels today as if all the bluebells are here in Waresley Wood. Through the gate, the bluebells are at their densest, on the up slopes, the down slopes, dominating the plateaus between. This is perfect product placement.

The National Trust chose the oak leaf as its emblem. It could just as easily and emphatically have gone for the blue-bell (*Hyacinthoides non-scripta*, the unmarked hyacinth). My German aunt and uncle were brought up surrounded by the forests that inspired the fantastical folk tales collected by the Brothers Grimm. In spring, those Saxon forests bloom white with ramsons, the flower they call Bärlauch – *bear's garlic*. But those Teutonic wonders cannot compare with Britain's greatest show. A quarter of a century ago, I brought my relations to Waresley Wood at bluebell time. '*So schön, so schön*,' 'So beautiful, so beautiful,' they whispered.

We enter the woods today and it is like being given an instant tot of schnapps, a quick draft through the nose, an indescribable sweetness, and then the fragrance is gone. Nobody can get drunk on bluebells. No amount of sniffing will recapture the first moment, that virginal sniff. I bend down to tilt the tip of my nose against a flower so that it swings at the touch. But there's the rub – there is nothing left to smell.

The bluebell is the epitome of ancient woodland, though it is also an open-air maverick. It may be a blue flag of antiquity here, but it ain't necessarily so out west. It grows perfectly well under bracken on Welsh hills without a tree in sight, for example. What of its name? Bluebell is both lyrical and prosaic. Those dangling cups are unquestionably bells, albeit elongated ones, with fairy curls lapping their fringes. But what about the colour? Are bluebells really blue? One patch on a rise is royal blue, another running down to the stream is garish mauve. Venerated naturalist Ted Smith called the bluebell show 'a purple haze' and, at 87 years old, he was possibly not thinking of the Jimi Hendrix song. We might ponder whether the glory of this display is in its uniformity. Perhaps there is a greater glory in near uniformity, a tantalising, unreachable almost. And then I find one of nature's curveballs, a pure white flower, one of the occasional colour variants dotted among the rest – the white sheep of the family.

We can think of the bulbs as something between a battery and a foetus. The plant's leaves first began poking their slender tips out of the leaf litter at the end of January, gathering what light there was percolating through the leafless trees, photosynthesising for all they were worth, drawing the sun's energy down into their globular under-ground stores. And for all the flowers' showy display it is the leaves that will decide an individual plant's future. From April until July, when the great green canopy above shuts out the light and the leaves shrivel to limp, weedy strands, they are building reserves for next year. And by July, just halfway through this year, next spring will be mapped out in the bulb, every flower bud created in embryo, the foetal shapes known botanically as 'initials'.

There is a pact going on beneath the carpet. Mycorrhizal fungi are treating the bluebells as if they were cows attaching their threads to the bluebell's roots and 'milking' the plant's sugars. It's a two-way suck though, and in return, the bluebells are gaining moisture and nutrients through these root extensions, including all-important phosphorus, an element that is sorely depleted in ancient woodland. Bluebells can't absorb phosphorus in its inorganic state. But the fungi can. Into our domestic gardens we tip expensive phosphates and probably kill the mycorrhizal fungi that we could have had for free.

A couple have wandered into the wood, swinging their heads from side to side in clear wonderment, giving audible gasps at the blaze of colour. They have lived four miles away for the last ten years and have never been here before. 'Nice, innit?'

Two elderly ladies approach. They are from Cambridge and, judging by their clipped, precise enunciation, are more gown than town. I'm all set for show-and-tell. I bend down and pick something up off the ground. 'Do you know what these are?' I ask them, offering each a weightless lump of what looks like shiny charcoal. The ladies look baffled, rolling them like pebbles in their fingers. 'King Alfred's cakes, a type of fungus', I say. They hand the cakes back, amused looks on their faces. I will take the cakes home and sit them on a piece of white paper. By tomorrow, the polished black leather will turn to suede, and the fungus will have a halo of black soot. Put the cakes next to a warm lamp and sometimes you can watch the spores spouting like little geysers.

One party trick done, I try another on my Cambridge

ladies. 'Feel this tree.' They have not quite reached the omigod-we-have-found-a nutter-in-the-wood stage. And my wife is present after all. 'Put your hands around it and tell me what you feel.' It is a path-side field maple, a tall straight trunk with no side branches below head height, the bark scarcely pitted. They embrace its coldness on a warm spring morning, chill winter still locked in the solidity of a tubular fridge. And it is solid, indescribably hard. Unshakeable. Hug a tree, though remember it is important to be choosy with your affections. An oak feels like big daddy – you can never get your arms all the way round and its rough bark feels like papa's unshaven chin. Hugging an aspen is like snogging a hedgehog. But a field maple is palpably dense, unyielding and just about smooth to the touch, a lullaby of reassurance.

We come to a stream in the wood, the parish boundary. We think nothing of parish boundaries. We don't even think of them. On a single trip out in the car, we might cross 50 or more with no awareness whatsoever. For our immobile ancestors, however, it was a big deal. The next parish had a different manor, a different church, a different community. It was other. For medium-sized and bigger woods, the division between parishes and thus ownerships of land were often marked with a physical barrier. Many a wood has running through it what seems to be an inexplicable earth bank. Waresley has a stream. There are actually two woods bolted together here, and their full combined name is Waresley and Gransden Woods. Geographically and geologically, they are as good as one.

For much of the year, the wild border of Dean Brook scarcely merits the name. Barely babbling, more of a sulky puddle, dry through the summer, it flows only after heavy rains. But with its steep sides, in the days before the land around was drained, it must have made an effective barrier.

There are plenty of bridges across the moat these days and foot traffic moves freely across. Gransden Wood is both similar to and very different from to its southern neighbour. Out to the east, the bluebell carpet flows from one wood to the other. Here in the west, it is still possible to go up a gentle rise and see evidence of what happened in 1928, when much of Gransden Wood, then under the ownership of Clare College, Cambridge, was felled. The woodsmen showed some creativity in their replanting, raiding nurseries for sycamores, turkey oaks, beeches, hornbeams, wild cherries, larches, grey poplars, hybrid poplars and even a Scots pine and Norway spruce, tall and isolated today among their broadleaved brethren.

Over 20 years, the Wildlife Trust acquired much of Gransden Wood, coaxing owners into leases, then buying when funds permitted. But it held back from buying the whole wood, leaving the northern part when it came up for sale to private purchasers, who promised wildlife-friendly management.

Today is Saturday. Had it been Sunday, we would have bumped into Graham the Warden, for he is here every Sunday without fail. Everyone knows him as Graham the Warden, because he wears a pin badge. It says 'Graham. Warden'. I suppose they might have added his second name to the badge, but then people might have thought he was a delegate at a conference. And if he'd hung it on a lanyard, they might have weighed him up as a visitor. Besides, dangly string, axes and saws don't really go together. As it is, the label feels right and somehow appropriately medieval. Hubert the Turner, Cedric the Cooper, Graham the Warden.

KING CONIFER

The children always tittered when the teacher announced the name of their guest speaker: 'Boys and girls, this is Mr Wood from the Forestry Commission.'

For Yorkshireman Brian Wood, school talks in Caithness and Sutherland were part of the ambassadorial duties of a man hand-picked by his employer for a job with enormous scope. Fresh out of university with a flying first, Brian had been offered a job as a district officer. He applied to work in Oxfordshire: he was sent to the far north of Scotland. Such apparent contrariness was done with the young man's future career in mind. The Home Counties were all very well, but an outstanding graduate could make a name for himself north of Inverness, where there was a vast area of near wilderness, a blanket bog of peaty soil, mosses and *dubh lochans*, the black pools. Future conservationists would lend it a romantic charm by naming it the Flow Country, after the Norse word *flói*, meaning wet. Brian Wood's mission was to fill this empty space with trees. He had a big tractor and many hundreds of thousands of trees.

Unusually among foresters, Brian Wood fell into his career almost by accident. As a teenager, like most of us, he had no fixed ideas, and was destined to be nudged and cajoled, drifting on a passionless whim into employment. Raised in 1950s Harrogate, he had a love of natural history and a vague desire for a job working outdoors. He knew nothing of conservation, National Parks, or anything that might harness his interests directly. It was only towards the end of a lower-sixth-form careers convention that a mention of the word 'forestry' gave him an inkling of a way to escape outside. He spent that summer hand-weeding plantations of Sitka spruce and liked the open air well enough to apply to the Forestry Commission for a job when he left school.

He served his apprenticeship in North Yorkshire's beautiful Nidderdale, a green valley filled with tiny copses and carrs, wet woodlands full of ferns, mosses and lichens.

One particular spot in Nidderdale stayed in Brian Wood's memory, a wood of downy birch and alder called Clarkes Carr. Perhaps it was an older forester who pointed out its dead past in the living trees. The birch trees had had a well-worked life, having been coppiced five to ten times before, but no woodsman's axe or saw had been near them for the best part of 50 years. Brian was assigned to a gang of four or five other boys of the same age. They set to work with chainsaws, felling the trees, one by one, cutting the trunks into six-foot lengths and loading them into a tractor to be taken away, pulped and turned into poor-quality Formica kitchen furniture.

One member of Brian's team was a farmer's son and he drove the tractor. The youths piled the smaller branches and twigs into great heaps and made bonfires of them. And having cleared the lot, they began planting Sitka spruce, scraping bare patches in the ground, cutting L-shaped notches and popping each bare-rooted seedling inside. They were supposed to plant 1,000 trees a day.

At 18 years of age, Brian's main concern was to work as fast as he could, since this was piecework. He was a young man earning his first pay packet and he wanted as much as he could get. He took no pride in what he was doing: for him it was just a job. But he enjoyed being outdoors doing vigorous exercise and was proud that, at the end of two years, he had reached a level of fitness and competence such that the area of weeding that had taken him a week as a schoolboy, now took him a day. Fifty years later, the older man, a retired lecturer in conservation, looks back at his younger self and reflects that today, Clarkes Carr, the wood he chopped down and remembered most of all, would probably – had it survived – be designated as an SSSI.

Unlike Brian Wood, most foresters proudly remember the formative experiences that would decide the course of their working lives. Today, Ray Hawes has overall responsibility for all of the National Trust's woods and forests – a huge job managing thousands of hectares. As a child growing up in the Buckinghamshire Chilterns, he sniffed his way into forestry. His father was a craftsman, making Windsor chairs out of local beech wood. The boy was intoxicated by the sweet smells of freshly cut beech. His passion for wood was evident to his father's workmates, old countrymen unbothered by new-fangled notions of health and safety, who would greet him by proffering their four- or three-fingered hands.

Lifelong forester John Voysey, who would one day restore the Grizedale oak woods of the Lake District, was a pupil at Bryanston School in Blandford Forum, where he had his imagination fired in the early post-war years by 'pioneering'. The boys were sent out to work in a wood with axes and bowsaws to carry out a spot of 'tidying up'.

Surrey teenager Peter Quelch, who would spend nearly 40 years working for the Forestry Commission, went on a Senior Scout camp in the Chilterns near High Wycombe, and completed the Forester's Badge. This was no small matter. At fifteen years of age, he had to:

1 Be able to identify, in summer and in winter, 20 varieties of trees. Know their uses as timber and fuel and be able to recognise them from a distance.
2 Have a general knowledge of the structure of a tree and how it feeds, breathes and makes timber.
3 Know the dangers to which a tree and woods may be exposed, ie, fire, snow, frost, insects, diseases, and animals. Discuss the methods of combating these dangers.
4 Prepare soil and successfully transplant a young tree (not a seedling). Know how to deal with wounds in growing trees.
5 Know how to select an axe, name the parts, how to take care of it and the safety rules of axemanship.
6 Know how to use a felling axe in felling and logging up. Use a cross-cut saw and wedges.
7 Demonstrate the general principles of felling, trimming, logging up, moving and stacking timber, and calculate the amount of useful timber in a given tree.

After three weekends immersed in a forester's world and with a badge to his name, he knew exactly what he wanted to do with the rest of his life. He fitted the profile of so many young men of the time. Forestry was then, and still is, a vocation. It is your first job, your last job and everything in between and beyond. Even after retirement, foresters still live for their trees. They buy a small wood to manage for themselves, or they manage someone else's wood. One told me that he was now 'living as the practical woodsman forester that I always wanted to be, with slowly failing strength, but still managing okay'.

The terrible irony is that thousands of men like these (and they were always men), tore the hearts out of tens of thousands of ancient woods over a devastating 40-year period between 1945 and 1985. Forestry was, without question, the biggest wrecker of ancient woodland, with almost a third of all ancient woods in Britain afflicted. In many places, the woodland edges would be left intact for aesthetic reasons. Great oaks along the edges of fields, marking the boundaries of something that was no longer there, shielded the public from the sight of conifer plantations. The official name was 'amenity belt'; critics called it 'picture framing'.

Leading botanist Sir Arthur Tansley saw it coming. A retired Oxford professor and pioneer ecologist, Tansley saw the end of the Second World War as his chance to set out a countryside manifesto, his own vision for peace in wartime Britain. Published in 1945, *Our Heritage of Wild Nature: A plea for organized nature conservation in wartime* correctly identified the greatest threat to ancient woodland:

In recent times the demand has been increasingly for coniferous timber ('soft wood'). At present soft wood is said to represent 94 per cent of the whole commercial demand. That is why modern planting, for example that done by the Forestry Commission, is mainly of pine, spruce, larch and firs of various kinds, nearly all alien trees.

So long as this state of things continues there is no prospect that the economic motive alone can justify the maintenance of British oakwoods. Unless a new point of view is taken they will be fated to disappear altogether, their sites being replaced with conifers. This is a course of events that no lover of the beauty of our countryside and no naturalist can contemplate with equanimity.

Tansley could not have known it but the war itself created the conditions and, just as importantly, the states of mind that allowed that dreadful course of action to be pursued. The driver of change was the government's own Forestry Commission. It was, and still is unlike any other government department. Lifelong employee Rod Leslie observed that: 'The absolute key was it was run by foresters – we didn't have some sort of detached layer of civil servants sitting on top of us. It also had an evangelical focus on its mission.'

Set up in 1919, the overriding purpose at its foundation was to address the question of pit props. During the First World War, a U-boat blockade had halted food supplies to island Britain. The stifling of trade had also turned a focus on the country's reliance on imported timber. A sparsely forested nation, used to importing most of its timber, was reduced to felling all available mature – and not so mature – trees to meet the demand for pit props. Holding up tunnel after tunnel in mines, those pit props would mean a supply of coal for an energy-hungry steel industry turning out guns, bullets and shells. Half a million acres of woodland were felled and the feeling in government afterwards was that Britain had been close to running out of timber. That close shave would be impressed upon decision-making minds for decades to come.

The future of the newly formed Forestry Commission was influenced by a number of factors. In the Victorian age, Britain had turned to Europe, and especially Germany, for guidance on how to exploit the forests of its Empire. 'Scientific forestry', practised by men in the huge forests of Germany, was applied to the teak forests of India and Burma, and

German theorists were sent to supervise the work. William Schlich was one of these men. Later the author of a five-volume *Manual of Forestry*, Schlich would be the guiding light for the foresters who worked for the new organisation. Many had seen service in the Empire, and many had fought in the First World War. Long-time Commission forester Paul Tabbush summed up the *modus operandi*: 'You recruit an ex-army man, give him an area, tell him to get an office in the middle and start buying land.'

From its very inception, the Forestry Commission had a military ethos, a strict hierarchy, firm objectives and set targets, a dislike of dissent and hence the characteristics of a giant ocean liner. Once the ship had been given its direction, it was an impressive, unstoppable force. Getting it to change course would prove exceedingly difficult.

Forest managers combined roles as tree farmers and gardeners of the countryside. In the former capacity, they would pay careful attention to the conditions under which their crops could grow; they would study soil types and the climatic conditions – how much rainfall did a site get? Where did the prevailing wind come from?

As farmer-gardeners they constructed a whole ideology, one that made complete sense to them. The basis of this thinking can be found in the books of forestry writers such as Herbert Edlin, a much-read and greatly respected publications officer for the Forestry Commission in the 1940s and '50s, who saw things from a particular angle:

> The native British flora includes remarkably few trees of timber value... Many species of conifers, formerly plentiful in Britain, were exterminated by climatic catastrophes such as the Ice Ages, and did not return. The forester only reintroduces what has been lost. By selecting the trees most

suited to our maritime climate, he is frequently able to
obtain faster growth than is found in the more continental
climate of the European mainland.

There was nothing new in complaints about the paucity
of tree species in Britain. They had been addressed by early
plant collectors of the eighteenth and nineteenth century,
men like David Douglas, who travelled to the New World
and brought back the Douglas fir, Sitka spruce and western
hemlock. These species had grown in a maritime climate, in
similar soils and at a similar latitude, and so, not surpris-
ingly, they thrived in Britain. Men like Edlin visited awe-
inspiring American forests and sought to replicate their
grandeur on home soil.

Foresters were happy to plant any species, of whatever origin, provided they got results. They loved trees and
delighted in seeing their nursed offspring flourish, admiring
fast growth, straight, broad trunks and a good crown.

Such single-mindedness led the new organisation
into making its first major public relations blunder in
1934, when it announced that it proposed to plant conifers at Ennerdale Head in the Lake District. It had already
bought parts of the Lakes and planted up whole fells at
Whinlatter and Grizedale Pike, with the trees in regimented lines like rows of cabbages. As the conifers grew,
so too did the criticism. Cherished views were disappearing
behind walls of spruce, the monotonous rectangular blocks
composed of a single species were seen as eyesores in a
landscape of rugged beauty. The Commission had struck
at the nation's Wordsworthian heart, defiling its national
identity with 'alien conifers'. They were, as one vociferous
critic put it, 'armies in serried ranks'. It was as if a sacred
part of the country had been invaded by the enemy, and

undertones of racism from some of the critics fuelled their fury.

One of the loudest pre-war critics of this affront to aesthetics was the newly formed Council for the Preservation of Rural England (CPRE). By the late 1930s, it had forced the Forestry Commission into a tactical retreat; making it agree to draw back from planting in the central Lake District. The whole episode opened up an area of vulnerability in the Commission that it would never really lose, and one which would again become apparent decades later.

The Forestry Commission's inter-war planting efforts were largely concentrated on 'marginal' land – the overgrazed, underpopulated uplands of places like Northumberland, where Kielder Forest was established, the all but abandoned heathland of Norfolk's Thetford Chase and the Isle of Purbeck in Dorset. Aristocrats inheriting estates without the money to run them gave up their land to the state in lieu of death duties. The Commission was handed Crown forests too, and eagerly set about turning open ground on Crown land such as the New Forest to plantation.

The Commission's attitude to deciduous woodland was not wholly negative – long-term chairman, Lord Robinson, for example, kept a fatherly eye on an oak coppice he had restored in 1912 and was a strong advocate of hardwood planting. In the late 1930s, the Commission had begun work on bulletin number 19, one of a series of instructive and influential manuals for foresters. Its title was *Cultivation of British Hardwoods*. The publication reached page proof stage... and then the proofs were destroyed in the Blitz.

Nobody picked up the earlier proofs of the lost manual Nor was anyone listening to forestry thinker Richard St Barbe Baker, who pointed out that the Germans were challenging their own methods of scientific forestry, and were shifting towards a more environmentally sensitive system that mixed conifer and broadleaved planting. His comments were made in 1942, perhaps not the time for Britain to be taking advice from Germany. The willingness to promote broadleaf woodland had largely gone, and would not resurface again until the 1980s.

The war brought about a transformation in official attitudes to woodland:

It is of the utmost importance that our home supplies of timber, of every size, should be available as and when they are required. Owners, therefore, can render the best service to their country by parting readily with their timber when asked to do so... even if the resultant fellings are far in excess of those which would be allowable under good forestry practice, and even if the timber in question is immature. It is hardly necessary to point out to members the immense importance of replanting felled areas with the least possible delay.

The Honourable Nigel Orde Powlett, President of the Royal Forestry Society of England and Wales, spring 1940

The government set up a Home Timber Production Department. Military foresters from the Dominions – Canada, Australia and New Zealand – were brought in to manage the felling, supplemented by prisoners of war, conscientious objectors and a workforce of 6,000 from the Women's Timber Corps (nicknamed 'lumberjills'). More than 50,000 people went from wood to wood, taking out the trees, and doing so in a great hurry.

Farmer, author and naturalist Frank Fraser Darling

wrote of the wartime tree fellers' impact in the Scottish Highlands:

> Our land is so devastated that we might as well have been in the battlefield. See the very windbreaks taken from the roadsides, see the wreck of Glenfeshie, the Rothiemurchus that is no more, the shearing of the Sutherland woods, the removal of shelter from the wind-ridden west and the immense landslips on the road from Tomdoun to Loch Hourn. That is what deforestation has meant in our time.

A senior employee and later official chronicler of the whole operation, Oxford don Russell Meiggs, estimated that 40 per cent of Britain's broadleaved woods had their timber taken out. Meiggs observed: 'The quality of home grown timber was very uneven and to meet the demands of war much scrub oak and other inferior timber had to be brought into production.' And so the younger, immature trees were felled too.

When peacetime finally came, the authorities took a long, appraising look at the plundered woods and saw a 30- to 60-year period ahead when these broadleaved woods would produce nothing at all in the way of timber. No output, no income. Foresters of the time would agree with Arthur Tansley's doom-laden comment: 'Today our oakwoods are economically almost worthless.' The tragedy for ancient woods was that foresters loved them, but saw them as obsolescent, a sad irrelevance in a world that was looking ahead.

Unproductive and unwanted, ancient woodland was tabulated in the Commission's national census of woodland of 1947, where all undesirables were bracketed together:

	Acres
Productive High Forest in Private Ownership (All Ages):	1,254,000
Productive High Forest held by the Forestry Commission (Mostly under 28 years old):	534,000
Total Productive High Forest:	1,788,000
Coppice, mainly under Private Ownership and largely unproductive:	350,000
Scrub:	497,000
Woods Felled before 1939 and not replanted:	289,000
Woods Felled 1939–1947 and not replanted:	373,000
Devastated Woods, mostly arising from 1939–1947 clearances	151,000
Total of Coppice and Unproductive Woodlands:	1,660,000
Grand Total, All Woodlands:	3,448,000

The word 'scrub' had been an accepted forestry term denoting small trees and bushes of a particular thickness. Now, it crossed a divide into more general use, along with 'felled', 'devastated' and 'derelict', denying the possibility of restoration or redemption. There was even a tendency to lump it in with 'waste', a loaded term that dated back to the Middle Ages, describing neglected land that landowners were under a moral duty to take in hand.

The proponents of 'productive forestry' saw change as an urgent economic necessity. Barrister Lord Merthyr addressed his fellow peers in July 1949:

I say without hesitation that from the point of view of the whole community it is economic and in every way desirable that much smaller areas of woodland – I am thinking of the steep dingles and dales and hillsides, of places which are covered with scrub and cannot be ploughed – should be afforested... if we are going to rely upon growing our own food and producing our own timber, as we pretend to be, we can no longer afford the luxury and extravagance of these small derelict, overgrown pieces of land.

(HL Deb 13 July 1949 vol 163 cc1212-70)

There were even those who would use aesthetic reasons to advocate their removal. Speaking disparagingly of the state of the Quantock Hills in Somerset, Earl Radnor said:

The mixed woodlands... are now practically entirely oak scrub, much of which is dying and none of which is beautiful.

(HL Deb 18 October 1949 vol 164 cc878-936)

The Commission worked its charm and influence on the politicians in power. A key target was Hugh Dalton, chancellor of the exchequer in the incoming Labour government. Incredibly, Dalton spent the critical days preparing his budget of November 1946 as a guest of the Commission in one of its forest lodges, and was wined, dined and, no doubt, courted assiduously. Here was a government body that could offer employment in impoverished rural areas, and a reduction in imports, something that weighed heavily on a chancellor obsessed with reducing Britain's postwar balance of payments deficit.

Dalton paid spectacularly for his room and board. In the House of Commons, he announced a package of £20 million over a period of five years for afforesting and replanting, declaring in his diary that it gave him more satisfaction than any other expenditure in the Treasury. Such a sum had been at the top end of the Commission's ask. The government was on board with a policy the agriculture minister declared would be 'pursued with utmost vigour'.

But a significant part of the proposed replanting was out of the Commission's control. More than three-quarters of the offending scrub woodland was in private hands. Landowners would need some kind of inducement to change. The Commission turned for inspiration to a scheme that had been set up with purely philanthropic objectives.

In the 1920s, philanthropist Leonard Elmhirst and his American heiress wife Dorothy had bought Dartington Hall in Devon, and had investigated how they might generate income for the rural poor in such an area of acute unemployment. They linked up with a forestry economist called Wilfred Hiley and, between them, devised a scheme whereby landowners agreed to 'dedicate' land for forestry planting, creating jobs in trees.

That idea would now be imitated: pondered during wartime, it was brought to life under a government dedication scheme. Those private individuals who entered their woods for 'rehabilitation' would receive state funding, in return for managing their land according to an agreed plan and dedicating it in perpetuity to forestry.

Initially, the scheme stalled. A Labour government embarking on a widespread programme of nationalisation was viewed with deep suspicion by those who owned lots of land. Labour peer Earl de la Warr defended the policy loudly in the House of Lords:

> We want it to be quite clear that any suggestion that landowners are holding back from the dedication scheme

because they do not want to join in some Socialist system of planning is just rubbish. The dedication scheme is not Socialist-planning; it was conceived by landowners who will still support it, provided that it is put forward in a form which they can accept.

(HL Deb 13 July 1949 vol 163 cc1212-70)

Once an acceptable form had been reached, landowners rushed to sign up. The biggest landowners did so on a grand scale. The Duke of Buccleuch dedicated 18,000 acres, the Chatsworth Estate 3,000 acres. The Country Landowners Association urged its members to 'press on with the task of rebuilding the country's reserves of timber with all possible speed and energy'. Over a 30-year period, around 5,300 landowners signed up. The puffy cloud symbols for deciduous trees on Ordnance Survey maps began to be replaced by pictures of Christmas trees. Many thousands of woods were affected: in present-day Clwyd alone, between 1,200 and 1,400 woods of varying sizes were transformed. In some counties, the results were devastating. Herefordshire, one of the greenest counties in England, turned a darker shade of green. It saw nearly half of its ancient woods coniferised.

One partial exception to this national trend was the heavily wooded Weald of Kent, Sussex and Surrey, where a market for sweet chestnut coppice products (especially fence palings) persisted. Today there are still small-scale enterprises that have passed through eight or more generations of the same family. The Forestry Commission conservator for the southeast declared in 1968 that sweet chestnut coppice was the only commercially viable hardwood crop. Even so, more than half of the ancient woodland under coppice was lost from this part of England in the 50 years after the Second World War.

Timber merchants sprung up all over Britain, enabling landowners to offload their troublesome burdens without fretting about what to do next. Many a farmer could simply sell their woods to a technically proficient middleman and someone else's heavy machinery would do the rest.

A great number of the landowners who turned to conifers had fought for their country and embraced the initiative with a strong sense of patriotic duty and an eye on a bob or two. Sir George Agnew recalled his father entering the dedication scheme to coniferise the woodlands of the Rougham Estate in Suffolk: 'He was a very enthusiastic forester of the post-Second World War school of forestry, which was based on a national resource of timber, the shortages and a duty to provide timber. At the same time, he had a strong belief that the new commercial approach to forestry would make money for the estate.'

Universities bought in to the dominance of conifer ideology. In the immediate post-war period, forestry students were stuck in an anachronistic trap. An Edinburgh graduate recalled: 'We were there to reconstruct the forests of the Empire. I knew more about the teak forests of India than I did about the forests of my own country.' By the 1950s, the Empire was fast becoming history and other views prevailed in education, some of them distinctly odd. Cirencester College would inform its students that broadleaved trees could not grow without conifers to help them grow straight.

Graduates of the 1960s forestry courses left university with a gaping hole in their education. Botany was only there to tell you what the soils were like, so that you could determine which conifers to plant. Nothing at all was taught about native trees; the words oak, ash and hazel had simply disappeared from the curriculum.

Within the industry, there were still vestiges of enthusiasm for the old ways. Even up until the 1960s, the Commission was planting some broadleaved trees and carrying out coppicing, although not much. It had joined up with a government body, the Rural Industries Bureau, to investigate the state of the hazel coppice industry. Their findings, published in 1954, revealed that barely a tenth of coppice woods were being worked.

In that same year, eleven-year-old John Barkham, later to become a professional ecologist, was going out on winter days with his big brother to play in Norridge Wood near their Warminster home. Four old coppicers (probably in their fifties and positively geriatric to a child of that age) were at work in the wood and had a charcoal burner, making fuel for the good people of Wiltshire. The boys 'helped' by moving wood around to exactly where it wasn't wanted. One of the kindly old woodsmen showed little John how to use a billhook properly. John flung his hook and managed to gash his knee. Such happy, fondly remembered times.

A decade later, the coppicers had gone from Norridge Wood and so too had the coppice, lost under a conifer plantation. By 1963, a repeat survey suggested there were perhaps no more than 100 full-time coppicers left in the whole of Britain. And those woodsmen were dying off fast.

Before the war, labour had been cheap and conifers were planted only after a gang had cut down the broadleaved trees, two to an enormous cross-cut saw. But now such labour-intensive work was judged uneconomic. A quick alternative used widely was 'ring-barking' big trees where they stood, earning the forester sixpence a tree. Ancient pollarded oaks, hornbeams and limes, two or three hundred years old or more, would have their trunks girdled with deep cuts, which sliced through the bark and the connective layer of cells beneath, stopping the flow of nutrients between leaves and roots. Some of the other methods adopted by landowners were, quite frankly, stupid. At Flint in North Wales, 'foresters' tried to kill oaks by strangling them with barbed wire. The wire marks are there to this day; the trees live on.

Thousands of young men, fresh out of school or university, were sent out to destroy ancient woods. How did they feel about what they were doing? These foresters did not understand the implications of their work. The idea of 'ancient woodland' and the recognition of its irreplaceable nature was still far off in the future. Most of the raw recruits simply followed orders unthinkingly. 'It was all new to you, you didn't question policy,' said one. Ray Hawes left the Chiltern beech woods of his childhood to begin his first job working for a forestry and landscape company in southeast England. 'I was not long out of university, I was doing what was agreed with the owner, and the Forestry Commission was paying grant aid. I don't remember any protests. You just got on with the job.'

Another new forester, born and brought up in the Oxfordshire Chilterns, was also cutting down the woods of his childhood. He had 'some misgivings', but did what he was told. At Appin Forest in Argyll, a nineteen-year-old new recruit witnessed a squad of men ring-barking old oaks to kill them. 'I didn't say much about it. I was a trainee, a new kid on the block. I was aware that there was a political hierarchy and certainly at that time you had to be very careful what you said.'

Others often did the dirty work for them. Hell Coppice, northeast of Oxford, was felled and cleared by inmates from the city prison, while the men from the Commission stood and supervised.

On the Cornwall–Devon border, Rex Cartwright was an experienced forester who had previously worked in Shropshire. He was awed by the conditions in the Tamar Valley, where the light soils were perfect for conifer growing.

The rainfall there was 55 inches a year at least. Some Douglas fir were felled and they were so big that I stood at the end of them and couldn't look over the diameter of the trunk. And they were 80 years old, which gives you an idea of how quickly they grew.

Unfortunately, I remember felling one woodland though. This was Greystone Wood, a mix of conifer and hardwoods, mostly oaks. I felt pretty awful felling this timber, a hundred and forty, fifty, sixty years of age. The thing that struck me, walking into this wood – they'd already started felling – I saw woodlarks. I'd never seen woodlarks before and haven't since. It made me very sad because we were getting rid of a habitat that suited that particular bird.

One rare and notable exception to this reluctant acquiescence was Peter Quelch, a young man who would go on to work for the Commission for nearly 40 years. Posted to the Commission's northern England office in Cumbria, his main task was planting up the open fells close to the border. But he remembered all too vividly Walton Wood, just a few miles north of his Brampton office.

They had a bizarre system where they would get in fairground men for the winter to camp there and, every year, they would fell an acre or two of oaks, split them and sell them for firewood. They were gradually clearing it so that the Commission could come in and replant with Norway spruce. I went to see the wood and immediately thought that this wasn't right.

To this day, Peter Quelch cannot explain why, as a guileless youngster, he went on to challenge what was being done. He had little knowledge and no particular interest in natural history at that time to inform his judgement. But something persuaded him to go to his superior and ask if the remaining oaks could be saved. The district officer, an old-fashioned forester, could not understand why his junior should ask, but he was a kind man, and it was within his favour to grant such a small request to a naïve underling. In Cumbria today, a tiny block of deciduous trees lives on, held within the embrace of a plantation of conifers.

A handful of older foresters with far greater awareness of the consequences of what they were being told to do simply disobeyed orders. The Forestry Commission worker who was instructed to plant up Leigh Woods on the western side of Bristol planted conifers, but not in the way he was told. He fooled his employer by planting them all around the edge of the wood, leaving its ancient deciduous heart intact. It seems he was never found out.

Global politics in the late 1950s threatened to dismantle the Commission's whole *raison d'être*. In the new nuclear age, long-held worries about a besieged island nation running out of pit props in wartime felt outdated. A push of the button and it would all be over. At the end of a government inquiry in 1957, the Zuckermann Report concluded there was no longer a need for Britain to hold what had been referred to as 'a strategic reserve' of timber. In future, forestry would have to pay its way. The Treasury demanded a return on its capital investment.

The blunt fact was that, in the way it operated, the Forestry Commission couldn't turn in a profit. Imagination was called for. Economists were employed to invent what they called 'a social rate of return', intangible benefits that, they argued, should be offset against costs. The Commission became creative in its attempts to justify its existence and, conscious of its role as a public body, it began to emphasise public benefits. Camping and other types of recreation proliferated within its National Forest Parks, and landscape designer Sylvia Crowe was taken on to make new forest plantings more attractive. The Commission was a far-thinking and imaginative pioneer – by the end of the 60s there were 92 nature trails and 104 picnic sites, opening up the forests to people.

Yet at the same time, it was employing managers with a single focus: that of attaining their productivity goals and running what were dubbed 'cellulose factories'. Long-term employee Paul Tabbush was well placed to describe what happened in the mid-1960s.

The military-minded, engineering, vertical-thinking types believed you just had to make everything cheaper and stick to your targets and do it right. If the trees misbehaved, then they were just naughty trees. They didn't have any biological understanding of what they were doing.

There was nothing quite as farcical as the situation the Forestry Commission got itself into in its Eastern Conservancy, a huge area stretching from Lincolnshire down to the edge of London and from Suffolk as far west as Oxfordshire. Paul Tabbush tells of an insane train of events:

I was taken to Rockingham Forest, where the economists

and high-ups were trying to work out what to do with the Rockingham clays. They had quite a big holding there. It had been planted up [by the Forestry Commission] with oaks, young oaks about 20 years old. They decided that if you did the economic sums using Treasury rules, the oaks would have a negative value. Not only that, even if you costed up killing the trees and removing them, it would still be worth doing that and replacing them with a crop of conifers, and therefore they decided that was what would be done. They set their research people the task of finding out how to destroy this oak forest.

Government scientists were put to work to devise ways to kill the trees. The common alternative to ring-barking, brought into play in the 1960s over thousands of acres of Commission land, was more brutal. A chemical defoliant called 2,4,5-T was sprayed from fixed-wing aircraft or helicopters over large areas of forest, or injected into the living trees by means of a pump-action device known affectionately as the Jim-Gem Hypo-Hatchet. Some foresters, refusing to kill perfectly good oak trees, resigned from the Commission.

The defoliant 2,4,5-T would go on to be used more widely, and not just in this country. It was passed on to the US army which manufactured it (badly, so that it contained high levels of dioxin) as Agent Orange, used to defoliate the jungles of Vietnam and – incidentally – maim a million Vietnamese civilians.

Good naturalists within the Commission did what they could within the system to promote conservation. A senior figure in southwest England, Morley Penistan, urged farmers on Dorset's Isle of Purbeck not to plant on the flower-rich downland, or to take out the woods hanging on the ridges above Corfe Castle. He warned off a forestry syndicate in Gloucestershire's Lower Woods from cutting down extremely rare wild service trees. Elsewhere, Penistan took sympathetic care in planting conifers in clumps, in an effort to preserve the overall character of ancient woods. He was an active voluntary conservationist too, serving on the national body as well as being chairman in retirement of his local wildlife trust. But his favours towards conservation probably counted against him: promotions within the Commission came slowly and he never received the official honours that others who climbed the career ladder to identical posts far faster gladly accepted.

In the mid 60s, the impetus for new planting shifted from the Commission to the private sector, thanks to stimulus from some creative accounting. A tax shuffle allowed investors paying high rates of income tax to reclaim more than half of their planting costs. Not only that, more juggling enabled them to avoid paying tax on any income from sales of timber. Private forestry companies sprang up, their senior staff ex-army men who had connections in the City.

University student Mike Martin had direct experience of the consequences. Returning to his parents' sub post office in Rotherfield, East Sussex, he discovered that nearby Hornshurst Wood, a familiar haunt of his childhood, was surrounded by high security fences, bearing signs that warned 'Permit holders only'. A forestry syndicate had bought the oak woods and was proceeding to remove the trees and plant up the Wealden sands with conifers.

Rachel Allum lived next to Athelstan's Wood in the Wye Valley, and used to ride her horse among the bluebells and wood anemones. King John had granted nuns the right to fell timber in the wood in the early 1200s. In 1973, the Economic Forestry Group felled the lot.

The rush to plant and avoid tax, heedless of the long-distant future, resulted in acts of sheer madness. Conifer seedlings were planted as a tax avoidance wheeze in a steep-sided, dead-end valley in Monmouthshire without any thought as to how fully-grown trees might be extracted half a century later. Nobody tended them, nobody thinned them. They are still there today, some standing, some leaning, some toppled over – ironically it is what some might deride as a derelict, non-productive woodland.

In Caithness and Sutherland, the man who had gone into schools as a paid evangelist was beginning to doubt the words of his sermon. The giant tractors that Brian Wood sent out into the open moorland to scar the landscape with deep trenches sank up to their cabs when the peat began to thaw out. He planted row after monotonous row of Sitka spruce in soil that was drained but refused to dry out. He was ordered to cover up what he had done, to plant Japanese flowering cherries where the plantations abutted public roads, to prettify and sanitise his work. Picture framing.

As he carried out all that trite window-dressing, it began to dawn on him that he was working against nature and that perhaps there might be a better, more sympathetic way. He turned to ecology, sending south for books that explained natural processes. They enabled him to draw up a picture of what he thought would have been the ecology and natural distribution of woodland in his district. If they were going to plant trees on the edges of plantations, he argued, they could at least grow species that belonged there. He sent a carefully considered paper to his big boss, the Forestry Commission conservator in Inverness. He got no reply.

Still he persisted, thirsting for more knowledge and understanding. He applied for a place at Durham University to take a one-year MSc in ecology and was accepted. He asked his employer if he could take a year's unpaid leave to pursue his studies and come back as a better-informed worker. The answer came back: 'The Forestry Commission doesn't want specialists, it wants generalists.' Brian Wood resigned out of boredom and frustration. He often wondered if he could have shaped things differently had he stayed. As it was, the great ocean liner carried on without him on its seemingly inexorable course.

Birds

I have my nose in a guelder rose. It gives off a spicy smell, but I've taken too sharp an intake of breath. My giant sniff sucks out a handful of pollen beetles from within and they spill out over a petal like a handful of thrown dice. They are up and righted almost at once, motoring back into the flower's heady bower.

Earlier in the spring, there was a great profusion of cuckoo flower here in the damp hollows. It has gone now, though the cuckoo that arrived when it blossomed is singing, maybe a quarter a mile out to the west. Under the canopy and hidden by leaves, song thrushes and blackbirds are in full voice. And what else?

We have a good idea of what was singing here when the Wildlife Trust for Beds, Cambs and Northants bought Waresley Wood more than 40 years ago. A man I remembered from my first days working for the trust as having a permanent beam on his face, came regularly all through that first year to survey the wood's birds. An architect by profession, volunteer Julian Limentani submitted his results to the British Trust for Ornithology. His list leaves a poignant record of how things have changed.

Limentani counted 44 breeding species and the numbers of pairs are given here in brackets: red-legged partridge (1); pheasant (1); moorhen (1); woodpigeon (3); turtle dove (2);

cuckoo (1); little owl (1); tawny owl (1); green woodpecker (1); lesser spotted woodpecker (1); carrion crow (1); rook (1); magpie (1); jay (1); great tit (2); blue tit (2); coal tit (2); long-tailed tit (2); treecreeper (1); wren (3); song thrush (2); blackbird (2); robin (2); blackcap (2); garden warbler (1); whitethroat (1); lesser whitethroat (2); willow warbler (2); chiffchaff (2); wood warbler (1); spotted flycatcher (2); dunnock (3); pied wagtail (1); starling (2); greenfinch (2); goldfinch (2); linnet (2); bullfinch (2); chaffinch (2); corn bunting (1); yellowhammer (1); reed bunting (1); house sparrow (2); tree sparrow (2).

A mere tally, a collection of names and numbers, it is nevertheless shorthand for a story encapsulating the strengths and weaknesses of a single, isolated nature reserve. A sizeable proportion of the species listed are here, there and everywhere; kitchen window birds which merit an annual entry in the top 20 of the RSPB's Big Garden Birdwatch. Great tit, blue tit, robin, blackbird, woodpigeon, chaffinch, dunnock, wren. Ubiquitous and adaptable, wide-ranging and common.

But then other birds pop up in the list that tell stories of vastly changed fortunes. Not one, but two pairs of turtle doves! A bird that – as I write this – is heading towards extinction in Britain at a faster rate than any bird in history. What can one wood do to save the turtle dove? Can it tackle disappearing and deteriorating habitat in Africa, or stop the hunters' guns on the bird's migration through continental Europe?

The lesser spotted woodpecker, breeding here in 1976, has vanished from a third of its East Anglian haunts within a quarter of a century. Lesser whitethroat – the wood was then bountiful and suitable for two pairs. A decade later, drought in the African Sahel would send this migrant's numbers plummeting. Wood warbler – now almost completely absent from southeast England, possibly because of changes in its African wintering grounds.

The tree sparrow was the very last bird on the list and low in the '70s pecking order too. While Julian Limentani was making his entries, the RSPB, at its headquarters just six miles away, was pondering how to keep over-abundant tree sparrows out of its nestboxes, in favour of brightly coloured blue tits – a bird much more desirable than these plain old ten-a-penny sparrows. Nobody then could have predicted a dramatic nationwide collapse in the tree sparrow population.

Waresley Wood is Everywood, typifying what has been happening right across the country. A decade ago, Rob Fuller of the British Trust for Ornithology helped lead a massive bird survey of British woods. Ornithologists – mostly volunteers – searched 406 woods across Britain. It was a repeat of a survey that had been carried out in the 1980s and – in many cases – the 1970s and 1960s too.

The results made for sober reading. Numbers of breeding birds had fallen by a fifth since 1976, the year Julian Limentani made his count in Waresley Wood. There were half as many bullfinches, lesser spotted woodpeckers, marsh tits, song thrushes, spotted flycatchers, tree pipits and willow tits as there had been in 1976. Dunnock, goldcrest, lesser redpoll, mistle thrush, willow warbler and wood warbler numbers had all dropped by a quarter.

Rob Fuller had begun to notice all was not well with woodland birds long before the survey confirmed his suspicions. Suffolk's substantial Bradfield Woods were within home reach for him, and he had begun going there in the mid-1980s, to count its breeding birds. After introduced muntjac and then fallow deer had begun to appear in the woods, he saw that the structure of the wood had started to change substantially. The undergrowth was being grazed out by the deer.

Over the same period, Rob Fuller was counting fewer and fewer nesting long-distance migrant birds, especially garden warblers and nightingales. The garden warbler, a species that, despite its name, does not breed in gardens and is famous for having no distinguishing features, arrives from Africa, slips into the anonymity of a thicket, sings like a clarinet and eats bugs within its leafy fortress. The male garden warbler makes up to 20 so-called 'cock nests' the female will build her nest and raise her young on one of these basic straw platforms, still within the shrubby under-growth. Everything for the garden warbler – and the night-ingale too – is geared to a breeding season of cover and concealment.

When Bradfield Woods' coppices were eaten out, there was nowhere for them to hide. Rob Fuller fenced an area to prevent deer entering, and carried on monitoring over the next few years. There were significantly more birds breeding within the deer exclosure than beyond the makeshift pale.

But does that tell the whole story? The Suffolk Wildlife Trust began culling deer to reduce the damage they were causing. Yet nightingales continued to decline. On a May evening nowadays, a visitor might walk into Bradfield Woods and listen for nightingales. Even after the last black-bird falls silent at dusk, there is not a single nightingale to be heard.

Perhaps we can console ourselves with good news from the nationwide survey. Eleven of the 34 species monitored saw their numbers increase, among them blackcaps, blue tits, green woodpeckers, robins and treecreepers.

There are the birds that didn't appear at all in Limentani's class of 76, new arrivals for which we give thanks today. He saw no great spotted woodpeckers at all during a whole year of surveying. It's a bird that is almost guaranteed to draw attention to itself on every visit today, chipping from a treetop. There were no buzzards mewing overhead as one did last week, when I could hear but not see it through the canopy. Their spread back from the west to fill the great blanks of eastern Britain, after gamekeepers lowered their guns and thought better of their traps, was still decades away.

A single sparrowhawk seen in the winter of 75 testified to the continuing nationwide dearth caused by chemicals such as DDT. How different things were the other day when I came with friends who had never visited the wood before. A great scattering twitter of small birds from one corner of the wood was followed by a gliding hawk. It provoked a knowing smile. But nobody said anything. It was a sparrowhawk. Not such a big deal these days.

* * *

A common bird with rare character calls from a little way down the ride. It seems to be leading me down the 'garden path', keeping just ahead, fluttering out into the open, slipping back into the wings, peeping out again. All the while, it gives its siren call – 'hweet!', by turns plaintive, yearning, coaxing. Out of the wood the bird and I go and around the outer edge. And there it is on a branch, barely an outstretched arm away.

It is a chiffchaff, a bird whose jingle bookends every summer, the random assortment of chiff and chaff a curtain-raiser for migrating birds, the September reprise of 'chiff chaff chaff, chiff chiff chaff' signing off the season as it heads south again. In the months when it is on the move, it keeps its distance. When it is settled in its territory, it can be unaccountably confiding. The sly robin says 'dig me a worm' and sidles up close in anticipation. But we have nothing to offer a chiffchaff. The bugs nestling in cracks and fissures high up in the trees are beyond the reach of human fingers.

This pert warbler, light-bellied and with a vivid mascara eye-stripe, calls to me, or so I fondly believe, moving so quickly that it appears to be running up the branches. It seems to follow a loose pattern – call, move, call, move, sometimes two moves to one call, up to the outer twigs of one bush, then down to the next. In these giddy moments when I imagine empathy between human and a wild creature, this wood is home and I am filled with indescribable happiness.

UNDER THE PLOUGH

'The land has to be used in a manner likely to produce something useful and not to breed butterflies.'

Major the Honourable Mountjoy-Fane
(in a letter of 1977 responding to a request to
preserve a five-acre oak copse in Lincolnshire)

On a low ridge ten miles south of Bedfordshire's county town, one of William the Conqueror's lesser nobles put up a motte and bailey castle. A descendant followed the medieval craze for creating deer parks; it was an obligatory status symbol for every knight of standing. It seems the whole family was wiped out in the Black Death, though the essence of the park lived on in its woodland. A map of 1711 shows Cainhoepark Wood as a tipsy rectangle. It was still there on the wonk in the 1960s.

Standing on the very top of the castle mound today, it is still possible to look out over the trees of that wood. But there are very few of them to see – they are but a thin green line and from this summit, we can peer between the trunks into daylight and open land beyond. An aerial view shows that what is left of the wood resembles corner mounts in a photo album. There is no picture in the middle, save a canvas of wheat or oilseed rape.

Britain is full of these odd little wooded shards that were once part of greater wholes, the pieces of jigsaws that are no longer complete. Balneath Wood, near Lewes in East Sussex, was once a great oak wood oblong; it has been left looking like a red deer's antlers. Immediately to the west of Telford in Shropshire is Big Wood Cottage. There is no big wood. Instead, there is a scatter of tiny copses edging irregular arable fields, the clumps still bearing the names that served them within a great wooded conglomeration. Today, in their shrunken isolation, they make little sense: the middle has dropped out of the once central part of the wood that was named Middle Wood. All that remains are two separate copses, both called Middle Wood.

Between 1945 and 1985, as Britain's hardwoods were being replaced by conifer plantations, one-tenth of all ancient woodland went under the plough, with southern and eastern England especially affected. Not that many woods disappeared altogether: thousands were only dismembered.

You might walk around Devichoys Wood in Cornwall today and look out over the small fields on its eastern boundary that used to be woodland. The old wood has left an impression on today's farmland. Straight edges between fields follow the exact course of its broad rides; the meandering border between two arable fields a path through a wood that, in 1945, was about three times its present size.

Many woods went in for a light trim. West of Stowmarket in Suffolk, Great Wood has a straight northern boundary. It was not always so; a humpbacked section was sliced straight off, like the top off a boiled egg.

I have gone looking for so many of these absent woods to seek their presence. But I find it impossible to turn a wheat field into a wood in my mind's eye, to imagine that the fine tilth of a field put to winter rest can ever have been anything other than cultivated land. Even lumpy, ploughed soil that throws up the past casts out no branches, no stumps, no clues to its previous life. Relics may still be there in diminished copses and thin belts of trees, but it seems only an old map can fill in the blanks where woodland once stood.

It is hardly credible to us now that, in the closing years of the war, most naturalists failed to see that this would happen. Sir Arthur Tansley, the ecologist who correctly foretold the coming of conifers, was less prescient when it came to agriculture. In his otherwise visionary book of 1944, he predicted: 'The great increase of ploughland that has been made during the war will probably not be wholly maintained, but a considerable part will rightly continue to be cultivated.'

Had Tansley (and many other experts who agreed with him) been a reader of *Farmer's Weekly*, he might not have been so certain. In its first issue of 1943, the magazine's editorial showed an industry hungry for continued expansion: 'We have seen during the war how infinitely responsive our land is and how resourceful our farming genius is, even when working under great disabilities of shortage of labour, of equipment, of supplies. But all of us know, too, that there still remain vast potentialities of production as yet hardly tapped.'

*   *   *

On a late summer morning, I am sitting in the kitchen of Norfolk farmer Chris Skinner. He opens the conversation by plonking a twisted lump of metal down on the table. It is the size of a guinea pig and the weight of a cat. He tells me that on a summer night in 1941, his pregnant mother was running for the air raid shelter when the German bombs came down and this great shred of shrapnel ripped right through the farmhouse's foot-thick outer wall and embedded itself in the wall of the nursery. Rock-a-bye-baby. Another lump dislodged all the apples from the tree over the fleeing Mrs Skinner, and she screamed in fright, thinking she had been hit by an exploding bomb.

For a generation of farmers who waited in the silence and heard the enemy planes come over their land, night after night, feeding a besieged and bomb-battered country gave them a heightened sense of purpose. Chris Skinner recalled: 'My father took his role very seriously. You were doing your war effort; it was the same as being a soldier on the front line.'

The farmer was there to feed the nation and the whole nation was behind him. That spirit of zeal and purpose continued long after the war was over. Every summer, the vicar of Caister St Edmunds took the whole congregation around the Skinners' farm and blessed the crops.

Everyone wanted an end to food rationing, everyone wanted more food, cheaper food. Governments saw it as a way to reduce the balance of payments deficit in a war-bankrupted country. They brought in the Agriculture Act of 1947. It did away with the economics of supply and demand: it guaranteed farmers fixed prices for everything they produced. The more they grew, the more money they would earn.

One side of parliament was filled with natural allies, the farming and landowning Conservative MPs with vested interests, but members on the government bench were equally supportive. Farmers were the nation's darlings. The first post-war Labour government expressed its unqualified

Derek Niemann

support and gratitude through the minister of agriculture, Tom Williams:

> Our present economic position requires that we should produce an increasing proportion of our food from our own soil and for the next few years we shall need to grow relatively high acreages of grain, potatoes and other crops. The Government greatly appreciate the voluntary response which farmers have made to the crop targets set for 1948 and are confident that they can rely on the great majority for a continuation of their efforts to meet the country's needs.

(HC Deb 21 June 1948 vol 452 cc106-7W)

There was no question that, in the minds of those with influence in the agricultural world, woods were one of the key obstructions to progress. 'Too often the hedgerows and small woodlands are mere nuisances to farming, harbours for rabbits, pests and weeds; the value of the timber is far outweighed by the damage to which they give rise,' complained Sir Alfred Daniel Hall, principal of the agricultural Wye College and director of the Rothamsted Experimental Station. People listened when he said: 'What angers one is the multiplicity of patches, perhaps no more than a few acres in extent, of neglected, overcrowded trees intruded on to good farming land.'

In a period of mechanisation, better and faster-growing crops, pesticides, herbicides and fertilisers, woods quickly became obsolete. The farming world developed a vocabulary in which there was a presumption that cultivation was the natural state of all land. There was much use of the word 'reclamation' – to *win back or away from vice*

73

or error or savagery or waste condition' (Oxford English Dictionary). The inference was clear: farmers were reasserting the natural order of things by 'reclaiming' fields.

Reporting the clearance of an ancient wood, *Farmer's Weekly* could say that 'after felling, roots were grubbed out and land restored to arable'. Restored? On land that might have been wooded since the last Ice Age, long before the first humans had even appeared, never mind planted their first crops?

The government commissioned agricultural researchers at Wye College to examine the potential for woodland 'reclamation' in England and Wales. They arrived at the colossal figure of 383,000 acres. 'The figures suggest the existence of a large acreage of woodland which is both unproductive and uneconomic for forestry management and which, if not put to some other use, will remain derelict and a harbour for pests.'

So woods were not only redundant, they even had a detrimental effect on modern farming. They had to go. How could it be done efficiently and cost-effectively? For years, agricultural scientists wrestled with field trials until they had answers. In 1957, the ministry published a booklet entitled *The Reclamation of Derelict Woodland for Agricultural Use*. The results from a trial experiment carried out on four Hampshire farms were laid out before the reader.

The booklet proclaimed nothing but good news for the improving farmer. Rates of return were:

...so high that it might be asked why farmers were not willing to undertake operations of this kind on their own initiative. The answer may be twofold. In the first place farmers may not have considered reclamation as a practical possibility until the provisions of the Marginal Production

Scheme brought it to their notice. Secondly, even if they had done so and were favourably impressed by the potential results, they might not have been willing or able to put up the full sum of capital required... The results of the investigation suggest that many farmers with isolated areas of derelict woodland on their holdings would be well advised to explore the possibilities of reclaiming it to agriculture.

By February 1959, the latest Ministry of Agriculture bulletin was published, and at twelve shillings and six pence for a dozen copies, it would have been popular with the government advisors who were touring farms and estates. Fixed Equipment of the Farm Leaflet No. 37 was entitled *Tree, Bush and Stump Clearance*. From 1960 onwards, the loss of woodland to agriculture intensified. The publication date can hardly be a coincidence.

* * *

An archivist from the Museum of English Rural Life has kindly pulled this potent publication out of the vault for my arrival. It is such a grimly matter-of-fact little booklet. A pen-and-ink sketch on the cover shows a tiny shadowy figure on a bulldozer, gamely attacking an impenetrable thicket of stems, as if he were an ant trying to weed a flowerbed gone wild.

The photographic plates inside are a machinefest of agricultural implements. Farmers would understand the images and the language – there is 'a heavy crawler tractor fitted with a long-reach arm for maximum leverage in pushing over large trees', and a man wearing a jacket pictured astride the tractor busy toppling an oak.

Various bits of machinery 'specially designed' for

'woodland reclamation' are depicted, such as the curved tines (teeth) that penetrate tree roots and lift them from the ground. A gaping hole in a morass shows where a farmer has dug out a tree, roots, stump and all. Better by far is the use of explosives. The results are shown in the picture below, where the hole is small, the land readier for crops, the stump of a giant oak shattered into smaller, removeable pieces.

Here was the means to an end, the indispensable guide for the man with a bigger, better bulldozer than ever before. And he needed to act quickly: 'It is advisable to get the clearance done quickly so that cropping can begin and income accrue as soon as possible.' There was, however, a cautionary note to guard farmers against trying to do too much clearance at once. And a warning against bothering on land which was 'badly drained and inaccessible'.

What land should the farmer tackle first? An answer was forthcoming:

> Derelict unwanted coppice, game preserves and amenity land are often ideal in size for reclamation. They frequently lie on land quite comparable with the remainder of the farm... although the initial cost of clearing is often high, good returns usually make this type of work attractive to the farmer.

There was a handy tip for clearing out the undergrowth of a wood before felling, one that the Mear family of Waresley probably followed:

> Grazing pigs in woodlands prior to reclamation will result in considerable destruction of small growth and an undoubted easing of the main task... Pig-running may lead to one or

two years' delay in getting the first crop from the site, but if reclamation is not contemplated immediately, this preliminary treatment is worth consideration.

The mechanics of clearance were covered in detail. Every type of tree, bush, wood, copse, hedge and spinney was examined. There was even a proposed order of clearance. Nothing was left to chance:

When all valuable timber has been felled, only misshapen trees which will not suffer unduly from rough treatment will normally remain standing. The only advantage in removing them without prior felling lies in the leverage provided by their trunks... Large stumps, often hidden in the undergrowth, may result from clear felling of timber trees, or they may remain after useless trees have been felled... After removal of trees and stumps many roots and pieces of wood remain firmly entrenched in the ground – particularly after bulldozing. These can be removed by the use of a special undercutter, which cuts the roots and brings them to the surface... One and a half acres of rubbish piled up to about 15 ft often remains after clearing 10 acres of woodland. Such a quantity can rarely be buried and should never be left on the surface, where it soon compacts into solid, pest-harbouring mounds. Burning is the only solution.

A tempting bait was dangled before the doubtful farmer or landowner on the last page: 'Grant Aid is available for this type of work under the Farm Improvement Scheme. One third of the cost may be paid to either landowners or farmers provided the work is deemed to constitute an improvement to a farm and approval is granted before the work commences.'

So, by the late 1950s, the farming industry, government and all, had created the incentives and the technical support to encourage woodland clearance. How did the various types of farmer and landowner respond to its exhortations?

Born at the stately home of Cliveden, the fifth child of Britain's first woman to sit as an MP, Michael Astor did not emulate his mother Nancy, but bowed out of politics after six unremarkable years as a Surrey MP, and followed his father's lead. Waldorf Astor had been a significant modernising figure in pre-war agriculture and his son showed a similarly progressive outlook. He bought the Hatley Estate near Cambridge and spent the rest of his life innovating. He took out the estate's hedges, straightened the fields, turned hay meadows into monocultures of ryegrass, lost a copse or two and listened intently to the views of neighbouring, equally progressive landowners. Animals were his thing: he bred pedigree Hereford cows, chickens and pigs, and converted much of the land into a stud farm. He eventually became chairman of the Agricultural Research Council. A 39-hectare ancient wood had come as part of the estate. The timber of Cockayne Hatley Wood had been taken out during the war to make Mosquito aircraft: the bulldozers were practically waiting for the rest. Yet when Michael Astor died in 1980, his son Micky inherited the exact same 39-hectare wood, and without so much as a conifer needle in the undergrowth. Sitting at a table in a stone-flagged farm office, with estate maps and pictures of racehorses on the walls, Micky tells me he can still remember his father's words: 'I'm not going to touch the wood. I can't go wrong by not touching it. It will survive like that.'

In his highly individual behaviour, Michael Astor senior epitomised the sheer unpredictability of large landowners' treatment of their woods. Curiously, there was an unwritten rule of thumb that ensured the survival of many: woodland should make up ten per cent of a good estate. Every land-owner should have his woods and, generally speaking, the bigger the landowner, the more likely woods were to survive.

The barons, earls, lords and ladies, whose families had owned estates for centuries, often placed a high value on traditions and continuity. They were also generally sensi-tive to their standing in the local community. The estate was part of who they were. There might be sentimental reasons for saving the oak wood visible from the windows of a country home. The old woods might provide a place to walk, a pleasant spot for guests, a screen from prying public eyes. Individual trees might be named; they could be dearly remembered landmarks from the owner's childhood.

For generations, the incumbent Lord Salisbury and his family at Hatfield House called the veteran trees in the estate's parkland their 'Grand Old Masters', and estate foresters traded acorns with Windsor Great Park to boost genetic diversity. They still do. Park foresters were under orders to shelter and cosset the mighty oak, hornbeam and lime pollards unto death and beyond. The tree under which the first Queen Elizabeth reputedly sat when she heard that her sister Mary had died raised its last green flag when an elder sprouted from its hollow trunk. The dead hulk was displayed at the entrance of the park, until it rotted away.

Landowners might – as we saw in an earlier chapter – take advantage of the government-sponsored dedication scheme to coniferise their woods. There was one major factor stopping wholesale adoption of the scheme for many – plantations would be cold places with bare floors. They would be no good for pheasants, ground-feeding birds of the woodland margins that rarely ventured more than 50 metres from the woodland edge. Pheasants like old woods; they love the sunny glades, the abundant seeds and insects in the undergrowth. Countless woods were valued enough to be saved for the shoot, though not necessarily in their entirety. You couldn't draw game out of the open heart of a big wood, so it could be advantageous to make woods smaller, or break them into pieces.

A sizeable rung down from the great landowners, most owners of small to medium-sized farms, lacking estate workers with forestry skills, saw no value in woodland. It could even be a source of annoyance. Eric Carter of the Farming and Wildlife Advisory Group pinpointed the reasons for their lack of enthusiasm:

I am not entirely convinced that farmers do clear woodland solely to increase agricultural production... I suspect the motives are mixed. For a farmer, it is easier to manage land under crops than under woodland, they do not understand it and see the returns, if any, as too long-term to be of interest. Woodland tends to be untidy and to harbour vertebrate pests so that clearance offers a solution to these problems.

There was every reason to conform to views that were buttressed by *Farmer's Weekly* and on farming programmes on the radio, and reinforced by peer pressure from fellow farmers at the cattle market, or neighbours over the soon-to-be-removed hedge. A farmer might, for example, do the next-door farmer a favour by taking out the wood that was casting a shadow over his crop.

In the post-war years, every farm received two kinds of official visitor. The man who turned up on his own once a month was welcomed universally. He came from the Ministry of Agriculture's advisory service (called ADAS after 1971). He was well educated; in most cases, far better educated than the people he was coming to advise, and he came with ideas on how to help the farmer make more money from his land. The advisor's primary role was to boost production and, from 1950 onwards, productivity was rising by an average of 2.5 per cent each year. Farmers were inclined to listen and act on what he had to offer. The Mear family of Waresley were certainly beguiled by promises.

Some of the schemes to increase output were, to say the least, ill-advised. Farmers in Mid Wales were strongly encouraged to create more grazing land for sheep, and were given grants to clear hanging woods, plough and turn land over to ryegrass, without any regard to topography. One farmer trying to plough a 45-degree slope was killed when his tractor toppled over.

They were offered incentives for making farm tracks, but without those tracks necessarily having any functional purpose. Many farmers in Mid Wales already had plenty of natural stone in their fields, so they could make a tidy profit from pocketing the money and creating roads to nowhere. They didn't want to put stony tracks through good farming land though – instead they ran them right through their woods. On a wooded hill under multiple ownership near Llanidloes, every farmer cashed in, driving roads up to the top. Ray Woods was the government's regional nature advisor at the time. He objected in vain to despoliation that turned the hill 'into a pit tip'.

There were perhaps mixed feelings about the second type of visitor. Leading farmers in each district formed themselves into county agricultural executive committees, successors to the dictatorial wartime committees known as War Ags. Periodically, these self-appointed committees would descend on a farm, to pontificate on how the farmer could fulfil his duty to maximise production.

A parliamentary question put to the agriculture minister by the MP for heavily wooded Horsham in Sussex in 1951 demonstrates not just the direction these committees were taking, but also hints at the prevalent, coercive attitude they displayed:

> Earl Winterton asked the Minister of Agriculture if he is aware that hundreds of acres of land, which had reverted to scrub or was derelict woodland, have recently been successfully bulldozed for reversion to food production in the Weald of Surrey and West Sussex by various owners; and if, in view of the amount of such derelict land still remaining, he will call the attention of the agricultural executive committees to the matter.

The minister of agriculture, Tom Williams, replied:

> Yes, Sir, I am fully alive to the fact that reclamation work has been carried out by owners or occupiers of scrub-land and derelict woodland during recent years in the interests of food production. The attention of county agricultural executive committees has already been called to the possibility of bringing this type of land into fuller production, and under the marginal production scheme a limited amount of financial assistance for this purpose is available to occupiers of farms.

> (HC Deb 01 February 1951 vol 483 cc1073-4)

For owner occupiers, there was the small, but

nevertheless real threat under the 1947 Agricultural Act, of compulsory purchase by the government if they did not demonstrate 'the full and efficient use of the land for agriculture'. In an eleven-year period, 5,000 farmers were put under supervisory orders, and 400 had their farms taken off them. Geoff Hearnden, who had farmed in both Devon and Lincolnshire, felt it had no influence on how he had run his farms. But it may well have weighed on others elsewhere, who may have had more demanding and less sympathetic agricultural committees bearing down on them.

Every farm and every wood has its own particular story. The Bedfordshire farmer who bought Cainhoe Manor Farm in 1972 had a bigger and more diverse landholding than the Mear family of Waresley. Within a year, he had assessed his land, and judged that he had more than enough woodland. In selecting one for removal, he chose Cainhoepark Wood. 'I cleared it to grow more food. I got a grant to clear the wood and a grant to drain the land. I enjoy hunting and it's better for sport now than it was. A big area of woodland is no good,' he told me.

In attempting to clear the wood, the farmer encountered an obstacle that was to partially thwart a number of such initiatives. Under the Town and Country Planning Act of 1947, local authorities were empowered to place Tree Preservation Orders (TPOs) on single trees, groups of trees, or even whole woodlands on the grounds of 'amenity value'. For reasons unknown, one such TPO had been placed by the local council on large trees in the north-east and south-west corners of Cainhoepark Wood. Over a two-year period, contractors simply hollowed out the wood as far as rides on the fringes, leaving the protected trees within the thin photo-mount edges, and allowing the farmer perfect cover and good sightlines for his pheasant shooting.

In 1992, early purple orchids flowered in Cainhoepark Wood for the very last time. Today, the farmer is open and matter-of-fact about what the government paid him to do: 'There's still plenty of woodland and we've planted more.'

What about the farmers who did not own the fields they sowed? Tenant farmers were responsible for two-thirds of England and Wales's farmed land. New legislation enabled them to hold farms for three generations; that continuity acted as a spur to invest in improvements. One such figure was Norfolk's Chris Skinner, the middle generation farmer in a three-generation tenancy.

If farmers were trees, then Chris Skinner would be an oak. He is stocky, weather-beaten, with thick boughs for arms and giant, acorn-brown hands. But there is more to this metaphor than the merely physical. This man grew out of the soil, was nourished by it and by the animals it fed. He seems to know every knot in every tree, every plant, every brick of the rust-red farmhouse. He talks to me while keeping a watchful, all-seeing eye on everything and everyone around. For those of us contemplating yet another house move, fickle flitters from place to place, it is worth considering that this man has spent his entire life rooted to the spot. He is, in every sense, from the land, and of this land.

There are two aspects of this farmer's life that are particularly relevant to this story. The first is that Chris Skinner breathes conservation. He grows wildlife – barn owls, hares, badgers, skylarks, reed buntings, solitary bees, grass snakes and orchids. He has turned over his whole farm to environmental objectives. And what do his neigh-bours think of what he is doing? 'They hate me. They say I'm not a real farmer.' Facing disapproval and hostility on all sides, he has the moral strength to act out of conviction. He deserves applause.

A generation ago, the wind blew from a different direction for Chris Skinner.

I can still remember Gordon Long. He was my hero. He would come to the farm with his bulldozer every year. I still remember the smell of the harvest, the bullocks and bales in the background. He would bulldoze round a large oak tree, a tiny bulldozer, about 50 horsepower, with tracks and a bulldozer blade on the front. And he'd dig all the way round these oak trees because oaks have a huge tap root that goes into the ground almost as far as the trunk goes upwards. He'd dig down, take all of the radial roots off and that caused the bulldozer to cough out black smoke. If it was raining he'd carry on regardless.

He must have taken out 200 oak trees. Some of them were sold, most of them were just put on a fire and burnt. You were creating more arable land and more arable land meant more profit. It was so dangerous what he was doing, but because he was so skilled, you didn't worry about it – he would dig down eight or nine feet and leave this oak tree on a pedestal – on one root. Then he'd push the soil in on one side so that he got some purchase and push the oak tree over. And to see a tiny little tractor 30 or 40 years old doing that – it was the bee's knees. Although it seems criminal today to think of it, you were a young man, you were helping the country, you were going to grow more crops. And if a conservationist had come up to me and said: 'Do you know that tree is 200 years old?' I would have said: 'I don't care.'

The young Chris Skinner was a zealous moderniser, even

spending time in New Zealand to learn more about how he could boost yields on the family farm. In those 'improving' years, model tenant farmers such as the Skinners, embracing the new ways with passion and skill, were congratulated and showcased; they were even asked to take on apprentices.

Tenants in hill farms had no incentive to protect the woodlands within the land they farmed, and good incentives to neglect them. The timber was not theirs to harvest and, had they kept their sheep out of the woods in the growing season, it would have given them less grazing land for no benefit. Since the tenants were encouraged by government payments to keep high numbers of sheep, they freely made use of the woods as 'barns with leaves'. All year long, sheep grazed the ground, nibbling out the woodland flowers and chewing up tree seedlings. There would come a time on plenty of farms when it would be near impossible to tell whether the scattered individual old trees had ever been ancient woodland at all.

At the bottom of the rural hierarchy were the agricultural labourers. Many a farm worker living in a tied cottage delivered the coup de grace to a copse or hedgerow. They had no alternative. The owners of rapidly mechanising farms had jobs for their hired hands in the growing season and at harvest time. But machinery had taken over their tasks during the winter months, and so they were set to tidying up, rationalising, bringing new land into production. When their work was done and there was nothing left for them to clear or do, they lost their jobs, their homes and their way of life.

Tunnel vision

On a hot Midsummer's Day, I am on Mear's Ride, the narrower of the two main thoroughfares that form a V-shape through the wood. I'm inching down the path on what the calendar deems an auspicious day, a hinge between spring and summer, a moment for enjoying flowers past, present and future.

The future is like a miniature cauliflower. It is a pathside plant with a vegetable bloom that will blossom in a few days into poetic-sounding meadowsweet. Meadowsweet? I sniff and smell sweet nothing.

The past is a crop of marbles on stalks. It's hard to remember that these were beautiful bluebells only weeks ago. Each seedpod is a cross between a lemon and a deflating balloon, dull green in the shade, translucent when pierced by shafts of sunlight. The overlong stems have grown straight and brittle. Before long, they will bow, keel over and look, dare I say it, untidy. Ragged robin too, clustering in the damp dips after moisture, is beginning to fade. The petals, twisting in on themselves as they shrivel, are sugarpink and look as if they have been through a strimmer. Ragged they are.

The present is everywhere, with every flower crowding in to share this open strip, bathed in sunshine. It feels criminal to go at anything faster than a snail's pace, lest I miss the snails with their striped coils, and everything else that glitters and glints, creeps and crawls. Each plant tells a story and a story within the story. There is cuckoo spit frothing under a meadowsweet leaf and a blackfly trapped in its bubbles. One insect, an infant froghopper, is cocooned safely in the foam; the other, the helpless blackfly, is on the outside, fatally pinned to the sticky mass. The wood is a cornucopia of superabundance and I could linger here all day.

There are common spotted orchids peeping out between grass stems, framed by buttercups. The orchid petals have a drizzle of mauve; the spots are on the leaves, uneven blobs dabbed by a beginner in watercolours. This year, there are about 200 flower 'spikes'; last year there were 50. Some of the flowers are shading in the direction of purple; some colour up cream.

At the ride junction, I take a left. This is where I'm sure I'll encounter it, as I have so often in summers past. The broad, straight ride acts like a pedestrian subway, a tunnel with solid walls on either side. Meet a stranger in the subway coming the other way and you cannot but be funnelled into acknowledging each other's presence. Even an aversion of the eyes is noticed. It is in this situation that it is possible to have the most meaningful encounter with one of Britain's most remarkable creatures. And if I were small enough to fit in my own pocket, I would be very scared indeed.

Down the tunnel comes a hawker dragonfly, an insect that combines the bulk of a Lancaster bomber with the speed and agility of a Tornado jet. The ride is a prime hunting ground for hawker dragonflies, and they are seriously big; the smallest dragonfly is 3.2cm long; this southern hawker measures 7cm. It is not strength that has brought it here though; it is weakness.

The pond is a dangerous place, full of fiercely territorial rivals that could be deadly to a newly emerged dragonfly, exhausted by the effort of metamorphosis. Some wise instinct tells infant dragonflies to get the hell out of there, to feed and build up their strength elsewhere, travelling as far as necessary to find a safer location. A wood offering a sheltered tunnel full of flying food and sunshine is perfect.

I watch it come down the ride with confident surges and sideways swoops. At the point of confrontation, I give it pause for thought. It stops in the middle of the path, facing me at head height, body absolutely still, wings thrumming. A series of jerky, robotic moves take the hovering insect up a bit, down a bit, to the left, to the right. The dragonfly is appraising me and, given the disparity in our sizes, it is unnerving, but safely so. Dragonfly experts say that a meeting of this nature is surely the most powerful experience a human can have of an insect actively thinking about us, weighing us up, making split-second decisions and choices. Is this an insect relating to a human being as a fellow creature?

What can this insect poised so expertly in mid-air see? A pigment in the human eye called opsin allows us to detect red, blue and green and make our rainbow out of those colours. Research suggests that a dragonfly, with its multi-lensed compound eyes, can see anything between eleven and 30 colours in the spectrum. That dragonfly is looking at a walking kaleidoscope. But am I predator or prey? It loops over my head and off down the ride, suggesting it has opted for the former. *But then it flies back* for a second look. Genevieve Dalley of the British Dragonfly Society offers a strictly scientific explanation for such behaviour: 'It's really nosey.'

Dragonflies display no territoriality in woods – they have

no reason to do so, and plenty of reasons not to. As a result of these winged truces, numbers can build up. I remember an August day in the beech hanger above Gilbert White's Selborne, where common darters were so numerous along a fence-line that they could have formed a dragon daisy chain. When this hawker has fed and grown strong enough, it will return to its natal pond, and challenge rivals for the chance to mate. In time, it will drive other dragons into the wood.

Scientists are still coming to appreciate just how important woodland rides and glades are to dragonflies. One of Britain's rarest dragonflies, the white-faced darter, once thrived on the meres and mosses of the Cheshire plain. What do they have to do with woodland? Our understanding today is that, historically, this weak flier would be able to find new pools and ponds by dispersing through woods, because it could take a series of sheltered short-hop flights from tree to tree. The loss of its breeding ponds will have been crucial to its decline. But so too would be the disappearance of the fringing woods and copses that would have provided the essential bridges. In Delamere Forest, the Cheshire Wildlife Trust and the Forestry Commission are restoring the mires and translocating darter larvae to the ponds. Such a scheme has already worked in Cumbria; surely it can work in Cheshire too?

The spectre of development

An enticing voice on the phone says: 'Take me to a wood and I will walk you through 2,000 years of history.' Ian Rotherham does a very good sales pitch. He tells me there are 80 pieces of ancient woodland around where he lives. These clusters of sylvan antiquity are not in some leafy corner of unblemished countryside, but in one of the most heavily industrialised cities in Europe. He is talking about his home city of Sheffield.

We have stopped the car on a busy road, with woodland on either side, a short distance from where Ian grew up. Sheffield is where he has spent just about all of his working life, first as the city ecologist and now as a lecturer in environmental history at Sheffield Hallam University. For me, he is a professor of bumps.

Ecclesall Woods is criss-crossed with paths. From time to time, we say hello to dog-walking women, pat their dogs, nod greetings to joggers. The kids are just back at school after their summer holidays. Shutting out the swoosh of traffic, it is quiet, calm, soothing.

People used to come here on Sundays. The day was well named for the locality; it was the only day of the week when the factory chimneys stopped belching smoke and you could actually see the sun. Ian rests his hand on a smallish young oak tree. It looks little more than a sapling. 'I'd say this is maybe 150 years old.' The trees here are stunted; those species that struggled with the smog of the industrial age simply died out. There are no limes here – there are whole woods of small-leaved lime 30 miles away, free from the pall of polluted air.

We have come to our first bump. Or rather a dip, a depression, a giant's thumb press, a Jacuzzi half-filled with leaves. With a bit of pointed-finger guidance from my tutor, I can just about make out its peculiar trademark, a trench-like slash running out of the lower end. This distinctive shape has given this crater its name – it is called a Q pit. Ian says there are about 150 in Ecclesall Woods. Historians know that these were the foundations of Elizabethan industrial kilns, used to turn wood from the surrounding trees into 'whitecoal', a type of charcoal for smelting lead made a a lower heat. But how exactly this was done is a complete mystery: the process was kept secret, handed down by illiterate fathers to illiterate sons and, when a better method was found around 1650, the secret died with the last workers.

Ancient wood experts overlooked Ecclesall. Where are the flowers? they asked. Where are the plants that would indicate this wood is ancient? They did not understand that the topsoil had been stripped, that the Elizabethan white-coal workers had cut turf to roof their kilns.

In one showery afternoon, Ian is training me to look for barely perceptible aberrations in the natural contours. A bump like a speed hump is the boundary marker between the Saxon kingdoms of Mercia and Northumbria. A linear hollow was the tramway where ponies pulled carts along wooden rails. There are flattened patches on the slopes where you might rake your fingers through the soil and find the blackened, weightless pieces of charcoal from one of about 350 charcoal-burning hearths. Museums in the city centre tell of Sheffield's industrial past, but you can feel it, smell it, touch it here too, the heritage preserved in a living exhibition.

*   *   *

Early naturalists feared the people of Sheffield. They dreaded the urban, fecund, aspiring masses, overflowing out of town and city centres to swallow up the countryside with housing and factories. It is not surprising that the Council for the Preservation of Rural England (CPRE) was founded in 1926, its main purpose being to control the unrestricted development that had resulted in four million homes being thrown up in open countryside after the Great War.

Pressure from the CPRE and others led to the first Town and Country Planning Act in 1932. Thereafter, prior permission would be required for built development. If there was to be post-war destruction of woods by housing and industry, then it would be officially sanctioned destruction.

Future wildlife film-maker John Burton lived through unchecked creeping urbanisation as London sprawled in pre-war Britain; indeed he was an unwitting part of it.

When I was boy living in northwest Kent in the 1930s, there was still a good deal of unbuilt-on countryside in the vicinity, including Coldharbour Farm, one of the last working farms within the old County of London boundary. The council estate where I lived with my family was itself built on open farmland during the mid-1930s. I remember new houses being built in the White Horse Hill of West Chislehurst in the couple of years before the Second World War began.

He also witnessed what came next:

After the war, much of the countryside to the east was
destroyed, including the southern part of Petts Wood
that was not owned by the National Trust. An extension
of Elmstead Wood contained, in the mid-1940s, among
other things, pearl-bordered fritillaries, grizzled skippers,
hawfinches, and wood warblers. In November 1948, I was
much saddened to find it being bulldozed for the construction of a sports ground.

Yet the statistics show that the overall picture for London
was far from grim. A third of the city's woodland today
is ancient; not only that, the great metropolis possesses no
fewer than 200 ancient woodlands larger than two hectares
in size, comprising some 2,600 hectares. Not bad for a big
city and not all that dissimilar a situation to that in Ian
Rotherham's Sheffield.

Why did so many woods in the cities survive? A century
before the war began, they had a clear purpose, essential in
providing firewood for the urban population. What value
did they have by 1945? There were as many factors involved
as there were woods. There was not the same simplicity of
control as in the countryside where, generally speaking, one
person would decide what to do with a wood and act upon
it. There were no threats from agriculture or forestry. There
were, however, common themes to a myriad of stories that
would determine their fate.

A significant number of London's ancient woods became
marooned as green oases within urban development. Some
were the spoils of Victorian battles. Highgate and Queen's
Wood were both the subject of hard-fought campaigns
which led to their preservation. Undoubtedly, some of these

middle-class defenders of woods valued them for their own sake. For others, there was more than a degree of self-interest: a leafy outlook kept house prices up. No Felling In My Back Yard was key to their survival.

Far more woods were secured before the war by local authorities, especially following the break-up of large country estates, for 'public recreation'. Both Oxleas Wood on Watling Street and Coldfall Wood in Haringey were typical, bought in 1930 on that basis. Thousands of Londoners strolled through these woodland parks. They may have trampled the bluebells (and picked plenty more), but they were an army of stakeholders who would ensure that no bulldozer came near the trees.

Other cities followed a similar pattern. Sheffield's Ecclesall Woods was bought by the city council in the 1920s. Tiny Gipton Wood was given to Leeds City Corporation in 1923, which managed it for the local community. Preserved for public access, such woods kept their status, if not necessarily their quality. Did urban wood managers see themselves as park keepers or gamekeepers? Croydon Parks Department staff shot 786 squirrels, 87 foxes, 160 jays, 72 magpies, 37 crows and 155 pigeons in Selsdon Wood over five enthusiastic years in the early 1970s. In the same period, they planted 10,000 larch and Norway spruce trees. There were proposals during the same decade to fell the whole of Sheffield's Ecclesall Woods and replant with red oak and other exotic trees. Thankfully, it didn't happen.

Some woods were untouchable. Steep-sided banks that had hitherto resisted development were still an impossible challenge to developers. They were triumphs of topography, riverside slivers weaving through Gledhow (from Old English 'kite's hill') in Leeds, the dingles of Dudley in the West Midlands, Boggart Hole Clough in Manchester, the banks of the Wear in Durham, Jesmond Dene in Newcastle and along tortuous loops of the river Clyde in Lanarkshire.

Larger woods close to an urban conurbation could be vulnerable if piecemeal clearance had already begun. Bishop's Wood had belonged in medieval times to the Bishop of London, and occupied an enormous expanse of what would become Hampstead Garden Suburb. A pioneering road had cut through it in the 1920s, with houses embedded among the trees along its route. It seemed to mark a fatal compromise of the wood's integrity, a 'divide and fell' policy. Once the first incursions of development had begun, it was all too easy for them to continue. By the 1950s, Bishop's Wood was completely gone.

Developers had snipped away at Southampton's sizeable Bassett Wood for the best part of a hundred years. This process accelerated after the war, leaving a copse surrounded by a well-treed estate of roads. Just as developers might name an ex-field Skylark View (i.e. no skylarks, no view), so they 'preserved' the lost character of the wood by naming the streets of the new housing estate: Aspen Holt, Woodview Close, Bassett Wood Drive...

Urban conurbations benefitted from a great post-war innovation, the so-called green belt policy: 'to provide a reserve supply of public open spaces and of recreational areas and to establish a green belt or girdle of open space'. Often bought by local authorities, the woods in these green ribbons served as playgrounds for city inhabitants. They had a purpose.

But even green belts were not sacrosanct when a government diktat decided otherwise. A remnant of the Forest of Arden in the green belt east of Birmingham was where city dwellers had traditionally gone on bank holiday excursions, taking the train to stroll through their 'bluebell wood' and refresh themselves in tearooms that had sprung up in nearby Marston Green.

Birmingham City Council did not have bluebells in mind when it bought Chelmsley Wood in 1963. It was looking for land on which to build an overspill estate. This was the heyday of social housing and, despite opposition from all four parish councils, housing minister Richard Crossman gave approval for the Solihull suburb that would be called Chelmsley Wood after the wood it paved over with concrete. The roads were built and named: Birch Croft, Rowan Way, Aspen Drive, Beech Avenue, White Beam Road. You start to see a pattern.

Plenty of big towns and cities still have the stubs and slices of bigger woods. There are single grand trees that once marked a woodland boundary but now stand on roadsides. Little pockets of woodland, barely copse-sized, are wedged among houses and schools. Some call these 'shadow woods'.

The Cardiff suburb of Cyncoed ('*coed*' is Welsh for wood), less than two miles from the city centre, has traces of the woodland that gave the suburb its name, woods that were still extensive at the end of the war. There are little more than names left to remind us of Queen Wood, Wern Goch, Well Wood, Chapel Wood, Coed Caegwyddau and the wonderfully named Coed Peggy Giles and Pennsylvania.

We might have expected one huge post-war development initiative to have heralded the end for many rural woods. Britain's new towns were laid out in the aftermath of the war to house thousands rendered homeless by bombing, and later to accommodate overspills and relocate communities in slum housing. They were the successors of a scheme dreamed up by Sir Ebenezer Howard, who created Letchworth and Welwyn Garden City in the 1920s, promising, in wholegrain prose: 'by so laying out a Garden City that, as it grows, the free gifts of Nature, fresh air, sunlight, breathing room and playing room shall be still retained in all needed abundance.'

In the post-war period, huge tranches of countryside were earmarked to fill with populations of up to 60,000. The land was allocated, taken out of local authority control, and given to newly formed corporations to map out. The planners were given a designated area of land where they could build low-density housing, factories, schools, shops and the all-important pub. The portents for ancient woods, those individual, unplanned, purposeless aberrants, were ominous: even as late as 1985, town and country planning did not take wildlife or nature conservation into account, at all. 'Trees are clearly – as far as town and country planning is concerned – a matter of amenity,' pronounced the Ministry of Local Government and Housing. Dog walkers and nice views from your window could be taken into consideration, but a primrose or an orchid was not worth a bean.

And yet, for all that, many new town planners showed some vision and sensitivity. Hemel Hempstead and Basildon held on to Howe Wood and Marks Hill respectively; they were both safeguarded in their entirety within estates. The same was true of South Wood in Glenrothes, Northerams and Tarnam's Copse in Bracknell, the Hawth in Crawley, the cloughs of Skelmersdale and Castle Eden Dene in Peterlee. Even when they were absorbed within Stevenage, Whomerley and Monk's Wood kept the irregular shapes they had possessed in open countryside. In the fields five miles to the east of the new town, Witnesses Wood was cut to half its pre-war size.

Not all new town woods kept their figure. A main road sliced through Hazel Wood in Corby, along the exact route of an old Roman way, an exchange of chariots for cars. A hospital and a boating lake dumped in the middle added to the ignominy. Housing estates and roads swallowed up much of Foxlydiate and Pitcher Oak Wood in Redditch. The odd copse and tiny wood in other towns would be trimmed or vanish under development. But such cases were unusual. If town planners were guided purely by 'amenity' and what they believed would constitute a pleasant environment for the new citizens of the new towns, then they did, for the most part, a reasonably good job of it.

*　　*　　*

Post-war Britain needed buildings and roads for its reconstruction, and if woodland happened to be on top of valuable minerals, it seemed that was just too bad. A fast-track piece of legislation in 1946 allowed for the creation of what were called Interim Development Orders (IDOs), giving indefinite permission for mineral extraction in perhaps as many as 1,000 locations.

In the Mendip Hills in Somerset, one such IDO saw limestone quarrying permitted over an area of 350 acres, virtually the whole of Asham Wood, the biggest woodland in the whole of the Mendips. Only in 1995, when the quarry had eaten a sizeable chunk out of the wood, did the eventual owners, the Amey Roadstone Corporation, surrender the quarrying permission. A few miles to the west, Cook's Wood was mostly lost to quarrying, though remarkably, the rock beds, sliced open and looking like a multi-layered piece of gateau, took on a new significance. They were given SSSI status for their all too apparent geological importance.

Through much of the post-war period, quarrying continued to bite into woods in other parts of the country. Breedon Cloud Wood in Leicestershire lost its left half to limestone quarrying. Poor Buddon Wood on the outskirts of Quorn ended up shaped like a horseshoe, with a moonscape of a quarry sunk into the centre. The *Loughborough Echo* reported that 350 protestors packed the village hall on a January night in 1972. The local wildlife trust stood up to say that the wood was home to more than 1,000 species of wildlife. It made no difference. Permission granted more than a quarter of a century before proved the deciding factor.

In north Lancashire, mineral operators leased woods for year-round grazing for large numbers of livestock, while they put in planning applications for extracting limestone, and waited for the inevitable approval. By the time the applications came up for consideration, the woods had been eaten out by the animals. The county planning officer noted: 'Any argument for retention of parts of the almost non-existent features is hard to sustain.'

* * *

It would be all too easy to assume that, in the heyday of motorway building, the routes chosen went through the middle of substantial woods, sliced off the edges of medium-sized ones and obliterated copses, for the simple reason that the landowners – faced with compulsory purchase – readily sacrificed what they considered to be their least valuable land.

We might also deduce that the transport authorities would have tried to resist; after all, it is surely easier to cut a road through obstacle-free farmland than to plough a route through tangled thickets, haul out great stumps and dispose of all the debris afterwards?

Both of these are logical conclusions, but when PhD student Charles Watkins sat down to interview a government official in the late 1970s, he discovered that the Department of Transport had a very particular way of thinking. They quite deliberately *chose* to put motorways through woodland.

> The official, a very nice man, said that we don't want to disguise the motorway completely; we will go *through* woods because it shelters the motorway. He said it allowed those in the vehicles a varied view from the road. You didn't want to make roads all the same in case people fell asleep at the wheel.
>
> There was this idea of the road driving as a promenade through the landscape, a bit like a squire walking through his park. Architects came up with schemes to run a road through the Malvern Hills along the bottom at Castle Malton Common, saying this could add variety to the landscape.

Charles must have seen the look of sheer incredulity on my face. 'Of course,' he went on, 'this was the 1950s and 1960s when roads were all positive.'

The car was king, and woods paid for it. The first of Britain's motorways, the M1, built between 1956 and 1968, cut through 33 woods over its 189 miles; one wood for every five miles. The M2 'visited' 15 woods in 25 miles of Kent countryside. The earliest stretch of the M3 between London and Winchester promenaded through 25 woods in 59 miles. The M4, constructed during the 1960s, picked off 45 woods in 135 miles. The M5, built between 1962 and 1977, went through 25 woods, while the M6 took in 26 between Gretna and Rugby.

This was the practice even as late as the early 1980s. Conservationist Nigel Ajax-Lewis recalls driving along the

> **M6**
> Penrith 19
> Brough 39
> Kendal 46
> Preston 86
> Ancient
> woods 3, 4, 6,
> 7, 9, 19

extension of the M4 from Cardiff to Port Talbot on the day it opened: 'I was very conscious and horrified that it joined up all the dots, slicing through every piece of ancient woodland and common land along its route.'

People remembered. An episode from her childhood in 1960s Berkshire left a deep impression on garden writer Susie White:

We would walk the dogs every Sunday afternoon, taking the car to favourite local places – to half-overgrown lanes, picking sloes or blackberries, walking amongst the Roman ruins of Silchester, where trees were rooted in the stones, to a wood surrounded by a leaf-filled moat and dog's mercury.

One of these favourite places was called Norman's

Shaw, a wood of oak and hazel, with primroses and early purple orchids. It was the building of the A33 that was to see a third of this special wood being felled. My mother was so saddened by the loss of the oaks and the plants growing in the wood that she dug up primroses and orchids to transport to our two-acre garden. I think it was with a feeling that at least something would be saved.

The new roads carving through the countryside also provided the means for incidental woodland removal. It was not just that road builders physically took out those that lay on their route; they also gave some landowners the wherewithal to take action that they probably would not otherwise have contemplated. In Northamptonshire, an opportunistic farmer got wind that there was some heavy earth-moving machinery lying temporarily idle not far from his land. During this lull in construction, he managed to divert it to his farm, and persuade the driver to power through the heavy clay, digging out stumps, turning 23-hectare Cotterstock Wood into history.

Northwest of Nottingham, the new M1 bisected Watnall Coppice, and earth-moving machinery pulverised five hectares of woodland to put in carriageways and embankments. While the bulldozers were on site, the owner persuaded the workers to clear another five hectares, level the land off, then shove all of the stumps and debris into the remainder of the wood, so that he could prepare the ground for crops, more than doubling the area of agricultural land on his holding.

*   *   *

The pre-war doom-mongers were, at least in statistical

terms, proved wrong. The bogey figure of development accounted for just one-tenth of all woodland losses. But numbers tell only part of the story. The first six motorways in the sequence cut through 169 woods directly. What of the scarred woods that were left? How many nightly badger beats were broken, how many woods were fractured into pieces, leaving too little habitat in each for dormice to survive? How could courting birds be heard over the roar of traffic? And who was speaking up for them? It is time now, after an almost unrelenting story of woe, to look at how the forces for conservation stood up. Or didn't.

Night shift

A little after dusk on a summer's night, a man is stealing through the farmyard, heading off on the path towards Waresley Wood. He is carrying a large rucksack, its top pushed out of shape by what looks suspiciously like a shotgun.

Sixty years ago, a brace of pheasants fetched 50 to 55 shillings, a tidy sum of money. An old woodsman at the time noted that 'current prices provide poachers with an incentive to work harder at night than they do by day at legitimate enterprises'. But this is now, the 'poacher' is me, and the gun is a folding chair of the decadent, open-air theatre kind that features a round slot for a wine glass that won't fit.

Ripening barley to the right of me, field beans to the left, I'm on a broken concrete track. A left turn and the wood is a dark-green mass directly ahead, swallowing up the sinking sun. I can barely see the entrance.

A couple of weeks ago, I met a lady and her teenage granddaughter as I was leaving the wood. I had just found a scatter of green woodpecker feathers on the ground. A predator must have zoomed in and plucked the 'pecker. So there I was, wearing shorts and brandishing one of these feathers with manic glee. Despite my crazed-looking appearance, I must have looked approachable, for the lady asked: 'Is there a path you can go on without getting lost?' I detected the slightest touch of apprehension in her voice; her eyes flickered with uncertainty, and the child cast me a hopeful, watery smile. It wasn't me that unsettled them; it was the wood.

So often, the words 'wood' and 'lost' go together. In stories and folk tales spanning different cultures and continents, the heroes become lost in the wood, physically and spiritually. I don't suppose Kenneth Grahame would have sent Mole out into a calcareous, herb-rich grassland and created the same mounting suspense as he did in the wild wood. You cannot fear a buttercup. And being lost, at night, in a wood, is a triumvirate of terror. But nobody can claim to truly know a wood if they have not stayed there for the night shift. And that is just what I plan to do now. In Waresley Wood, there are no bears, no big bad wolf, and you will not exactly be mauled by a hedgehog.

I have reached a tiny scoop of grassland around the mouth of the wood, a harbour of preserved wildflower meadow. St John's wort stands out as a faint yellow beacon; the yellow rattle below has lost its flower but not yet gained its rattle – the loose, ripe seeds that shake in the dried out case. This is the purple time of the evening and rosebay willowherb glows more intensely than any other flower in the twilight. I'm at the entrance stile and a cloud of midges is circling over my rucksack, over my head, under the leaves, into the gloom. Welcome to the wood.

On a broad-daylight recce last week, I decided that my all-night-wide-awake vigil would be in a small clearing called 'the box junction', where two rides and two paths meet. I stop before the wooden bench that makes me think of a bus shelter. It is directly in front of a screen of hazel bushes. I set out my folding chair, as if for a performance of

A Midsummer Night's Dream, and sit down, wrapped in a blanket, fleece, gloves, a wide-brimmed hat and a mosquito net draped over it, made to repel Canadian mozzies, blackfly and no-see-ums. Called no-see-ums because you don't see 'um coming.

9pm
In this first half-hour, I am drawing comfort from familiar sounds out of my own, diurnal world. A robin, a burst of blackcap song, a bumblebee behind me, a warm confiding buzz. A whole flock of sheep are bleating a baa fugue far away. Then a duet. Then a soloist.

Two crows spar with throaty calls, one high-sounding, one low. Traffic on the main road, a mile distant, will be audible all night long, though later the constant whoosh will break up into comings, goings and echoing silences between.

Everything green has gone grey. A rabbit shuffles into the clearing from the left, stops and nibbles, then moves a foot or so. It sees me or smells me, and runs. Exit stage right. Tawny owls have started up further along one of the rides. So far, they are sticking to the script.

'Tu-whit!'
'Tu-woo!'

9.30pm
A song thrush was singing overhead just now – a four-minute variety act that has no prelude and no finale. Various blackbirds have been scudding across the rides giving that nervous 'tuk-tukking' they make around nightfall. Now there is one settled a little way off in full song. A blackbird never sounds more elegiac than when it marks the end of

the day. Is it raging against near invisible rivals? Or is it just enjoying itself? Blackbird sings the blues.

The wind lifts and the uppermost branches are shivering, the leaves hissing. Down here, it's only a soft puff of cooling air and a waft of meadowsweet, a delicate scent, scarcely perfumed, like a dab to the wrist. Then comes a still cooler smell of damp earth, cold clay and sodden flowers. And from time to time, an in-breath of honeysuckle. These smells do not mix. Each takes its turn.

10(ish)pm

The mosquitoes are frantic, clinging to the mesh in front of my face, spearing the holes with their probloscises, but each thrust of the lance leaves them still 5cm from fresh blood. Yah boo suck all you like, mozzie! I'm squinting at one with my left eye, when a badger walks into the clearing. It's very small, one of this year's young. It turns its stripy snout to face me, takes a couple of slower, considered steps, then thunders off at a Newmarket gallop, splashing through a puddle.

It's the night after new moon and should be dark (and is) but gradual acclimatisation means I can see more than blurred shapes – I can pick out the flower heads of meadowsweet, individual leaflets on tall ashes. The trunks are so light and vivid. I imagine them as dead totem poles.

Every so often, there are sharp cracks as if a heavy animal has trod on a branch. But I think it's high branches clashing in airborne percussion. There are little furtive scuffs in the bush over my shoulder. A mouse or a bank vole?

Midnight

There are no sounds, no movement.

1am
A sweeping breeze is blowing cool air down the ride. The mosquito whine has stopped, so it's off with the net. Tawny owls have been on the move. They have been making sharp calls and longer, quavering ones. One bird very close to me has just given a scarcely believable, hoarse-throated cock-a-doodle-doo. I think it has just passed overhead.

1.30am
I have noticed before on all-night watches elsewhere that there comes a point when nothing happens, a great big downtime when all the world's asleep. This may be an original observation. Or perhaps I fall asleep without realising it. But surely even badgers need a lunch break or a midnight snooze?

2.20am
I can see the starry heavens through a gap in the treetops. Cassiopeia is visible, a splayed W for 'wonderful'. The waves of honeysuckle that have scented the night air are stronger than ever. And I have the certainty that first light is only an hour away. It is chocolate time.

3.50am
I caught each incremental moment as day broke. The miracles of colour and form came slowly and almost imperceptibly. When did grey foliage resolve to green? When did muddy blurs become individual leaves again? When did I start to feel hungry? Someone turned the little lights above out: the stars dimmed then disappeared altogether. A song thrush started the day and now every blackbird in the wood has opened its beak wide. Out with the apple, start crunching, accept that the pretence of cover is blown.

4am

I sling on my rucksack, leave my bus shelter perch and take the winding path towards the badger sett, pacing very deliberately, for they may still be about. It is still twilight here under the closed canopy. There are black holes of the sett in bare soil. Something wrenches at my rucksack and I am gripped with momentary panic, until I swing round and find the 'gun-toting' top of the rucksack has collided with an overhanging branch.

4.40am

Emerging into the open field again, suddenly filled with joy at broad daylight. Like I say, you cannot fear a buttercup.

MILLIONS LIKE US

'The countryside which is so much a part of our nation now stands in real danger of destruction. I am in no doubt that the loss of our countryside would be universally perceived as the unprecedented catastrophe it would undoubtedly be. Yet there is almost universal ignorance of the imminence of this catastrophe. If people knew what was happening, they would rise up and stop it.'

Henry Moore, sculptor, 1980

Millions of people over the age of 50 remember the trees coming down. In many cases, profound and traumatic changes to the landscape are still deep within people's memories, and so when I sent an appeal to all of Britain's 52 Wildlife Trusts for recollections, it stirred some poignant responses. But it was not ancient woodland they remembered.

In the extreme winter of 1962–63 my family moved to the Wirral, not far from the Lord Leverhulme estate at Thornton Hough, where there were wonderful avenues of elms. I left home for university in 1967 and was horrified on a visit home to find they had been felled because of Dutch elm disease. I felt a keen sense of grief like a bereavement.

I do remember, with great sadness, the disappearance of our

Cornish elms, which used to sucker prolifically along our Cornish hedges, the latter being actually two lines of stone, in-filled with earth and rubble, which, in time, become colonised with whatever trees and herbs come along. In the area centred on Wadebridge, either side of the Camel river and away from the immediate coast, these elms were almost ubiquitous along hedges. Because of the small size of the fields, this gave the whole countryside, viewed from a distance, an appearance of being wooded. After the elms were gone, this was lost forever and the land took on a two-dimensional aspect, the hedges merely lines across it.

I was living 20 miles outside Oxford at the time. I remember a sea of elms, an 80-foot hedge. You couldn't see from one field to the next. Ten years later, you could see Oxford itself.

We have them in old family photos because there were some in the fields behind our house in Staffordshire. Nothing really matched the old English elm for its clouds of branches punching up to the sky – the cumulonimbus of trees.

Of course Dutch elm disease left a huge impression. Arriving in Britain in the late 1960s, it swept through like a plague and, within 20 years, 90 per cent of England's elms were gone. Tall, majestic trees, they weren't simply part of the landscape; they *were* landscapes. Elms were still there along country lanes after the lanes became streets and the fields were filled with houses. Elms were the puffy accompaniment to every train, bus and car journey. Here today and gone in only a few tomorrows. People grieved for old friends suddenly stripped of their leaves, their bark falling off in sheets, a chainsaw performing the last rites. When the disease struck a town or village, every elm was dead within two years.

There is simply not the same welling-up of memories when it comes to ancient woodland. Why is that?

Partly, it can be down to geography. In the mid-20th century, there was precious little left in much of Scotland, especially in the lowlands, substantial populated parts of Wales (Pembrokeshire being particularly denuded of cover) and English counties such as Lancashire, Cheshire, Derbyshire and Warwickshire. Some of the keenest post-war naturalists have no recollections because there were simply no woods around their childhood homes.

Then there was the issue of mobility; in the 1950s, only a seventh of all households had a car. Passengers on the 11.30 train did not generally alight at a woodland station. Bus stops were not located beside a countryside copse. But even if they were, the chances are you would not have been allowed inside.

The 'Keep Out' signs first started being nailed to trees in the late nineteenth century. As woodland industries such as coppicing and charcoal-making declined, there were fewer people in the woods and so fewer people with a 'legiti-mate' reason for being there. In many areas, particularly the arable-dominated east, pheasant-shooting landowners wanted exclusive access. The perception of public exclusion was captured in popular literature such as H.E. Bates' autobiographical *Through the Woods* of 1936 and Rudyard Kipling's poem 'The Way Through the Woods (1892):

Only the keeper sees
That, where the ring-dove broods,
And the badgers roll at ease,
There was once a road through the woods.

As late as the mid-20th century, there were still areas where the gamekeeper's word was law: conservationist Ted Smith recalled that while a university student during the war, he would return home in the holidays to the Lincolnshire Wolds where 'most of the woods were jealously guarded and heavily keepered'.

The post-war period was the age when the farming community's suspicion of 'townies' reached its height. In the eyes of government and many rural inhabitants, the biggest threat to the countryside came from the ignorant hordes pouring out of urban areas; the careless, thoughtless weekend trippers and pillagers. The Countryside Code, with its exhortations to shut gates and avoid dropping litter in case it harmed animals, had been devised in the 1930s to teach the common people proper behaviour. National Parks were set up as honeypots to keep them away from the rest of the working countryside. The Countryside Act of 1968, placing an emphasis on the creation of semi-urban country parks, served the same purpose. The farmer's fields were a factory floor and outsiders were simply not welcome. No wonder the stereotypical 'Get off my land!' image of the farmer gained currency.

Such a broad generalisation does not take account of differences – the relatively free access to the countryside in Scotland and a more extensive network of footpaths through parts of western England, for example. But in much of lowland Britain, the vast majority had little direct knowledge of their local woods. The few naturalists who ventured into woods in search of wildlife did so with a strong awareness that they were breaking rules. Lifelong butterfly enthusiast Matthew Oates grew up in the 1960s on the Hampshire–West Sussex border. He confesses with glee: 'I trespassed like mad.'

Ordinary people did, nevertheless, see the countryside changing. The extraordinary thing is – they didn't believe their eyes. Hundreds of thousands of hedgerows were ripped out and woods vanished or shrunk, but there was a cognitive gap in the minds of millions. There was an ingrained perception that farmers were the custodians of the countryside, the wise tenants of the land who could be relied on to do what was best. Such trust persisted well into the 1960s.

Indeed, in the welter of post-war legislation put through by a Labour government, farming was deliberately excluded from restrictions on development imposed by the Town and Country Planning Act (forestry was the other exception). It was unthinkable – and it really was unthinkable – that landowners could be destroying the countryside. Would you trash your own garden? Politicians, especially in the House of Lords, stood up for farmers and foresters; a fair percentage of the parliamentarians owned farms and forests themselves.

Ordinary people simply did not see in a conscious, thinking, rational sense what was happening or else disbelieved their memory. I know, because I was one of them. I vividly remember a sense of bewilderment during my teenage years in Hertfordshire, when I looked across a bare field at the exact spot where there had been a copse the summer before. No amount of looking at the neighbouring wood to the right and following the shape of the whole field to get my bearings could convince me I was wrong. But it couldn't convince me I was right either. I remember feeling puzzled, but not angered or sad. I said nothing to anybody.

Northumberland poet Katrina Porteous had a similar, though profoundly upsetting experience:

There was one particular wood on the Derwent banks which

I loved as a child. It was a couple of miles from my house, and I used to go there alone, to sit in the leaflight under the trees and write. Sometime while I was away at university, it vanished under conifers. I couldn't believe it when I came home to find tall conifers where my beloved mixed woodland had been. I had no understanding of environmentalism, or the science behind plantation versus natural woodland: just an instinct that the beauty and diversity of the place, its birds, beetles, mushrooms, butterflies, its animation, variety, colour and life – its song – had been replaced by something dark and sinister. The conifers were huge: I couldn't believe that they had grown in so short a time. The ground beneath them was sour and dead. All the light had gone. They seemed haunted by a very different spirit and made me question whether that enchanted wood of my childhood had ever existed.

Nobody was disabusing the public of its self-deceptions, connecting each individual experience with wider patterns of loss, enabling them to understand cause and effect. Those who could see and at least partially understand events unfolding before their eyes nevertheless belonged to a generation that had experienced war and the privations of rationing (and food rationing only ended in 1954). They had known what it was like to go hungry.

Even for most conservationists, farming represented progress; they saw the new technology of machinery as part of a modern drive to feed the nation. The wartime experiences of farmers told to plough up marginal land, and owners forced to cultivate commons 'for the war effort' provided powerful evidence of the need for home-grown food, and the need to sacrifice. Necessity was the mother of blindness, for it overcame thoughts of aesthetics and general concern for the greater countryside. The national pride in productivity and a belief in progress was so strong that it could defeat the internal resistance of even those with a wider understanding of what it meant.

One of those was a Cambridge-educated biology master from Oundle School, who stood at a farm gate and watched the complete removal of 23-hectare Cotterstock Wood. He had explored the wood only the summer before, slipping into the trees cautiously because he knew it was private. He had found a white admiral butterfly there – the only one he had seen in that part of the county. So was he now aghast at seeing this precious wood and all its wonderful wildlife disappearing? Not a bit of it.

I was impressed at the way this awful boulder clay was being converted into agricultural land,' said 88-year-old Ioan Thomas. 'It took them three years to get a crop off it. I was fascinated at what they could achieve. It shows you how much my mind has changed that I should have thought of it in that way. I didn't get any sense of the loss of a wood.

Not all farmers agreed with what was happening in the countryside around them. Wherever he stood on the family's south Devon farm, ten-year-old John Comont could see the wood on the skyline, an ever-present character. Their own farm had plenty of copses, but no wood, so he would play in the neighbour's, though he was too frightened to go deep into its dark, dense interior. Every day, he would take a short cut through the wood on his way to school.

It disappeared over a period of about three years. It was a slow process, cutting down some quite big trees and bull-dozing sections of it. Now if you go there, it's just a corn field. It had had a memorial in a clearing right in the centre, with rides radiating out. The memorial's still there, standing in the middle of the corn field. The whole family thought it was a crying shame. Fifty years later, we still do. It made a deep impression. But this was our neighbour, a fine neighbour aside from that, so we weren't going to complain.

The wood's disappearance brought physical changes to the family's own farm. With the sheltering trees gone, cold winds swept down from the north and east and the crops in the adjoining field would never grow as well again.

How did people in the livestock-rearing north and west feel about their woods turning dark green? A very large number of sizeable woods in parts of Britain were coniferised – for example 163 in Yorkshire, 46 in Cornwall and 51 in Shropshire. There were certainly some rumblings of discontent. In 1951, Lord Addison, the leader of the House of Lords commented:

> The complaint in the countryside is that the conifer forest destroys all the wild flowers, entirely revolutionises the fauna of the country and entirely changes the face of the landscape. I suggest that with a little more tact and latitude, and a little more hiding the conifers behind wide belts of hardwoods, the Commission could have overcome a large part of the opposition which they have aroused against themselves.

> (HL Deb 20 March 1951 vol 170 cc1177-240)

Perhaps the 'picture-framing' broadleaved screens were enough for the majority of the public. The woods were still there, after all. Most people laboured under the misapprehension that all woods were planted. You cut a wood down; you planted another. As yet, there was no general understanding of the actuality of an 'ancient woodland' – the phrase was not even used until the mid-70s – and so few appreciated that they were unique, rarer, or even different from any other place with trees. Millions enjoyed holidays in the Forestry Commission's Forest Parks, where the Commission urged them to 'help to safeguard Britain's new and growing forests – the forests that are becoming, as the years go by, ever more beautiful and valuable'.

Conservation: missing and misguided

In the month when Pearl Harbor was attacked, a group of ladies of a certain age were gathered in the drawing room of Miss K.I. Butler. She was always Miss Butler. One year, the Reading and District Natural History Society made the cardinal sin of calling her Kathleen Butler in its annual publication. The indiscretion was never repeated.

On that day in December 1941, the ladies were addressing a matter of some importance: 'The Group should endeavour to bring up-to-date the Natural History Society's List of Flowering Plants published in 1900.' At the end of a year in which 296 bombs fell on Berkshire, it was a beacon of hope held out for the peace to come. In the meantime, Miss Butler wheeled her bicycle down the drive of her Edwardian semi-detached and set off to meet up with Miss Cobb and Mrs Simmons. The three ladies spent wartime summers cycling around Berkshire together picking poison. As stalwarts of the Women's Institute-led County Herb Committee, they collected deadly nightshade and henbane, as well as foxglove leaves, which they laid out to dry. All three plants were accepted by the authorities for use in medicinal drugs.

In the summer after the war ended, Miss Butler was in flower heaven, walking on a chalk downland slope, 'so thickly sprinkled with *Orchis pyramidalis* [pyramidal orchids] and *Orchis maculata* [heath spotted orchids] that it was scarcely possible to avoid treading on the blossoms'.

Peace may have come but another war was about to begin. Miss Butler was one of dozens of county plant recorders who were ground barometers, a select band who patrolled the woods and fields, noting the minute year-by-year changes in the flowers growing there. Like botanist Terry Wells in Waresley a generation later, they were best placed to assess the health of the wild countryside.

Poor Miss Butler; her plant report for 1949 tells a woeful tale:

The Snowdrop wood near Arborfield is in the way of land drainage operations and trees have been felled and hauled away over the plants – thereby destroying many of the bulbs. A few plants remain unmolested on two small islands in the nearby Loddon and along the river banks... The Pasque Flower *Anemone pulsatilla* on the Downs is doing well despite its blasting by shellfire during the War. It remains practically confined to one small area although it used to grow on Streatley Hill... Ashridge Wood near East Ilsley is an isolated wood amid fertile cornfields. It is a locality for several rare and local plants, but their continued existence is made doubtful by extensive felling of trees. It would appear that the land is to be cleared and made into arable.

Faced with a sustained attack on wildlife in all habitats, the Reading district naturalists responded with heroic ineffectuality. They wrote to a farmer who was ploughing extremely rare orchids on the downs; he ignored their letter and carried on. One unknown individual saved a clod of earth containing two of the exceptionally rare monkey orchids and tucked it into a hedge. The society pinned a note of thanks to the anonymous rescuer on the hedge, gathered the turf, packaged it up, and posted it to Kew Gardens, hoping the plants could be saved. There is no record as to whether they were.

The society's delight in good news among the gloom is pathetically touching. A group of members visited what was left of the grubbed-up remnant of Ashridge Wood, which was now going through the indignity of coniferisation, and managed to find a lone flowering spiked star of Bethlehem.

Their joy over an event in Coronation year was unbridled: 'The year 1953 will ever remain a memorable one for the botanists.' Britain's rarest and most elusive plant, the ghost orchid, had been found by a member in the dappled shade of an Oxfordshire beech wood. A doctor happened to be in the finder's party, and, being male and of a profession, was given pre-eminence when the society bulletin reported:

> Dr. Graham and Mrs. Paul are to be congratulated on their pertinacity in searching and on their ultimate success. The very few colleagues who have been entrusted with the secret of the exact locality have each respected the responsibility and continue to safeguard the growing plants in the dense beech woods.

In 1962, Miss Butler's last year as plant recorder, she made her final report and signed off with a valedictory line: 'Inroads of civilisation continue to take toll of many of our local wild plants.

Three years later, one comment in the bulletin provided an insight into the essential but limited role of natural history societies at that time. It was something of a proud lament: 'If our wild life is declining, our knowledge of it continues to increase.' For the most part, naturalists, and the societies they belonged to, were busy recording the path to extinction.

Any impetus for addressing woodland losses could not come from the dedicated, expert, extremely specialised individuals of this society and others like it. Their erudition and apparent eccentricity tended to repel lesser mortals. They would, after all, go out to lure purple emperor butterflies armed with 'the customary bait of putrid fish-heads', and respond to a request to collect and post snails in a tin box cushioned with blotting paper to a Dr Quick for identification.

These self-selecting groups were naturalists, but they were exceedingly small in number, and they were not, with very few exceptions, conservationists. It was simply not what they did within their clearly defined remit. Ted Smith, a leading figure in post-war conservation, stood up at the annual meeting of the Society for the Promotion of Nature Reserves in 1954 to say: 'Only too often one finds naturalists strangely unaware of the need for conservation or indifferent to it.'

So where was the conservation movement? Where was the resistance, the fight, the marshalling of troops, the igniting of public indignation, the call to action? What were the RSPB, the CPRE, the Wildlife Trusts, the Woodland Trust and the National Trust doing while the chainsaws and bulldozers went to work?

A prescient voice in the RSPB had sounded the alarm in the society's magazine in the summer of 1942. In a forward-looking editorial entitled *Wild Bird Conservation and Post-War Reconstruction*, the unknown writer warned:

The enhanced value of timber, together with high taxation, make an irresistible temptation to many small, and some large, owners of land, to turn standing timber into money... Little imagination is needed to appreciate the inevitable impoverishment of our tree-haunting birds, such as Woodpeckers, Nuthatches, Wrynecks, Tree Creepers and Owls that must follow. The question will naturally be asked, what can be done about it?

And the answer, as far as the RSPB was concerned, would be practically nothing. For three decades and more, the RSPB sat on its hands while the woods fell around it. The RSPB was based in the ravaged southeast of England, and the organisation's director lived in tree-starved Cambridgeshire, a county that still managed to cut down nearly two thirds of what it had left at the end of the war. How could the RSPB fail to see the signs and how could it fail to act upon them?

One answer could be that it was too busy. Up until the mid-1960s, it had a membership of less than 20,000 and a very small number of staff. To a large extent, those few concentrated on the issues that shouted loudest. In the years leading up to 1954's Wild Birds Protection Act, they battled for legislation to safeguard birds' nests. Not long after, they discovered that thousands of birds at a time were dropping dead out of the skies. As the effects of farm pesticides such as DDT on wildlife became known, the RSPB joined a protracted struggle against institution-alised resistance to doing anything about it. The effects of oil pollution on seabirds were also apparent, more visceral evidence of an injustice against nature, brought into sharp focus by the *Torrey Canyon* tanker disaster of 1967. The organisation also channelled resources into tackling egg thieves, bird trapping, illegal shooting. Dead birds demanded action.

There was no such sense of urgency when it came to

woodland. The fact was, woodland birds could not play the extinction card and herein lay the fundamental reason for inaction. The future of the blue tit was never in doubt. There would always be tawny owls, blackbirds and willow warblers, and plenty of them.

There was also a question of attitude. The men who ran the RSPB were products of a Victorian mentality geared towards collecting and recording, old-style naturalists who were obsessed with their own particular passions, whether birds, butterflies, beetles, or lichens and mosses, seeing everything in terms of protecting threatened species. The new philosophy of ecology linked to preserving habitats, expounded by Arthur Tansley immediately before the war, certainly registered, but it was not built into their conservation DNA, and it was not what drove them. Those men born before the Great War or just after still clung to their old ways and looked for species to save.

And so the RSPB's rare forays into protecting individual pieces of woodland were tied to understandable but myopic objectives. The RSPB's interest in the pinewoods of Loch Garten, the acquiring of a nature reserve and the enormous energy and time spent on nest protection there, were all geared to ensuring the survival and breeding success of a single pair of ospreys. The RSPB's leading lights wanted the osprey to return to Britain. The last bird had been shot before they were born or during their infancy, and in their desire and single-minded purpose, they lost a sense of perspective. The pinewoods of the Highlands were almost incidental; no effort was put into safeguarding those endangered habitats of Scotland until almost quarter of a century later.

An organisation that had fought the Forestry Commission tenaciously over coniferisation of the Lake District in the 1930s was rewarded with a seat at the top table for decades afterwards. The CPRE, together with its Welsh counterpart, met the commissioners in a joint informal committee right up to the Commission's reorganisation in 1965. However, the CPRE was a shadow of its pre-war active self; the founders had died off without having done much succession planning. As the years went on, and the rate of ancient woodland loss increased, so the committee met less and less often. The police sat down for the occasional chat and cup of tea with the gallery owner, while all the paintings were carted away.

The Forestry Commission's deputy director-general claimed in 1969: 'Today, these councils [the CRPE in England and Wales] recognise, in the main, that the Forestry Commission's work has generally, if slowly, added to the scenic beauty of their two countries.' It would appear that the Commission's picture-framing policy worked. A belt of deciduous trees left around the rim of a wood was, it seems, enough to satisfy the leading lights of the charity. Beauty really was skin deep. During the 1950s and '60s, the CPRE addressed green belt legislation, National Parks and planning issues. Broadleaved woodland was certainly not high on its agenda.

At the end of the war, the Wildlife Trust movement was still in its protracted infancy, its county structure virtually non-existent. Founded in 1912 by wealthy naturalist Charles Rothschild, the Society for the Promotion of Nature Reserves put its energy into urging others to buy and manage nature reserves. It spent far too many years failing to give parental support to its own fledgling brood. In 1945, Norfolk was the only county with a naturalists' trust. West Wales, Yorkshire and Lincolnshire followed in the 1940s, but, until the late 1950s, there was a curious reluctance on the part of the national body to support those eager pioneers by encouraging the formation and direction of more county trusts.

When agreement to do so was reached in 1959, a plethora of new Wildlife Trusts appeared. Even so, in their formative years they were weak organisations, with no – or very few – paid staff, often driven by strong-willed volunteer naturalists inclined to bend a trust towards their own pet interests. Wildlife Trusts had the unfortunate characteristic of being land hungry and cash poor. Many of their acquisitions were of mediocre quality – small donations or scraps of land that came cheaply.

Before the late 1970s and the great rush of government-funded employment schemes, there simply weren't the resources, either at local or national level, to campaign. Tim Sands came to work at the national headquarters (by now called the Royal Society for Nature Conservation) in 1975. He may well have met all his new colleagues on his first day: there were just four of them. There was little understanding of just how serious things were. After his retirement as director of conservation, Sands rued: 'I don't think woodlands figured anywhere near as much as they should have done.'

What about the Woodland Trust? Where was the organisation whose very raison d'être was at stake? Quite simply, it didn't exist. There is a long history of wildlife groups being set up as disaffected, frustrated or single-minded splinters from bigger conservation bodies – Butterfly Conservation, BugLife, Plantlife and the Marine Conservation Society are all modern examples. The Woodland Trust was one of these offshoots. But it was not created until 1972.

The National Trust had been founded at the end of the nineteenth century, its aim enshrined in law 'to promote the permanent preservation, for the benefit of the Nation, of lands and tenements (including buildings) of beauty or historic interest; and, as regards, to preserve (so far as practicable) their natural aspect, features, and animal and plant life'. It has always, as its director-general Sir Angus Stirling admitted at a centenary gathering in 1995, struggled to reconcile its wide and sometimes conflicting interests.

The Trust was hampered in a way that other conservation organisations were not; it was split by multiple objectives and money had to be found in the post-war period to fund the upkeep of new estates and rundown stately homes that were being offered at such a rate that it seemed there was a great countryside closing-down sale. Looking back over a century of its work in 1995, Sir Angus acknowledged, quite laudably, that when it came to judging whether it was safeguarding nature conservation too, 'there have been times in the past when we could not make this claim'.

The National Trust happened to be the only conservation body with significant holdings in the post-war period. It became clear that its loosely federal structure, widespread ignorance of wildlife, pressing need to generate more income, and the professional background of managers locked into particular ways of thinking, resulted in mistakes being made, again and again.

In managing its estates, the Trust judiciously employed the best people for the job: land agents who were used to running a range of enterprises – properties, parks and farms. When it came to ancient woodland, they cleaved to one book, *Practical Forestry for the Agent and Surveyor* by Cyril Hart.

Its advice was authoritative: 'Today more than ever woodlands must be run as a business, and if an agent is failing to get the best financial return from them, their management should be entrusted to professional supervision of high efficiency, whether it be to a fellow agent specializing in forestry or someone outside his own profession.'

And the way to do this should be by throwing aside the old methods of woodland management: 'The system has long gone out of favour, and many areas have been and are being converted to either high forest... Where coppice is inferior or growing from almost worn-out stools, or is not of a timber species, such as hazel, it is usually clear-felled and the area replanted.'

The Trust decided to mark Queen Elizabeth II's accession to the throne in 1952 with a project that would leave a legacy for future generations. On the slopes of its flint-strewn Ashridge Estate in the Chilterns, it created a new wood, and erected a sign, complete with its classic oak leaf emblem: *Queen Elizabeth's Wood: Planted 1952.*

Except that it wasn't new. The plantation was superimposed on a wood that had been old at the time of the first Queen Elizabeth's accession. A large area of Great Frithsden Copse was cleared to make way for the planting. Frith is a medieval word for wood. In with the new, out with the old.

Three years later, the Trust became embroiled in another messy affair. Before the war, it had been given the sizeable residue of a royal hunting forest in Essex by a number of landowners. In 1955, the son of the owner who had given the largest bequest wrote a letter of complaint to *The Times*, revealing that the Trust was planning to lease part of Hatfield Forest to the Forestry Commission, with the intention of removing existing old woodland and replacing it with plantations. Debate raged through the national newspapers. The Trust appeared to relent, not wanting to offend the family of major legatees, or stir up bad publicity, and so the proposal was abandoned.

Except that it wasn't. In 1959, the Trust received a Forestry Commission grant to grub up 50 acres of coppice woodland and replant it with conifers, oak and beech – pretty much the same scheme that had been withdrawn four years earlier.

Even the Lake District, the mountainous jewel in the Trust's crown, could be the subject of blinkered thinking. In the late 1960s, head forester Philip Hardman was given instructions by his regional manager for managing a wood in Borrowdale.

Johnny Wood was a picturesque, boulder-strewn steep oak wood, whose stones were clad in luxuriant mosses and liverworts, known as bryophytes, some of which were exceedingly rare (the mosses are called oceanic mosses – an appropriate name since it feels on the rainiest days as if half the Atlantic's rainclouds are dumped on Borrowdale, the wettest place in England). The wood had been designated as a SSSI for its bryophytes in 1960.

This fact did not appear to register in the mind of the National Trust's regional officer, who ordered Hardman to plant fast-growing conifers in the gaps between the oaks, telling him that it would be cheaper to grow their own timber than buy it in. The forester, a good naturalist, knew that this crowding and shading would have disastrous consequences for the site's sensitive wildlife. But his objections were brushed aside, and it was only when he raised his doubts with certain influential people, who then lobbied privately on his behalf, that the instruction was rescinded by a higher official in the Trust.

In acquiring numerous country houses and stately homes, the National Trust was amassing more pasture woodlands, the open-grazed woodlands and deer parks that dated back to Norman times, than any other conservation body in Britain. Much of the pasture was ploughed and reseeded to produce faster-growing grasses. Ploughing often damaged the roots of ancient pollard trees and sometimes killed them. Artificial fertilisers killed the fungi associated with tree roots and probably killed yet more trees. The dead trees and deadwood, crucial to the survival of a whole host of invertebrates, including rare beetles and hoverflies were tidied away or removed for safety reasons. The Trust's own invertebrate expert Keith Alexander later complained that its precautionary approach was 'often taken too far by property managers, with zeal for making trees "safe" despite a notably poor understanding of what constitutes an unsafe tree'. Parkland was being managed as if it was a town park. Much of the damage, though, was done by tenant farmers, and the Trust – tied to long tenancies – could do nothing about it.

But everything could have been so much worse. In John Workman, the Trust had a wise head, an experienced forester, to oversee its woodland management. Workman was in the unusual position of being respected by both foresters and conservationists. But he was under great pressure, not only from his peers in forestry, but also from the Trust's land agents and even members of the Trust's own council, who bought into economic arguments for clearing out the 'old, derelict woodland', and would proclaim in meetings that it should only be necessary to have a few broadleaved trees on the outside of a wood for the sake of appearances. Workman devised a ratio of planting that would be applied to the Trust's woodland: one-quarter broadleaves, three-quarters conifers. It was not ideal, but a compromise was better than nothing.

Workman's successor, Bill Wright, who would go on to

shift the Trust's policies in the more enlightened early 1980s to align with nature conservation aims, said diplomatically of those postwar years: 'The Trust did not abandon its primary objective of preserving its woodlands, but, regarding itself as a responsible landowner, felt bound to place more emphasis on the secondary objective of timber production and developed a system of mixed planting best suited to this compromise.'

It would be unfair to criticise using hindsight. There were plenty of people at that time who would argue that the conifers were no worse for wildlife than the broadleaves that had gone before. In fact, some said they could be even better:

One may hazard the suggestion that systematic forestry favours wild life conservation. The habitat is varied with the successive operations, so that while some groups may suffer temporary eclipse, others have a chance. A mature oak wood offers a single monotonous environment to both plant and animal life: it is relatively dull. The introduction of other forest trees, including a range of conifers, undoubtedly creates a range of environments and in consequence more varied wild life. It would be hard for a naturalist to range himself wholeheartedly against afforestation, or against the variety of species now used by the Forestry Commission.

We might expect this quote to come from a forester or someone connected with forestry. It actually appeared in a prestigious book *Nature Conservation in Britain*, and the content was checked and approved before publication in 1966 by a panel of eminent conservationists. The writer was Sir Dudley Stamp, chairman of the England Committee of the government's own Nature Conservancy, the body that was there to stand up for wildlife.

Ground control

We met Graham the Warden for the first time in Waresley Wood last summer, and I remember standing on the bridge and looking out over an ocean of flowering field beans. My wife and I were taken to the southern edge of the wood, the outer limit, with only a shallow ditch separating us from open farmland. 'This is the critical bit of the wood, always the highlight of my walk when I come to this,' he said, with what I detected was a trace of grim relish. 'I bring visitors to this point and I say to them, "here we are, in the middle of the wood."'

Graham raised his finger like an Old Testament prophet and pointed to a hedge way off in the distance. He drew an imaginary line from right to left, as if he was tracing along that thin green line, and said, 'That marks the old boundary of the wood.'

'Oh my goodness!' exclaimed my wife, looking out over the vast expanse of beans. Graham's showstopper had worked again.

Over the winter since we first met Graham, I have looked at a lot of ploughed fields, the ghosts of woodland past, and I am looking at one now, standing in that same place where we gazed out over the field last summer, their sweet smell mingling with the wood-bound scent of trailing honeysuckle. Could the huge expanse that the Mear family call Woodland Field not grow trees again? Could the wood reclaim its own from fertile land? If only it were that simple. I have feet of clay: when I stand here in the wood, the earth a metre beneath my boots is identical to the tractor-chewed claggy soil ahead of me. The difficulty for those trying to recreate woodland lies in reconstituting that first metre-thick band of earth that is so thin yet so fundamental.

About 2-4,000 years after the last glacial period – we are talking perhaps 8,000 years ago – the soils in Waresley Wood settled into their present state. On top of the clay cap, laid down when dinosaurs walked the earth, and on top of millions of years of wind-blown dust, the forested earth had taken on its own character, formed according to the following recipe:

ANCIENT WOODLAND SOIL
(Serves numerous trees and characteristic plants)

Ingredients
Dead leaves (billions)
Twigs and small branches
Plants
Worms
Fungi
Micro-organisms (including mites)
Dead foxes, badgers, stoats, weasels, mice, voles, birds, etc
Caterpillar poo (and poo of everything else)

Scatter leaves, twigs and branches over surface and allow to stand. Let worms, fungi and micro-organisms break them down. Add other ingredients and repeat breaking down process for roughly 8,000 years.

All this time, the soil in Waresley Wood had built up

relatively undisturbed. Woodsmen cut down trees, but they did not dig them up by the roots, so there was very little mixing up of the layers of deposition. The odd earth bank dug by villagers and the excavations of a badger sett would make little difference to the overall stability of the woodland floor, an established, settled habitat.

Nature's composting did certain things to the soil. The boulder clay of the farmed fields around Waresley Wood is slightly alkaline, with a pH of about 7.8. Waresley's plants are nourished by the remains of their ancestors – the dead vegetation producing mildly acidic soil with a pH of about 6. Over time, the soil in the settled wood became less fertile: as trees were felled and removed, and coppiced bushes were cut and their stems taken away, the levels of nutrients – nitrates and phosphates – began to fall, and continued to fall during more than a thousand years of human exploitation.

Situated on a plateau equipped with a giant clay pond liner, Waresley Wood retains water. It's damp or worse for up to ten months of the year; more in a wet summer: no wonder this land was left as woodland by the Saxon farmers. The gloopy mud on paths like linear buffalo wallows caused the daughter of a friend to question why she had left London for the country, and the lady who turned up in the car park the other day wearing little suede boots with gold-tipped tassels, to look aghast when we suggested that such footwear might not be quite *de rigueur* off piste.

Any plant grown in waterlogged soil will discover to its cost that oxygen diffuses through water to its roots 10,000 times less effectively than through air. But that is not what kills plants in a wood – it is the chemical reaction that causes otherwise inorganic and harmless iron and manganese compounds in the soil to become soluble and poison the plants. The wood is often at its wettest in April and May, drenched by winter rains, but not yet drained by the transpiration of billions of leaves. And that is just at the time when spring flowers are in bloom.

Oxlips are great survivors of such conditions. They can sit for two months at a time in completely waterlogged soil and they can tolerate its active metal compounds, while dog's mercury, the dense and prolific woodland plant that might otherwise overwhelm it, dies off. We know, without ever having seen it, that the huge part of the wood to the south that was lost in the 1970s would have been one of the soggiest parts of all, because it was said to be the best place for oxlips. But oxlips cannot survive the plough.

A single ploughing destroys all. It mixes the clay, the silt and the humic layer in one great, undifferentiated mass. Historically, minor damage could be repaired, in time. Long ago, farmers might claim more land for their crops by 'assarting', felling the trees and bushes at the edge of a wood and ploughing the virgin soil with a light cattle- or horse-drawn plough that barely raked the surface.

The 200-year-old enclosure map for Waresley shows three sticking-plaster strips on the side of the wood labelled as 'stockings'. These strips had been cleared for farming some time before ('stocks' meaning tree stumps) and were, by late Georgian times, naturally regenerating. But even now, more than 200 years later, the one remaining stocking has a slightly different composition to the rest of the wood, still lacking flowers that are prevalent elsewhere.

The ditch at my feet tells yet another part of the story. On other sides of the wood, the boundary is marked by humped banks, the soil shovelled up in medieval times to keep foraging pigs and other livestock out during the growing season. But in 1973, farmer Stephen Mear wanted to dry out the field he had newly 'reclaimed' from the wood and keep it dry. So this steep-sided ditch in front of me now was dug as a drain, part of a network to ensure that the winter rains would soak away from his fields. Any present-day attempts to restore the wood on this land would involve blocking the drains and bringing back the water.

In March, an elderly dog walker in the car park told us we needed some good drains in the woods to get rid of the puddles. No, sir, the wetness is exactly why the wood and its oxlips have survived, and exactly why it is so special today. Lose the water and you will lose the very essence of the wood itself.

The older fields beyond the wood may still contain traces of the pulverised bones of soldiers of the Napoleonic Wars and the guano of Chilean seabirds. The battlefields of Europe and the seabird breeding cliffs of South America were plundered in the nineteenth century to fertilise crops for an expanding nation. Our fertilisers today are more targeted, and more effective at boosting soils deficient in chemicals. Not always that targeted: wind and rain have blown fertiliser spray into the northeastern corner of the wood, and those arch-invaders, stinging nettles and goosegrass, have crept in to exploit the enriched soil and overwhelm the ancient woodland plants such as prim-roses, which cannot compete with well-fed, fast-growing opportunists.

For more than 40 years, the soil of Woodland Field has been drenched in fertilisers, year after unfailing year. It would be perfectly possible to plant trees there and watch the flowers grow beneath – a rank harvest of nutrient-hungry nettles, thistles, brambles, hogweed, cow parsley, ivy and goosegrass, thriving in the fertile soil, and mimicking the uniform, standard, predictable character of thousands of plantations just like it. Nonetheless, though it may be impossible to recreate ancient woodland, there may be some merit in secondary, lesser-quality woodland bolted onto ancient woods. It may provide a buffer against the drift of farm chemicals from fields that are hostile to wildlife, a green coat that protects the precious edges from harm.

Not so very far beyond the fertilised fields around Waresley Wood are the green hummocky shapes of another ancient woodland. Roman farmers probably cleared the land of trees between Waresley and Gamlingay Wood about 1,800 years ago. Gamlingay Wood is slowly creeping back to touch trees with its neighbour again. More than a decade since the Wildlife Trust bought a field on the northeast side of it, the wind has done the rest, blowing the trees, shaking the branches, loosening the seeds to fall far out in the field to the west.

This bridge between has a name but no adult trees. Sugley Wood is still open country, filled with skylarks by day and barn owls gliding out for the night shift. Not for much longer. By some kind of miracle, seedlings have sprung from the rough grass: ash in profusion, oak, field maple, hazel. Sallow bushes have sprouted in the marshy, puddled patch at least a hundred metres from the main wood. Black-headed reed buntings flit from branch to branch and, on cold winter mornings, snipe shoot out at the sound of approaching feet. And on the paths where summer-cut hay from rides in the old wood was laid, there are flowers appearing with poetry in their names; hedge bedstraw, meadow vetchling, bird's-foot trefoil, creeping jenny, germander speedwell. It is a start, but unless human ingenuity finds ways to quicken the process, the transformation of this field towards anything resembling ancient woodland will be measured not in years, but in centuries.

A GOVERNMENT CHAMPION

After the outbreak of peace in 1945, it seemed everyone was at war with ancient woodlands. In this story, we have so far followed the merciless charge of forestry, agriculture, housing, roads and industry, despaired at the weak, misguided and distracted conservation movement, and witnessed – at a 50-year remove – a general public blissfully unaware.

It was not until 1949 that the nation's first official organisation to support nature conservation was created. It was given a good start. Canny civil servants ensured that the newly minted Nature Conservancy was set up through a Royal Charter. As constituted, it was an independent body, free from the constraints of being within a government department, answerable to no minister for its actions. The downside was that it was friendless in Whitehall, and, for at least the first decade, it battled to justify its very existence.

The initial main purpose and thrust of the Nature Conservancy was to acquire land that it would manage as National Nature Reserves. It sought the best examples of different habitats across Britain, but not simply with the aim of seeking to protect them. This new organisation had to persuade the Treasury to support its acquisitions on the hard-nosed basis of value for money. It had to counter prevailing prejudices. One conservationist had warned that nature was perceived as being associated with 'a somewhat childish and eccentric form of botanizing, bird-loving and butterfly-hunting'.

Right from its beginnings, the Conservancy had a cred-ibility issue, and so it set out its stall as a body conducting scientific research. It argued that its reserves would be used as experimental outdoor laboratories. Why, they could even benefit the nation's farmers and foresters.

Though it had shopping lists of sites, the Nature Conservancy was poorly funded right from its inception. It had to rely on finding a bargain, making opportunistic purchases of places it hadn't necessarily targeted, as well as collecting others through a mixture of leases, gifts and management agreements with private landowners. 'National Nature Reserve' was a big title for what was often a small piece of land.

'Derelict' ancient woodland came relatively cheaply, and the Conservancy began to build up its holdings. Beinn Eighe in Cromarty, its pinewoods subjected to heavy wartime felling, was its first reserve, purchased in 1951. Over five years, the Conservancy took on Ham Street Woods and Blean Woods in Kent, Yarner Wood on Dartmoor, Monks Wood and Castor Hanglands near Peterborough, Roudsey Wood in the Lake District and Kingley Vale in Sussex – complete with a forest of yews, like nothing else in Europe.

Two men, both now nearly 90 years old, give vivid portrayals of those early reserve-accumulating years, when being a jack-of-all-trades was a necessity for an organisation short of staff as well as money. Eric 'Robbie' Roberts had come from the Forestry Commission in May 1954, to become the Conservancy's first ever forester for England and Wales. He was told his job would be to roam the two countries, advising on management for reserves as it acquired them. It would require a great deal of travelling.

Not unreasonably, he went to ask about getting a car. 'You?' spluttered Colonel Manley, the former army officer in charge of transport. 'You're not important enough to have a vehicle. We only have two at the moment.' And so Robbie began his life as a roving civil servant using public transport. He got on a Green Line bus at Victoria Station, got off at a Huntingdonshire village on the A1 and walked to the new reserve at Monks Wood. Though his job was to manage reserves, there was, in the beginning, only one person around to do the practical work. Robbie took off his rucksack, pulled out his hatchet and saw, and began clearing rides and coppicing the long-neglected hazel bushes.

Carrying his office in his rucksack, Robbie was in charge of all the Conservancy's woods. At first, he was encumbered with responsibility for marshes and lakes too. He graduated from buses and trains to a 350cc BSA motorcycle, pootling out from HQ in London's Belgrave Square to each new reserve.

Each expedition was, as he recalled, 'an evangelical odyssey'. Wherever he went, the locals were puzzled. The idea of nature conservation had to be explained and they simply couldn't grasp the concept of a nature reserve, especially when it was applied to the plain old wood down the lane.

Robbie was required to contact local authorities, find out who needed to be told about a change of ownership and what needed to be done. He sought thatchers to do coppicing, volunteers to manage the sites, and paid friendly farmers a pittance of an honorarium to bring in their tractors for any heavy work, such as moving timber.

Two years earlier, James 'Archie' Archibald had been

one of the Nature Conservancy's earliest office recruits. A forestry graduate of Edinburgh University, he served out his two years of National Service by working for the Forestry Commission in Dumfries and Galloway and the Borders, trudging over moors to survey new plantations. Archie remembered the Forestry Commission's response as the Conservancy began to take on woodlands. 'They weren't happy at all. They were talking about dividing woods up: they would come back to us to say, why don't you have part of the wood and then we can manage the rest properly?'

Government foresters had decades of experience in planting and nurturing conifers. Archie and Eric were stepping into trashed woods, inheriting decades of neglect, with scarcely a woodsman left to tell them how things should be done. Archie went on a steep learning curve in Ham Street Woods in Kent.

> Sweet chestnut was still valuable, but most hornbeam coppice hadn't been cut for more than 20 years, so we were trying to get it reinstated and finding old coppice workers to advise us. I did a lot of standing around talking to them and learned quite a lot. We employed an old chap in his seventies who had never been out of Kent. I would trot along behind him with my notebook, tramping many a mile through the coppices of east Kent.

By the 1960s, the Conservancy was employing full-time professional wardens. There were even fewer old woodsmen left to give advice by then, and their modern counterparts would discover with hindsight that the slightest deviation from long-established practice could have profound consequences. In 1962, Ray Collier came as the new warden for

Castor Hanglands, near Peterborough. It was the last refuge outside Scotland for the chequered skipper butterfly:

> When I arrived, there had been just over 40 species of butterflies. Within five years of me leaving, it was down to the mid-30s. A few years later, I came down from Scotland to give a talk on dragonflies and some cheeky so-and-so said: 'Are you the Ray Collier who saw the extinction of the chequered skipper on Castor Hanglands?'
>
> 'Yes, I said, but one thing you have to bear in mind, one issue that most people overlook, is that in those days we did not know how to manage woodlands for butterflies.' I used to mow the rides twice a year as per instructions and everything seemed fine. What we didn't know was that things were gradually deteriorating. You were not aware of the optimum width of rides; you were not aware that the undulating margins of rides were important. You underestimated the importance of glades. And of course, you underestimated the importance of coppicing hazel. We weren't doing it right.

Doing it wrong could be down to something as specific as the height of the grass. Ecologists discovered – too late – that chequered skipper caterpillars spin three or four blades of grass together to make themselves a winter hibernaculum. Ray Collier's close-cutting mower along the rides was leaving them nothing with which to build their survival bivouacs.

Though the founders of the Conservancy cherished their National Nature Reserves, in retrospect, they would be – as far as woodland was concerned – but a small flotilla of life rafts in a very big sea.

A less highly rated task, a desktop Domesday, had the

potential for wider benefits. The Conservancy was working up a B list, a second tier of special sites. Each would be given an official stamp of recognition 'by reason of its fauna and flora, or geographical or physiographical features'. The call went out to every expert and every organisation they could possibly think of – natural history societies, entomologists, ornithologists, conservation groups, land agents of estates – and by a huge and impressive process of assimilation and selection, the Conservancy began to designate SSSIs.

Formal notification, lodged with all local authorities, did make landowners aware of treasures in their possession, and almost certainly encouraged many to look after their sites, or at least avoid harming them. However, SSSI status offered precious little protection. When the Conservancy (total annual budget – £7 million) lined up against the Ministry of Agriculture (annual budget for improvement grants alone – £540 million) there was only ever one winner. Farmers could apply to the Ministry of Agriculture for a government grant to grub up a wood that had been given SSSI status, and it would be given because of the overriding 'national interest'. Big money talked and the Conservancy, with nothing more than advisory powers, could do no more than shake its toothless head in disapproval.

Woods, wetlands, meadows, heaths – all were under attack from an 'improving' nation. In a single year, one in twelve of all of Britain's SSSIs was damaged. Staff fighting to save threatened habitats had too much to do – one regional officer spoke of keeping an eye on 120 sites, with more than half of them at risk: 'The telephone never stopped ringing.'

The perennially beleaguered Conservancy developed what its chief scientist Derek Ratcliffe called 'a monumental inferiority complex about itself and its worth to society. We behave as though we accept without question that our rightful place is at the bottom of the pecking order, and the result is that we are pecked hard by everybody else to keep us right down there.'

Waresley Wood

The woodsman

'So what tools do you use? Bowsaws? Billhooks? Axes?'

'Nah,' says Graham the Warden, with a grin. 'I use a chainsaw.'

Last week in neighbouring Hayley Wood, I saw a modern, professional woodsman in action, a lone figure wearing a safety helmet, ear defenders, goggles and steel-capped boots, just like a biker, brandishing a chainsaw that growled like a Kawasaki. Graham the Warden dons the same garb for quick-fix work and tree felling, but today he is a computer programmer in civvies, clad in khaki and steel-capped boots, a volunteer like the rest of us, carrying hand tools that allow for conversation and the calls of birds. All five of us in our work party have chosen to come here on our day off, for a morning of coppicing, to enjoy ourselves, to feel good about doing something useful.

Earlier in the autumn, I spent a full weekend coppicing in Hayley Wood. It was raining redwings: as we crouched over hazel bushes, we could hear them streaming through. We were told we would be cutting a coupe, a rectangular block of the wood that had last been coppiced fourteen years ago.

We didn't need to be told the time frame; every cut end showed fourteen rings radiating out from the first tiny circle of seedling growth. There were rough slashes across the flat oval disc, the marks made by each slice of our bowsaws. We could feel the weight, the bulk, the length carted away in every sawn stem. In no time, we had cut a cord. A what? Woodsmen love their specialist vocabulary; it saves so much time (see Appendix II for more). A cord is, quite simply, according to *Coppicing and coppice crafts: a comprehensive guide*, a stack of 1.2-metre-long logs, held in place by posts rammed into the ground 2.5 metres apart, and piled up to a height of 1.2 metres. The rule of thumb is that two metres cubed equals one tonne.

Fourteen years to grow so much firewood. And fourteen years in the growing cycle before that. And so on and so on for a thousand years or more. No fertiliser, no manure, a limitless, sustainable supply of fuel.

On this short, wet, winter's day, however, I am sawing and pondering at the same time, my brain working, my nose dripping with cold. A woodland historian made calculations for Hayley Wood, working out how much wood could be cut out each year and how long it would take. I guess that for the best part of a thousand years, two men were gainfully and fully employed here in Waresley Wood as woodsmen for the six colder months of the year, when there was no work for them on the farms.

Today, I can sense their spirits in the trees, observe their handiwork at the mossy base of the broadest ash stools, and make out where they cut stems and left the stumps for another generation to work after they had hung up their billhooks. I can feel history here, a sense of belonging to a lowly lineage of woodcutters, a continuity stretching back to 1086, when Swein of Essex was overlord, and the surrounding fields were good for nine ploughs.

Such musings should be put aside in favour of getting

my arse in gear. Graham the Warden has set us, as our task for this morning, a small, ride-side area of hazel, one that was last coppiced when he took over the wood about a dozen years ago.

One of the great unexpected joys of coppicing is that it's easier than it looks – at least to begin with. Another is that you can get quick results. A huge, splayed-out bush can be reduced in minutes to a knobbly stool and in no time the trimmings (the 'lop and top'), still in leaf, can be piled up over the stool to dissuade deer from biting off the first growth of spring.

The bowsaw is sharp, and one hand without a weapon quickly learns where its armed twin, wielding a jagged blade, is cutting. The stems are no more than 10cm in diameter and come down with just a few sweeping, satisfying slices. The uppermost branches, entwined with those of neighbouring bushes, disengage from their fellows; a whole stem, perhaps three metres long, is brought down to land on my neighbour's head. Oops, health and safety instruction number two. Cut stumps show accusatory yellowing faces, but the tree will revive; the coppice is a sustainer of life. The words 'vigorous regrowth' get used a lot.

And while we are stomping around off the path in our boots, inadvertently scuffing and scraping the ground, we are creating the conditions for next year's flowers to grow. Andy Byfield of Plantlife explained to me with the glee of a scientist who is revealing something wonderful, the random, accidental scars on the ground that will give rise to the next generation of flowers.

A single oxlip can live for years, shedding its seeds every spring. However, the seeds fall on the previous year's leaf litter and mulch, and are suspended without purchase for their roots in a loose pile of rot, so cannot grow. But the seeds can find a roothold in the exposed patches of bare earth that have been scraped clear. Coppicing roughs up the ground, just as wild, extinct animals would have done in millennia past. We coppicers have taken on the natural function of old boars.

The roar of a vehicle engine is unexpected here. A man comes down the ride towards us on a quad bike, a jaunty rural Steve McQueen plucked out of *The Great Escape*. Graham barely looks up as this vehicle slews off the ride and through the clearing. We give polite greetings, eyeing the churned-up tracks in the mud, tutting inwardly as he goes past. He has come to feed his pheasants and I doubt the access agreement covered ATVs when the wood was bought in 1975.

But far worse must have been done in the past. Heavy shire horses brought in to extract timber were not wearing slippers. Laden wagons did not have soft tyres on their metal-rimmed cartwheels. In some of the bigger woods, there would have been mudbaths in winter: a Victorian-era advert displayed in a pub close to Herefordshire's Haugh Woods announced that 40 acres would be coppiced that winter. That's cutting and clearing by a big gang of men on a messy, near-industrial scale.

There are parts of the wood that no coppicer's blade has touched in living memory. There appears to be no word in the medieval manager's vocabulary for the places where active management has been abandoned, because, in an age where every bit of the wood was worked, that simply did not happen unless, perhaps, plague reduced the workforce. Modern foresters tend to call it old growth forest.

The other day, I let my eyes wander through the trees in one of these abandoned parts of the wood and they rested on a three-pronged ash leading an interesting life and death. Maybe a century since it was last coppiced, its stool was like a hollowed-out cauldron, lined with moss. The three trunks, each as thick as my waist, growing out in different directions, had met with varying fortunes. One leaned outwards steeply as if on the point of collapse. Another had toppled to the floor decades before and was in a crumbly state of advanced decomposition.

The third fallen trunk appeared dead too. All but detached from the stool, it was specked with white fungus at its broken end. A rack of bracket funus was growing on it, and there were six finger-sized puncture holes in the wood. But some way down the rotting beam, there was new life: two side branches had shot up at right angles to the dying log, and thickened to become new trunks with their own branches and twigs full of leaves, raised in response to gravity, sustained in the earth by an invisible resurrection of roots out of the old trunk. The tree had effectively walked.

The pinewood story

As a wee boy looking out of kitchen window of my grand-parents' first-floor flat in Lanarkshire's new town of East Kilbride, what I could see were 'native pinewoods'. Their pointy bright tops were visible far below on the day my grandparents moved into their pebble-dashed new home, a day when their pet budgie cheeped 'Sydney's a good boy' from his cage. By the time the budgie dropped off his perch, and the pebble-dashed walls had turned a greyer shade of grey, the trees had grown tall, and they carried on growing until they rose above the window sill, blotting out much of the light as surely and as oppressively as any *leylandii* hedge.

The ground beneath the trees was not much fun for this child explorer either. Never thinned, the spruce plantation – for that is really what it was – had too many pokey side branches and resin-coated trunks to warrant more than a cursory intrusion. For years, that was my idea of a pine-wood, or any collection of conifers for that matter. I suspect my ignorance of native pinewood as a child is shared today by millions who think nothing of a trip to Thailand, or a weekend in Budapest, but for whom those incomparable lands towards Inverness are a complete unknown.

Native pinewood. It is such a tame, insipid phrase. Conservation-rich, imagination-poor. It needs a Scots bard, a Robert Burns of the 21st century, to raise its spirit and lift it out of its perfunctory, non-descriptive blandness. Scotland's native pinewoods are, as anyone who has been there knows, a territory like no other, places where mythology is overwhelmed by reality.

I remember my first time; stepping off the train at Aviemore, heading out for Loch Morlich, rucksack on my back, map in map case swinging to and fro, to and fro, tangling straps in straps. I entered Rothiemurchus Forest, a genuine native pinewood, and was enveloped in green, a shagpile carpet of blueberry, heather and moss. And that was what struck me most, the paradox of verdancy over ground that is subjected to such climatic extremes – snow in winter, snow in spring, snow in autumn, and a few wet summer weeks in between. I was drunk on the pine resin that filled the air, on dippers, sandpipers and wagtails along the burn, on chaffinches and crossbills in the canopy. I still am.

* * *

As the emblem of a nation, the Scots pine is as Scottish as the Costa Brava. Despite the name, it is the most widespread species of pine in the world. You can find it at the tundra border in northern Norway; it stands above Spain's holiday resort coastline. The Russians, Chinese and everyone else know this familiar tree by its scientific name as *Pinus sylvestris*, 'the pine pertaining to a wood or forest'.

Within the British Isles, Scotland can claim the tree as its own. Probably. Although a few tree experts argue that there may be some bog-dwelling remnants in England, the prevailing view is that a warming climate here 4,000 years ago drove the Scots pine out of all places south of the Scottish Highlands. The surviving native pinewoods,

referred to (with some degree of scientific licence) as 'the
lineal descendants of those of pre-glacial times' were identified as a sub-species of the parent body. *Pinus sylvestris
scotica* is a short-needled, stubby-coned variant of a tree
that shows more global variation than any other conifer.

A much-respected naturalist helped its case within its
Highland domain. There is no greater Scottish nationalist
than a resident Englishman, and Derbyshire-born Frank
Fraser Darling (plain Frank Darling until he tagged on
his wife's maiden name) boosted his Celtic credentials by
unwittingly perpetuating an anti-English myth. In his 1947
work *Natural History in the Highlands and Islands,* he
gave credence to the rose-tinted view of a Great Forest of
Caledon that had clothed the entire Highlands of Scotland
until the invading 'Auld Enemy' swept in. In his opinion, it
had been 'the English [who] have been the greatest agents of
destruction in Scottish forests'.

Long before the Romans coined the name of the 'Great
Forest of Caledon', the truth was pleated in a patchwork
of mixed forest and open land. Great clearances had been
carried out by farmers in the Bronze Age. But the story of
English villains pillaging Scottish land and cutting down its
trees was irresistible. It was even reiterated by Richard Mabey
in his authoritative *Flora Britannica*, published nearly half
a century later. Speaking in 1994, Magnus Magnusson, as
chairman of Scottish Natural Heritage, commented on 'the
rash of romantic pseudo-historical effusions which have
deluged us regarding that mythical forest'. He nevertheless
recognised that 'what matters is that they touched a chord
deep within the public.'

National pride played a significant role in ensuring
that the story of native pinewoods in Scotland would be
completely different, and on a different timescale, from

that of broadleaved woodland. The authors of *The Native Pinewoods of Scotland* declared in 1959 that the pinewoods 'can be considered to be not the least important of the historical monuments of Scotland'.

'Native' was an important aspect of their appeal. Many argued that 'genetic purity' gave the Scottish Scots pine particular strengths. Forestry scientists talked imaginatively of special 'strains' of Scots pine; observing a type in the windswept west that could tolerate salt spray and nearly two metres of rain on 240 days of the year, a hardy strain in the east that could grow at 900 metres. Scots pines were generally considered by those in forestry as 'important and valuable tree material which should not be contaminated by non-indigenous strains'.

The Forestry Commission showed its belief in this tree at its foundation, though this unswerving devotion didn't last long. In the 1920s, almost half of all the trees planted throughout Britain were Scots pines. However, it was soon discovered that they didn't do as well in the wetter soils of the west. The Commission's research scientist, Henry Steven, looking for viable alternatives, considered that he did not know 'a species... which gives greater promise than Sitka spruce'. It was a supreme paradox that the same scientist would go on to carry out a piece of work nearly 30 years later, that would, more than anything else, help to protect native pinewoods from Sitka spruce plantations.

Right up until the 1950s, the Forestry Commission was still carrying out projects to grow Scots pines on the estates it had acquired before the war, principally at Glenmore, Glengarry, Glen Loy and Guisachan (the name means 'little pinewood' in Gaelic). All sorts of methods were tried in the hope that pines would regenerate naturally, including stripping back competing vegetation and feeding seedlings with fertiliser. The results were, in the Commission's opinion, 'extremely disappointing'.

Meanwhile, Henry Steven, the dour, stern Forestry Commission researcher, the foremost pre-war advocate for Sitka spruce, embarked on work that would have far-reaching consequences. Steven had jumped the fence and now occupied the professorial chair of forestry at Aberdeen University. For whatever reason, he had embarked on a mission to identify and catalogue all of Scotland's native pinewoods. How many were there and where? Nobody had ever found out. In 1950, Steven advertised for someone to take on a research fellowship, a field worker who would have the daunting task of exploring every inch of the Highlands.

An ex-RAF man who had newly qualified with a forestry degree from Bangor stepped into the role. Alan 'Jock' Carlisle soon discovered that Highlanders were an extremely tough breed. He was sent off to serve an open-air apprenticeship under the tutelage of the head forester of Glen Tanar, a man who walked and walked and walked over rough ground, leaving the Lancastrian in his tweed jacket and hobnailed boots to keep up as best he could. Duncan Ross was an exceptional field tutor – Jock marvelled that he was able to predict the size of a cone harvest four years ahead.

His practical training complete, Jock headed into the Highlands, with the instruction to 'go and find the pinewoods' ringing in his ears. He rode on his ancient RAF bicycle, parking it up when he could only go so far on it, until one day it seemed a stag mistook the bike's handlebars for a rival's antlers and trashed it. He had no more success with his next mode of transport, a little car that was too much for a decrepit Highland bridge. The car, and its occupant ended up in a burn. Car number two kept breaking its axles.

Mostly, Jock walked. For up to a week at a time, he tramped over rough, boggy terrain, picking his way up mountainsides and gazing out through his telescope into the next glen for signs of pines. He carried a gun, so that he could shoot down seed-filled cones from the trees to examine them in the lab later. Sometimes he encountered gamekeepers who suspected he was a poacher. Since Jock had an appalling stammer, protestations of innocence could be painfully protracted. He joked that Steven had employed him as a field worker only because it meant he wouldn't have to talk to anyone much.

Sustained only by dried fruit and biscuits, Jock often slept out under rocks or trees in pouring rain, waking at dawn to find himself surrounded by herds of red deer, and eagles soaring above his head. He walked in winter as well as summer. There were times towards the end of a long slog when he became dangerously exhausted, and popped an amphetamine tablet to keep himself alert.

One day, he nearly died. Writer John Fowler travelled to Canada, where Jock had emigrated, to capture the elderly forester's memories in an interview for a wide-ranging and perceptive book on Scotland's trees and forests called *Landscapes and Lives*. Jock recalled the life-threatening incident:

> I had decided to hike up to the end of Alladale. It was icy and there were snowstorms, but I decided to hack on and see what was up there. So I carried out a rather superficial survey and then I thought, people had said there were still remains of pines in Diebiedale. So I decided to go over the hill and see what was there. When I got over the hill I encountered a terrible, terrible storm. I said, Jock, this is

being very stupid, turn back, go home.

I guess I must have been tired, I slipped on ice and fell over a cliff. When I woke I was paralysed from the waist downwards. I reckoned I'd smashed my spine. This was one of the few times I hadn't told anyone where I was going. There wasn't going to be any help. You're dying. Then I remembered deer I'd seen in the forest and how the foxes had eaten their entrails whilst they were still alive. Jock, you'd better damn well do something!

I started imagining. I remember looking at my toes and saying: Move, you bastards, move, wiggle, wiggle... I was on my hands and knees and then I graduated to stumbling. Quite soon I had to go over a river. It was icy. I took off most of my clothes and with great invective and cursing and swearing and howling and yelling, stumbled across, waist deep in places, half falling in it all the time.

I ended up lying on my side beside a road and I feebly tried to signal some cars to stop but they all thought I was drunk. Eventually a very elderly gentleman halted his ancient vehicle and he took me to my room at a temperance hotel in Ardgay. Temperance! – they'd never heard of temperance. They filled me full of hot whisky, tea and aspirins. I was fairly badly injured, actually.

The funny thing is, nobody thought of calling a doctor. In those days you didn't. I could stagger to a potty to relieve myself but I couldn't scrub myself. The two old women who owned the hotel decided I needed a wash. So they stripped me stark naked, these two old girls, and the ribaldry was very entertaining.

During several foot-slogging years, Jock developed an instinctive ability to assess whether a wood was ancient or not. He would return to the city, its libraries and its archives, to find he was invariably right. Jock was identifying and demarcating the bounds of 35 places that were to become universally accepted as Scotland's last pinewood remnants. Later research showed minor additions but Jock's basic list of 35 significant pine forests still holds today. Steven was simultaneously following the historical path. The professor shaped their combined findings into a book published in 1959 as *The Native Pinewoods of Scotland*.

Steven and Carlisle's magnum opus was an instant success, a landmark, a benchmark, a guide for those who wanted to give pinewoods a future. It won widespread respect, having been steered by Steven, one of Scotland's leading foresters, an unquestionable authority based in one of the country's most revered forestry institutions. And the authors were gifted quote makers. The most famous line in the book is a simple, evocative tug at the heart. Why should we save the pinewoods? They answer: 'To stand in them is to feel the past.'

In measuring the size of the task before the nation, the authors had done what it would take their counterparts in England another quarter of a century to achieve. They had quantified and defined the threatened habitat. It was established, beyond doubt, that native pinewoods occupied an area less than one-tenth of the size of Fraser Darling's native Derbyshire, and all were confined to the Scottish Highlands. It was surely possible to protect such a small, unique remnant?

There was one major snag. The forests were dying. Huge gnarled trees, hundreds of years old, were the only pines left standing – the great gaps between them created by two centuries of living lawnmowers. First came the cattle, then the sheep, and finally, an explosion in the numbers of deer – sustained for shooting on the moors, their populations were allowed to balloon unchecked.

Golden eagles still nested in the huge trees where they had nested half a century before, wildcats still sheltered their young in the hollow trunks, but there was no youth and no vigour left in these geriatric forests. As things stood, there would come a time when there would be no trees for the eagles, no hollows for the wildcats. It was becoming all too apparent that the patient was in a critical condition.

Steven and Carlisle's book provided the stirring words to spur a recovery. Countless authors and speakers would quote them to justify the need for change. A large part of the book's effectiveness lay in its direct call to action: 'The first thing needed to ensure the future of the native pinewoods is the appreciation by as many of their owners as possible that they are a unique natural heritage.'

Some longstanding and seriously landed estate owners took up the challenge. The Grant family of Rothiemurchus, owners of a four-mile-long stretch of forest on the River Spey since the sixteenth century, was restoring native forest devastated by wartime fellings. The head forester said the laird wanted his estate to 'look nice, look right'.

In Glen Tanar, the easternmost pinewood in Scotland, the laird had met with a happy accident when he fenced deer out of the forest and adjoining moor to prevent them spreading disease-ridden ticks to his precious red grouse. The unplanned by-product of this deer exclusion was the finest natural regeneration of all Scots pinewoods.

Worthy deeds did not, however, pay the bills. Basil Dunlop, head forester for the Seafield Estates, which owned Speyside's Abernethy Forest, said the forest was managed as a business on commercial lines. The owners had entered into a dedication agreement in 1956 to 'recognise the importance of the area as a native pinewood'. But, as Dunlop said, they failed to keep up with the fine sentiments of the agreement. Ten years later, they ordered him to begin piecemeal felling. Big pieces too – 200 acres one year, 50 acres another, 200 more acres elsewhere. And roads were bulldozed through virgin forest to get the trees out.

Dunlop would spend the rest of his working life (and his retirement) fighting to protect native pinewoods, but he gave an honest retrospective view of his time as a working forester on a private estate:

> Timber is valuable, it is worth a lot of money. The owner, quite rightly in my opinion, wants to cash in on his resources. It is up to us if we want to stop this felling of every last piece of timber to make sure that some sort of grants are provided, some sort of payment is made to induce the owner not to fell.

Steven and Carlisle write about 'a considerable area of almost pure Scots pine towards the upper limit of Amat Wood… on the upper slopes, there are small pure stands of pine that are well stocked and contain good timber.' But this has long gone. In 1964, away went the pines. You could call pinewoods 'magnificent', but standing trees made no money.

Who would take the initiative to stem the losses of pinewoods and promote their recovery? Steven and Carlisle were clear about who they thought should take control: 'Perhaps the two government departments interested, the Forestry Commission and the Nature Conservancy, might take the lead.'

The new Nature Conservancy already had some history in pinewood protection: its very first National Nature Reserve, a whole mountain, Beinn Eighe on Loch Maree, included a small pinewood, Coille na Glas Leitire ('the wood of the grey slope'). When the owner announced he had been made an offer for its timber, the Conservancy director broke Treasury rules by purchasing the estate outright. In 1951, he paid the bargain price of £3,300, which worked out at eight shillings and three pence an acre. Some rules are just meant to be broken.

The following summer, a site meeting involving all interested parties splintered into disagreements about how the reserve, ravaged by wartime fellings, should be restored. It was then that the Forestry Commission's director for Scotland made his pitch: 'The Forestry Commission too, have an interest in these woodlands because it is their duty to achieve the maximum productivity of the woodlands of the country of which this forms a part.' In his view, it would be too expensive for the Conservancy to manage. Wouldn't it be far better handing it over to an organisation that was set up properly to do so?

The Nature Conservancy was incensed by what amounted to an attempted takeover of its first purchase. An eminent Scottish committee member called Professor Yonge simmered with indignation: 'There is a gulf between the outlook of the botanical ecologist and that of the forester.'

The Conservancy's director-general in London shared his outrage over:

> ...the tacit assumption that the Conservancy's function should be so to modify the pinewood at Coille na Glas Leitire so as to make it, as nearly as possible, by silvicultural standards, a good wood. A good wood, in forestry terms, being plenty of tall, straight trees ripe for the sawmill, a plantation by another name. That this provides a valid basis for considering the regime of biological management which

should be applied to one of the Conservancy's few first class national reserves, I must categorically deny.

The Commission's proposal to carry out large-scale replanting on the estate was foiled when the Conservancy sent in a scientist to survey the wood, which was still studded with stumps where Canadian lumberjacks had felled during the war. The findings seemed to indicate that there was potential for the forest to regenerate naturally, and so the Conservancy wrested back control to promote that style of management. It was, however, a short-lived victory. By 1958, the Conservancy lost its nerve at a lack of growth and began planting thousands of seedlings, just as the Commission had recommended in the first place.

All through the next 30 years, the Forestry Commission played its role in the Highlands as a Jekyll and Hyde character. After the publication of the book known ever after as 'Steven and Carlisle', it went on to carry out restoration work under the guidance of some of the finest conservationists of the era. It went wholeheartedly into measures to promote natural regeneration. It welcomed the public into its forests, some of the most beautiful in Scotland. But at the same time, it was contributing to so much forest destruction, even in the pinewoods that it owned.

A future board member of the Forestry Commission, Sir John Lister-Kaye, recalled an episode that summed up the dual nature of the organisation at that time:

I vividly remember, back in the early 1970s, going to Glen Affric to hear Raymond Baxter [former presenter of the BBC's *Tomorrow's World*] announce on national television, the Forestry Commission's first Caledonian pine reserve. All too well do I remember driving back that afternoon to

[Forestry Commissioned-owned] Guisachan where I lived in those days, because as I drove home so I met the lorries trundling out the great noble trunks of the Guisachan and Cougie pinewood which at that moment was being clear felled for replacement with Sitka spruce and lodgepole pine.

Great things were possible within the Commission, if strong individuals were prepared to push for them. Red-bearded Finlay MacRae was an acclaimed piper from Skye and a former student of Henry Steven at Aberdeen University. He was sent to run the Commission's biggest forest at Glen Affric and quickly appraised himself of the errors of the past and the potential for the future. Three of the glen's lochs had been dammed for hydroelectric power, drowning parts of the forest. A decade before, the Commission had denuded Glen Cannich, a spur of the main glen, and planted lodgepole pines. There was still a scattering of birches, alders, rowans and aspens on the slopes. MacRae, with a fine appreciation of broadleaved trees and beauty in the landscape, left them standing. He said they softened the glen's appearance. They certainly brought a dazzle of autumn colour.

Before MacRae arrived, the main part of Glen Affric's pinewoods had been fenced right down to the shore of Loch Benevian to keep deer out. They hadn't allowed for Highland winters. When the deep loch froze over, deer trotted across for pine seedling breakfasts. In one exceptional winter, MacRae recorded surface ice to a depth of 27 inches.

He began in earnest a practice that is carried out today by all large pinewood owners, from the National Trust for Scotland to the RSPB: he and his men began culling deer systematically to bring their numbers right down. MacRae drove over the frozen loch in a Land Rover to collect the carcasses and then drove back, not worrying about what might happen if the ice broke under his wheels.

Other foresters had planted pines in Affric before him to regenerate parts of the forest, but the seed used had been collected from all over the Highlands. MacRae insisted on local provenance, creating a precedent for other foresters in other locations. He sent young volunteers up a ladder to collect cones and shake the seeds out, and then the seedlings were raised in a Black Isle nursery.

Eight million pines were planted in Glen Affric in three years, but that feat was exceeded by something far more impressive. Under the right conditions, the existing pines would do the work for them. The men had lowered the deer population to such an extent that enough pine seedlings were able to spring up from the forest floor unbitten. And MacRae allowed broadleaved trees to flourish between the mature pines instead of cutting them down and filling the gaps.

Thanks to an inspired and enlightened individual, the Forestry Commission's Glen Affric had become a glorious showcase for pinewood restoration, and still is today. When he retired after 25 years, Finlay MacRae promised that he would 'return in a hundred years' time to see how it looks from a different angle'. Let's hope he brings his bagpipes.

Another Commission forester ahead of his time came to turn round the fortunes of the Black Wood of Rannoch, west of Pitlochry. The organisation's chairman, Lord Robinson, had visited in 1947 to open the newly purchased site, stating that 'this piece of old Caledonian pine forest should, if possible, be preserved.' The word 'possible' hung precariously over the forest for the next quarter of a century, as 5,000 old pines were felled and exotic plantations were sited on wetter ground.

Rescue arrived in 1973 in the shape of Gunnar Godwin. Half Icelandic, half Danish, Godwin came fuelled with Scandinavian zeal for blending forestry with nature conservation. Doubtful about the long-term security of the Black Wood under the control of future Commission foresters, Godwin met up with Nature Conservancy Council (NCC – the successor to the Nature Conservancy) staff and concluded a radical joint agreement with the Commission. The Black Wood was to be managed in perpetuity with nature conservation as its prime objective. A plaque at the foot of a Rannoch pine today testifies to Godwin's perseverance and vision.

All too often, the great achievements of individuals were counteracted by the Forestry Commission's driving ethos of maximum production. Foresters were conditioned to abhor a vacuum: if there was a space, they had to fill it with trees. In his retirement, John McEwen, a past president of the Royal Scottish Forestry Society, reaffirmed his belief: 'I am not satisfied with woodlands unless they are highly managed, 100 per cent of every acre under trees'.

In the western pinewoods especially, the trees, ancient and stunted by Atlantic storms, were often far apart, the ground between them more characteristic of moorland than forest. Working for the Nature Conservancy in the late 1960s, Martin Ball recalled visiting forests where most of the pines had been left standing, but the land in between had been ruthlessly infilled with North American conifers. The growing crop would overshadow and often kill the veterans. Worse still, deep ploughing before planting had wrecked the soil. Instead of the complex mosaic of gravels and peaty hollows that had developed over millions of years, creating and encouraging pines here, a damp patch full of bog asphodel there, the ground had been chopped up into a homogenous mass.

Mindful of exhortations to maximise the potential of the land under their ownership, staff worked around the existing pinewoods, corralling them within plantations, denying them the opportunity to spread out and recolonise. 'These highland fir woods shift their stances,' said an eighteenth century sage. By the second half of the 20th century, there was nowhere for them to shift.

Ten years after the publication of Steven and Carlisle, Henry Steven was dead and Jock Carlisle had emigrated to Canada. The pinewoods the two men had documented were in trouble. A Nature Conservancy survey begun in 1969 showed that, in 58 out of 416 plots sampled, the pinewoods had been converted to exotic conifer plantations. As a consequence, a government-funded symposium was set up in Aviemore to form a plan of action.

Winners get to write history. Conservationists are always ready to tell the story of how the Forestry Commission's northern office banned its staff from the symposium. But less well known is the fact that when two men from the office local to Aviemore turned up for the symposium, unaware that their colleagues had been banned, they discovered that a summary document outlining future actions had already been written by a cabal of conservationists, before it had even started.

Late-night discussions to restructure the done deal resulted in a document outlining ways forward that met with everyone's approval. There was even agreement to create buffer zones to allow pine forests to expand naturally. At last, there was a plan for pines.

Or was there? For seven years, nature writer Peter Marren attended meetings to agree management for pinewood SSSIs on behalf of the NCC. These were supposed to be partnerships between the landowner, the NCC and the Forestry Commission. There are partnerships and then there are partnerships. Invariably, the meetings would follow a set routine; the landowner would decide what should be done, and the Forestry Commission man would agree. Not that their sewn-up agreement would make much difference – the estate's foresters would do what they thought was best regardless. Marren recalled that 'natural regeneration' often meant cutting down all of the mature pine trees and then seeing what came up.

Private forestry companies had no need of a public conscience and worried less about ecology than profits. When Irvine Ross took over from his father as head forester of Glen Tanar Estate in 1977, a senior manager in one of the large forestry management firms told him the only thing to be done with the native pinewood was to 'cut it all down and start again'.

Richard Ogilvie of Fountain Forestry, a company man who met regularly with the conservation lobby and understood them, was forever teasing the 'opposition' and, in his jesting, gave glimpses of the views of others on his side. He once half-jokingly remarked that the terrain under pinewoods was:

> generally hummocky with a fearsome growth of heather, blueberry and moss, with the juniper thrown in so you can't see where you are going. I often feel that those people most vociferous in demanding that we retain the pinewoods should be taken for a walk through them some time. It would harden the case of the foresters who wish to plough them all up with nice even furrows.

In Abernethy Forest today, you can look over an area of land and make out dips and rises that – if you were in a different place – you might think were signs of old ridge and furrow farming. But those lingering plough lines are a lasting reminder of something far more recent, a conifer plantation. It was at Abernethy that the whole issue was set to blow up quite spectacularly.

SMALL VICTORIES IN DEFEAT

Even in the darkest period of woodland history, there were individuals with sufficient strength of purpose, determination, even bloody-mindedness, who fought to preserve what one of them expressed eloquently as 'something permanent in today's world, in which so much else is subject to unpredictable change'. Those saviours are now elderly or no longer with us. The stories of the woodlands they rescued are half remembered or all but forgotten. Not quite. They offered crumbs of hope at the time. They still do today.

* * *

If you want the bloody place...

Cambridgeshire, 1946
The first of these stories begins little more than a mile and a half from Waresley Wood. A new student at Cambridge University was thrilled when his tutor, a lecturer in forest botany in the least-wooded county in England, planned a study trip to a local wood. Humphrey Gilbert-Carter was one of Cambridge's most entertaining dons, famous for taking his pet sheepdog into lectures and training it to bark every time he slipped in the word 'Ovina!' (the scientific word for sheep). Undergraduate Donald Pigott, a firm devotee, took

Gilbert-Carter's advice: 'When entering a wood, first look up at what is above you'.

The following spring, however, Donald could barely keep his eyes off the ground, for there was a flower he had never seen in his life. Thousands and thousands of oxlips were in bloom on that memorable day in Hayley Wood, in what was recognised as one of the finest and most abundant displays of the flower in Britain. Through his student years, lecturer Alex Watt would lead Donald and a Sri Lankan fellow student with the wonderful name of Bartholemeusz Aristides Abeywickrama to Hayley Wood, for it served as one of the university's outdoor laboratories and Donald would get to know it intimately. It was, in the words of a woodland historian, 'probably the only remaining feature of its parish that would be instantly recognisable to a resident of Domesday times', preserving its shape, its banks, trees and flowers, an extraordinary time capsule of richness and antiquity.

Years later, and by now a university lecturer himself, Donald Pigott returned to teach in Cambridge and resume his love affair with Hayley Wood. Often, he and his research students would chat with the family who lived in the railway cottage at the entrance to the wood. The day came when they learnt the farmer was planning to fell the wood and replace it with conifers. 'If you want the bloody place, then buy it!' roared the farmer when Donald went to see him. He was keen to be rid of the wood as it harboured woodpigeons, and told Donald he was planning to sell it to a timber merchant in the nearby town.

Donald, a council member of the Wildlife Trust, went to the next meeting with a proposal to buy the wood (the asking price was all of £5,000) and was dismayed at its response. 'They told me "we can't afford it, we'll have no funds to do anything else and even if we buy it, we will have no money to manage it."'

For a few dreadful minutes in the meeting, Hayley Wood looked doomed, fated to become yet another Norway spruce plantation. Donald fought a rearguard action, fired with passion. He spoke of the scientific value of the site, painted word-pictures of the great spring displays of oxlips and bluebells, the green tunnels of the rides in summer. Stirred by his oratory, a fellow member of the council, a chap of honour, spoke up: 'You obviously love this wood and hold it in very high regard; I think we should back you.' With that, the chairman added his support and the wood's future was secured. The privately uttered words of another council member stayed with Donald: 'If we can't do this, then what are we here for?'

*　　*　　*

A hill fit for goats

Lancashire, 1963
Remarkably, Donald was the prime instigator of another famous flagship reserve rescue at the other end of England. He had gone to Lancaster tasked with setting up a biology department at the new university. A geologist as well as a botanist, he decided to visit an extraordinary site close to Morecambe Bay he had heard of called Gait Barrows. He had seen it in photographs, a natural, smooth limestone pavement laid down by shallow seas 100 million years ago, and then raked, split and shaped by glaciers in the last Ice Age.

When he got there, he found a dwarf woodland growing on parts of the pavement: bonsai ash, yew and rowan that added no more than a couple of millimetres' growth a year. The sparse, scrubby bushes had given the site its name – Gait Barrows, a hill (barrow) fit only for goats (gait). Donald discovered deep fissures in the pavement, called grikes, that sheltered dark red helleborine orchids and limestone ferns. He was captivated by what he saw.

He had arrived in the nick of time. At the eastern edge, he found that the farmer was quarrying the limestone, slipping gelignite into the grikes to shatter the pavement, then sending lorryloads of rock down the motorway to end up in garden rockeries. He tried to explain the geological significance of the limestone pavement, pointing out what is known by the wonderfully apt geological term as an 'erratic', a giant boulder that a glacier had carried down from the northern Lake District. The farmer listened, then blew it up with explosives. Further negotiation seemed pointless.

Donald was – as we have already seen – a man of determined character. He took up the case with Lancashire County Council and embarked on what would become a drawn-out battle. Long after he had first contacted them, a reply came, asking him to survey Gait Barrows, and to state exactly why he thought it was so important. Very helpfully, the council loaned him a landscape architect, Roger Cartwright, who surveyed, and then wrote and submitted a paper with him. The council agreed to hold a public meeting.

Donald recalled his disbelief at what happened next: 'The Nature Conservancy Council official stood up and said "I don't see why a farmer shouldn't be able to remove limestone from his land, and if he can sell it, good for him." I was absolutely astounded that this could be said at a meeting that was being set up to save the place.'

It was perverse, inexplicable behaviour on the part of

the government official. Nonetheless, Lancashire County Council came to the temporary rescue by agreeing to put a time-limited stopping order on the farmer to prevent more limestone being removed, subject to Donald finding someone to buy it. History was repeating itself; again he needed money, this time £6,000. He asked the Lancashire Wildlife Trust, of which he was a council member, but knew it was an optimistic request. They said what he expected, that they could not afford that kind of money.

There was one last chance. Donald was also a member of the NCC committee, so he travelled down to London's Belgrave Square to sell the case for Gait Barrows, but met with a lukewarm response. However, rather than dismiss it out of hand, the committee agreed that their chief scientist should take a look. Derek Ratcliffe came up to Cumbria and the two men – who were good friends – carried out a full inspection over two days. Ratcliffe went into raptures over the limestone pavement and agreed it was a high-priority site. The wheels were set in motion and in 1977, fourteen years after the battle began, Gait Barrows was declared a National Nature Reserve. Patience was indeed a virtue.

*   *   *

Armfuls, literally armfuls, of flowers

Suffolk, 1966
One of the most shocking and celebrated woodland battles took place in the gently rolling landscape of Suffolk, east of Bury St Edmunds. The lands that had been owned by Bury St Edmunds Abbey before the dissolution of the monasteries were still substantially wooded. John Barker was local to

the woods, brought up during the early 1950s in the tiny village of Bradfield St George.

> We used to walk in the fields and the farmer would wave at us. We would never get up to any real mischief, because the farmer knew who we were and where we lived. In the spring, I used to perform a kind of social service. The old people in the village would send me into the woods to pick armfuls, literally armfuls, of oxlips and other flowers. They were too infirm to go to the woods any more, so they sent me to bring the woods to them.

There was no official access to most of these woods for the general public, but the locals in these still close-knit communities had walked in them for generations. They felt that they had some kind of connection with the view from their cottage windows. The largest – known as Bradfield Woods, which resounded to the song of nightingales in spring – had been studied by a Cambridge academic. He speculated that some of the gigantic ash coppice stools, measuring twelve feet in diameter and sprouting multiple stems, could be the oldest living things in Suffolk.

The area of Bradfield Woods known as Monks Park Wood had been just that – in 1252, Bury St Edmunds Abbey's monks had been tending it as an open park woodland with small meadow clearings. Coppicing had continued in Bradfield Woods until after the war; the woods had been owned by a nearby rake factory, which coppiced 30 acres one winter in the early 1950s. By the mid-60s, however, there was little demand for wooden hay rakes, the factory closed, and Bradfield Woods was included in a plot of land bought by a farmer down from Scotland.

In 1966, a bulldozer was sent in to grub out the wood.

The aftermath was not a pretty sight – trees, branches and twigs were simply stacked up and set alight. Over the next three winters, an area equivalent to 80 football pitches disappeared and the smoke from wood fires billowed up through the air all though spring and summer. But there was local resistance. A couple spearheading a campaign to stop the wood's complete destruction managed a holding exercise, by persuading the council to put a Tree Preservation Order on the mature trees. The farmer's son went in to clear the last area he was still legally entitled to bulldoze. As he pushed forward on his tractor, a sapling whipped back and struck, killing him instantly.

Would anyone step in to save Bradfield Woods? The Suffolk Wildlife Trust looked at its financial reserves and decided it was beyond them. They appealed to their parent body for help and the Society for the Promotion of Nature Reserves lived up to its name, stumping up £10,000 to buy the woods.

The Trust found its new reserve to be a site of unbelievable natural wealth, a wood unrivalled in East Anglia. A geological mosaic, ranging from heavy boulder clay to pockets of acidic, sandy soil, it hosts 370 species of plant, including more indicators of ancient woodland than any other in Britain. Those of us who want to get a sense of what it would be like to walk through medieval England might pass through the Shambles in York, or process down the nave of one of our great cathedrals. But there is perhaps nothing quite as 'authentic' as Bradfield Woods. Today its 82 hectares are a National Nature Reserve; at the time of its purchase it was not even an SSSI. It was a very close shave.

*   *   *

Cowman saves the day

Norfolk, 1965

A wood in the neighbouring county of Norfolk owes its survival to a farm worker who happened to go on a day trip to the seaside. In March 1965, cowman Alec Bull had just bought his first car at the age of 38, and had gone with his wife on an outing to the North Norfolk coast. He noted in his diary that, returning home across country, 'between Themelthorpe and Foxley we passed a large wood with a wide verge stretching for more than 100 yards, packed from end-to-end with huge oak trunks awaiting collection en route to the sawmill'. He recalled going inside and seeing 'a scene of devastation as it had been a very wet season and the deep tracks made by tractors pulling the trunks out were filled with vast pools of water'.

Alec knew exactly what this meant. Humble origins were no bar to this self-taught accumulator of knowledge and expertise. He mixed with the university-educated middle classes of the local natural history society, co-authored the *Flora of Norfolk*, and acted as the county representative of the British Trust of Ornithology, but kept his kind humility and Norfolk burr.

At that time, living 30 miles away, Alec felt he was in no position to do anything about what he had encountered. Quite by chance, when he changed jobs two and a half years later he moved to the village neighbouring the devastated wood. The following spring, Alec slipped surreptitiously into what he now knew to be Foxley Wood, to see if any flowers had survived the felling. Amazingly, the scars were healing well and the tracks and rides were already coming into bloom with primroses, bluebells, wood anemones and wild garlic. He wrote to the Nature Conservancy at once and received a reply saying that Foxley Wood had originally been designated as an SSSI because of its 200-year-old-plus trees. But since they no longer existed, the wood had been stripped of its status.

Undeterred, Alec sought and received permission to visit the wood. Over a period of two years, between milking and mucking out the cows, he recorded birds, bees, flowers, mosses, liverworts – everything. He made friends with the old gamekeeper-woodsman, who recalled seeing purple emperor butterflies there, flying round 'as big as bats', and said that the wood had a 'king oak'. Distinctive individual trees would often be given a name. This tree would, presumably, have been the biggest in the wood. In his book *Beechcombings*, Richard Mabey recalls the Praying Beech and the Queen Beech in the Chiltern hills near his Berkhamsted home.

Alec Bull wrote to the Conservancy again after completing his survey and this time it acted. He was invited to meetings in the wood with its representatives, sympathetic local staff from the Forestry Commission and the owner, an absentee businessman from Peterborough who thanked Alec for his work, and confessed he had been unaware of the damage caused since he had sold a lease on Foxley Wood.

All parties agreed on a management plan. The site was given a respite from conversion to conifer plantations, and, in due course, was bought by the Norfolk Wildlife Trust. Typically, Alec gave all the credit for its salvation to others. He went back to finding new species of bramble. At the last count, at the age of 89, his tally stood at 130.

* * *

A dying wish fulfilled

Ceredigion, 1966

A little to the north of Aberystwyth, the Ynys-hir estate overlooks the Dyfi estuary. It was bought in 1928 by Hubert Mappin (of jewellers Mappin and Webb) and, for decades, this gentle man and his wife Patricia managed it as their own private nature reserve. They were passionate and determined conservationists; the elderly Hubert had once seen off an otter hunt from his land. But now the dying Hubert feared for the future of Ynys-hir. He fretted about Coed Penrhyn, the wood on the slope, as well as the estate's water meadows and saltmarshes. The couple turned to their tenants for advice. They had given a cottage on the estate to empathetic souls, writer-naturalist Bill Condry and his wife Penny. Now the couple offered to repay their kindness by seeking a sympathetic owner to safeguard Ynys-hir.

The local wildlife trust was evidently an impoverished non-starter. What about the RSPB? suggested Bill Condry. The Mappins were dubious. Could they afford it either? Were they financially secure? Hubert Mappin's doubts were expressed in his last act, when he signed a deed of covenant with the National Trust. It gave the Trust overall management control over whoever bought the site. Shortly after, forestry companies heard about Hubert's death and, with vulture-like haste, began making enquiries about buying the estate.

Condry invited the RSPB director Peter Conder for a site visit.

He arrived on a March day of raw east wind. The world was grey and shrivelled; there was no sky; the oakwoods were black and lifeless; a dismal haze hid the estuary and its flocks of wildfowl; and the Dyfi-side hills that should have stood up as a splendid background were lost in the filthiest murk. Not a day we would have chosen to show off the charms of the estate. I took Peter round, trying to make up for the gloom and absence of birds by giving him a word-picture of what Ynys-hir is like on better days.

As we got near their clump of Scots pines, our pair of ravens rose and circled impressively, proudly trumpeting their ownership of the site, for after eight years they were still using their old nest. We watched them as they flew across the sky at speed to chivvy off a buzzard that had floated too near. Beyond the pines, as we walked along the ridge of Ynys Feurig, a lovely pale hen harrier sailed closely past. And, final touch, when we went to look at the heronry, there was a peregrine perched on one of the herons' tallest pines. Maybe these fine raptors helped the cause. For despite the east wind and the gloom, Peter Conder had no difficulty in seeing the possibilities of the place and went away full of enthusiasm.

Patricia Mappin was still not convinced. She asked Bill Condry to describe how he thought the reserve would look after the RSPB had bought it, and Condry gave her as clear a picture as he could manage. A few weeks later, she came to his cottage carrying a framed painting. 'Is this how it would look?' she asked him. She had produced an impression of Ynys-hir, a visual interpretation of Bill Condry's word-pictures. The painting still hangs in Penny Condry's cottage and the scene shows the reserve just as it looks today.

The RSPB had work to do. It appealed to its members to help it buy Ynys-hir, and unashamedly used approaches that reflected the times.

Calling all housewives – few in these rather trying times can squeeze £5 from the housekeeping money, let alone £20, but if five hundred bold spirits will each embark on just one good fund-raising effort there is a good chance that the Appeal will benefit by as much as £10,000.

It would seem that there was enough coffee money to go round, for the RSPB succeeded in buying Ynys-hir. The West Wales' Naturalists' Trust showed its support with a contribution. But even now, half a century later, the RSPB has to ask the National Trust for permission before it does anything on the reserve. 'Frankly, it's a bit embarrassing for everyone,' rues David Anning, the RSPB manager for the site.

* * *

The spy and the camera

Hampshire, 1970
Politeness and deference were wrecking a great swathe of the New Forest and it took an act of amateur espionage to stop it. When archaeologist and medieval historian David Stagg visited the Forestry Commission's library at its Alice Holt research station in the summer of 1970, he quite by chance discovered a document that shouldn't have been there – a paper that for seven years had been deliberately withheld from public view on the grounds of 'commercial confidentiality'. He could scarcely believe what he was reading, but had the presence of mind to take out his camera and photograph the pages, one by one. And then, when he got home, he had his pictures developed, sent them to the right people and watched Hampshire erupt.

All through the 1960s, the Forestry Commission had the New Forest in its pocket. A Commission employee acted as managing director under the title of deputy surveyor. A supposedly independent body, the Court of Verderers, whose role was to 'conserve the traditional landscape' and act as a management group, was chaired by a former Commission chairman. A lifelong New Forest inhabitant and former verderer talked of a prevailing attitude of acquiescence, the general opinion being: 'If that's what the Forestry Commission thinks, then it must be right.'

The Commission had manipulated a New Forest Act in its favour into place in 1949 and the deputy surveyor commented with relish that it 'gave us an opportunity at long last of putting these woods into production'. The Commission spoke airily of 'regeneration', when on the ground that generally meant felling all the old trees and planting new ones, turning rides into machinery-chewed quagmires and thinning so heavily that the wind came through and blew exposed trees over. Open heathland went under conifer plantations.

Forestry Commission staff continued to be blinded by the imperative to make money. To earn income from selling firewood, they judged ancient beech pollards as fair game for the chop on the grounds that they were dangerous, even though they were a long way from any public paths. The Nature Conservancy's representative for the New Forest, Colin Tubbs, pulled no punches by calling the 1960s 'an ecological disaster' for the forest.

All through that decade, Tubbs lived in a house in the grounds of the Forestry Commission offices. He saw, better than anybody, what was happening. He got on well with individuals on the staff, but was dismayed by what they were being told to do. However, his official hands were tied.

His wife Jenni said the only action he could take was to give others the bullets to fire. In 1970, David Stagg presented him with the pictures he had taken. It was, in effect, a whole ammunition box.

The secret paper photographed by Stagg contained the Commission's undisclosed plans. On the vast areas of land known as inclosures, the intention was to eliminate the 'unproductive' broadleaved trees altogether, apart from thin screens around new conifer plantations. Colin Tubbs made sure the paper's contents fell into the right hands. When they were revealed in public, there was an outcry. The minister of agriculture, Jim Prior, was sent down to mollify the people of the New Forest in September and, within months, had laid out a mandate, a policy paper stipulating that 'the New Forest must be regarded as a national heritage and priority given to the conservation of its traditional character'. The Commission is an exemplary manager of the New Forest today; it is hard to believe that this murky episode ever happened.

*　　*　　*

A townie in the country

Dorset, 1972
Strong-minded, forceful individuals could sometimes wield disproportionate power and break through contemporary conventions. They could be loose cannons, but they also had freedom to act without being answerable to anyone. Unencumbered by committees or memberships, pains in the arse to the establishment and any kind of authority, they shook, stirred and got things done.

One such figure was Kenneth Allsop, a celebrated

London-based journalist who sought an idyllic life in rural Dorset and discovered, after a blissful couple of years, that someone was in the process of trashing his demi-paradise.

Most locals knew of Allsop by reputation when he moved into the old mill, two miles from Powerstock Common, near Bridport, in 1970. He was a pugnacious current affairs TV reporter and presenter, an eloquent, charismatic and extraordinarily persuasive personality. He was so forceful in argument that he once persuaded strong-willed John Lennon to change his approach to song writing and make it more autobiographical. Had it not been for Allsop, we might not have had such lyrical pearls as 'Strawberry Fields Forever'.

As a columnist for *The Sunday Times* and *Daily Mail*, papers which at the time commanded readerships of millions, Allsop was listened to by people with influence. He also happened to be a gifted nature writer, combining the journalist's pacy delivery with vibrant, pithy observations. Few realised, though, that this sometimes belligerent man was goaded by constant pain – a wartime accident when he was training to join the RAF left him with a tin leg and perpetual, grinding discomfort, which he stoically endured.

Allsop was stirred into outrage following a visit to Powerstock Common, where he found the Forestry Commission had laid out a new metalled track close to a boggy interior of oaks, which he described as 'squat, gnarled trees, twisty as those in a fairy story picture of a witch's haunt. Writhing boughs are festooned with mosses and feathery lichens, and ferns hang green tongues from their crevices, licking the fungi and velvet sphagnum of the clayey ooze'. Yes, Allsop could do purple prose when inspired.

Fearing what the new road presaged, he raised his concerns with the Commission's forester, a sympathetic man who claimed he was helpless as he was 'at the bottom of the ladder'. Allsop began to climb the ladder. He badgered senior officials, who reluctantly disclosed a plan to afforest three-quarters of the common. Allsop threatened to expose the Commission's intentions in the media, and drummed up a New Year's Eve meeting at a local pub where he managed to bring various Commission and local officials round to his way of thinking, and then rounded on the hapless – and by now drunk – conservator who had insisted that planting must go ahead. The blustering official caved in, cowering in his seat.

Uncertain that he had the government's nature conservation body fully on his side, and frustrated by its refusal to answer his letters and calls, Allsop drove his E-type Jaguar onto the pavement outside the NCC's London office and demanded to see the director-general with the ominous words 'You know who I am'. Polite, reserved Britain did not know whether to tut or cheer.

Allsop continued to press, writing columns and urging his *Sunday Times* colleague Brian Jackman to do likewise, and embarrass the Commission. The felling stopped, and, in time, the whole of the site was given by the Commission to the Dorset Wildlife Trust. It is a beautiful spot today, free of conifers. Everyone should be happy.

Somehow, the key role played by a courageous man was conveniently lost. As Allsop's biographer David Wilkinson points out, the Dorset Trust had been blind to Powerstock Common's plight. It was then a purely voluntary organisation, run by people living in the east of the county. Rather shamefully, senior officials, understandably uncomfortable with this headstrong, sometimes abrasive individual, tried to brush aside and even denigrate Allsop's part in its rescue afterwards. The poor man, who took his own life a year later, deserves to be brought out of the shadows and acclaimed for what he accomplished.

* * *

A national trust for woods

Devon, 1971
A holy terror tore down the country lanes of Devon in the early 1970s: 'There's a wood I'd like you to see. Hop in.' The petrified and exhilarated passenger would be subjected to the rural equivalent of Monte Carlo. Some remembered gripping the seat of a yellow Ferrari, others a Lamborghini. The driver liked cars. Fast cars.

Petrol-head Kenneth Watkins (known as KW), very deaf, unable to hear the roar of his own engine, had been sent as an asthmatic child from smoky London to Devon, and had stayed there. He became a millionaire by setting up a successful business with his brother importing agricultural machinery and introducing just the kinds of vehicles that were ideal for ripping out hedges and grubbing up woods.

KW had developed a great passion for woods, perhaps fuelled by seeing so many of them disappear. The ladies of the county's Women's Institutes had collaborated with Devon County Council to carry out a rough survey, which indicated that a third of the county's woods had disappeared in ten years. Not inclined to idly bemoan the losses, KW responded with action. His obsession drove him, and drove others faster than they desired. As its honorary secretary, he urged the Devon Naturalists' Trust to take on woods, woods and more woods, tearing around the county's narrow, hedgebanked lanes and combes to spot potential purchases.

At a trust council meeting in 1971, KW arrived with

details of yet another threatened wood for sale. It was too much for the majority of the committee – they wanted to hold back in favour of marshes, meadows and other equally endangered habitats. The council hesitated, with nobody wishing to speak, until the embarrassing stalemate was broken by a member who said words to the effect of – well, Ken, it looks like you're going to have to set up your own national trust for woods.

A determined KW did just that. The Woodland Trust was founded in his house near Ivybridge in 1972 and, for five years, it was a voluntary Devon-based operation with the modest, shy and unassuming KW in charge, and some of his old pals from the Naturalists' Trust on its council. The same bunch of enthusiasts would go out at weekends with their bowsaws to manage their new acquisitions, often little copses, unwanted by their previous owners.

KW had thought that landowners would donate unwanted woods. It didn't happen. The Trust soon needed money and support to pay for them; it was also outgrowing its southwestern core, as more woods came on the market in other parts of the country.

With the self-made man's talent for doing the unexpected, KW played an ace. He had never dipped into his own deep pockets, believing that the Trust should be self-supporting. Rather than appoint a conservationist as his first member of staff, he persuaded the grant-giving Countryside Commission to pay for a marketing whizz from cigarette giant John Player to galvanise the Trust into professional fundraising. John James brought commercial innovation to the tiny charity. Potential donors received personalised letters at a time when direct mail was virtually unheard of. Oooh, a letter for me! Snappy slogans such as 'Plant a tree for 50p' filled the Trust's literature. They tugged people's consciences with affordable requests.

Celebrities were coaxed to sign up as patrons: sculptors Henry Moore and Elisabeth Frink put their names on the letterhead. Lord Bradford, a big name in private forestry, lent his name and donated a couple of his own woods for good measure. Sometimes, celebrity backers needed soothing: Elisabeth Frink once contacted the Woodland Trust in great distress – her Dorset neighbours were up in arms about its desecration of 'their' local wood. Nobody in the village appeared to have ever come across coppicing before. Such protests were not infrequent in the days when both locals and newcomers to the countryside came across stark methods of management that had not been seen in decades.

One of the biggest names on the radio, the *Today* programme's Brian Redhead, fronted a Radio 4 public appeal: 'Since the Second World War, we (or rather they – because it probably was not you and it certainly was not me) have destroyed half the broad-leafed woodland in Britain'. Every one believed Brian; the donations poured in, membership rocketed, the Woodland Trust was gaining a huge profile. It even made its own programme for BBC2, with John James interviewing an earnest, denim-clad young naturalist writer called Richard Mabey.

The Trust took on its first conservationist. KW had a vision of what he wanted, a man who would be equipped with a four-wheel drive, a chainsaw and a caravan. The 'man' who outshone the others at interview was Elizabeth Driver, a tall, confident young woman who would go on to win over the male-dominated woodland world by exuding calmness and good sense.

Liz Driver arrived at a time of great expansion. Increasingly well financed and adept at drawing in grants, the Trust was buying bigger woods. Aversley Wood in Cambridgeshire came complete with its 'armed' pond, a starfish-shaped pool that had given whole herds of drovers' cattle a drink in medieval times. Wormley Wood in Hertfordshire followed, a hornbeam wood with the earth bank remains of Bronze Age farming and a plantation of tiny Christmas trees. Hoddesdon Park Wood was bought at the same time. The Trust launched a new slogan: 'a wood a week'.

Even if the Woodland Trust had succeeded in buying a wood a week for the next 20 years or more, it would not have been enough, for woods were being lost far faster than they could be saved. Something fundamental needed to shift in the corridors of power. The woods needed someone with the imagination, verve and nous to change influential minds as well as public hearts. They got a double act.

THE WOODLANDERS

A man in red socks and the descendant of a Jacobite soldier are universally acknowledged as the people who played a critical, pivotal role in saving what was left of Britain's ancient woodland. Everyone who was there at the time – conservationists and foresters alike – agree that these two visionaries, different and complementary, working separately and in partnership, achieved a seismic change by combining dogged determination with creative brilliance, making the leaps of imagination that leave ordinary mortals wondering why such simple thinking is beyond us. Their names are distinctive, memorable, old-fashioned sounding, even. They are Oliver Rackham and George Peterken.

Oliver Rackham burst into public consciousness at the age of 36 with a book that shook accepted 'facts' out of their cosy pigeonholes. It was an iconoclastic blast. He was a genius let loose among the understudied archives, decoding truths that had been hidden for centuries, scouring old woods for the physical evidence that would render his eloquent prose both irresistible and authoritative. Here is the opening salvo of that first major work, *Trees and Woodland in the British Landscape,* setting out his stall:

> The literature on the history of trees and woods is very unsatisfactory. Some scholarly works have been written

by foresters, whose interests are in plantations rather than in alternative and older methods of handling trees. Others have been written by historians who have worked among archives and are reluctant to put on their boots and discover what the land itself, and the things that grow on it, have to say.

Oliver Rackham was an exceptional talent who rose from very modest beginnings. Born in 1939, the son of a Suffolk bank clerk and a housewife who died when he was in his early teens, he gained a scholarship to Corpus Christi, Cambridge, intending to become a physicist. Persuaded to take botany as an element of his degree, he devoted his entire final year to the subject. Professor of Botany Peter Grubb supervised a brilliant student who was 'extraordinarily curious and very demanding', so demanding, in fact, that his previous tutor had been unable to cope with him. As a PhD student, Oliver studied how plant leaves work, and why an inability to absorb carbon dioxide quicker than they do limits their rate of growth. In his findings, Professor Grubb said Oliver was 'three decades ahead of the field'. Not bad for a student just 25 years old.

Oliver could have had an illustrious career as a plant biologist and indeed, for several years he worked for the Plant Breeding Institute, studying the effects of drought on barley. But he had already developed a spare-time passion that would completely change the course of his life.

Another Cambridge don, Donald Pigott, who, as we saw in the last chapter, arrived in the nick of time to save not one but two woods, remembered sparking what he viewed as Oliver's moment of epiphany. They had gone to Hayley Wood, and the tutor was showing his students a triangle of a former field adjoining the wood, one that had been isolated from farmland when a railway was driven through a full century before. At first sight, the triangle of woodland that had been planted and grown up in the former farm field over a period of 100 years was indistinguishable from the rest. The tutor brought enlightenment. 'I showed him how minimal the migration of bluebells and wood anemones had been into it. He was totally fascinated by this. He could not understand how plants could be so immobile.'

An enraptured Oliver (who could not drive) became fixated on old woods and eagerly bagged the passenger seat, travelling with Donald Pigott to see others in west Cambridgeshire. However, Hayley Wood became the primary focus of his interest and for one immediate practical reason. When he left for Bristol, fellow postgraduate student Mike Martin passed the role of reserve management committee secretary on to Oliver. How should the wood be managed? wondered Oliver. He consulted his father, who told him to look to the past for guidance on the future.

Oliver travelled back in time in a way that nobody had attempted or managed before. He had a rare gift for learning languages, once conducting a conversation on a bus with a Croatian priest about woodland management in Latin. This talent enabled him to translate seemingly impenetrable thirteenth century documents written by monks in an anglicised form of Latin, to make sense of Hayley Wood's history. His encyclopaedic mind absorbed everything and forgot nothing. A master of botany, he also became an authority on fungi and a self-taught expert in woodland archaeology, interpreting bumps and depressions, never accepting anything as fact without gathering the supporting weight of evidence.

When he drew together the accounts of various specialists and his own original work in a book on Hayley Wood, the then professor of botany at Cambridge, Sir Harry

Godwin, praised his achievement:

> It is the good fortune of the Hayley Wood research that it has found, in Dr Rackham, a scholar with the remarkable combination of scientific training with linguistic and historical aptitude to exploit and interpret a mass of documentation from the time of Domesday onwards.

Somewhere, in this tumult of research, Oliver made the decision to jettison his career in plant biology and, in a way that was typically Cambridge, managed to secure a research fellow post at Corpus Christi, sustained by a succession of grants that gave him the freedom to follow his own inclinations. Possessing only a bicycle and a knack for cadging lifts, Oliver began to work his way into every wood and archive in East Anglia, venturing further afield when the opportunity arose.

Nobody could sum up the role that Oliver carved out for himself and its purpose better than Oliver himself:

> Historical ecology seeks to interpret the natural and artificial factors that have influenced the development of an area of vegetation in its present state. It is the history of particular woods, especially of those that are still extant, rather than the history of generalisations about woodland... Although historical ecology combines the specialized techniques of the field, the archives, and the laboratory, most of the results are not too remote from ordinary experience. My object has been to write for both botanists and historians and for amateurs as well as professionals.

It is hard for us to appreciate today just how firmly half-truths and misconceptions about ancient woodland were held before 1976, because history was rewritten by Oliver, and preached by his disciples in the subsequent decades. The research that gave rise to his first groundbreaking book transformed its author: the devout Anglican boy who had always deferred to those in authority discovered that accepted beliefs were mere shibboleths. By the age of 35, it was as if Oliver Rackham believed in God and nothing else, unless he could prove it for himself.

The book that was launched as a modest addition to a series on archaeology was seized on by conservationists and foresters alike and became enormously successful. In *Trees and Woodland in the British Landscape*, Oliver showed both his prodigious talent for plain speaking and a powerful authorial voice that often had the ring of a sermon.

One by one, he knocked myths off their shaky perches. In the years Before Rackham, most people vaguely assumed that the bulk of woodland clearance had been carried out in the Middle Ages or later. Not so.

By AD 1200 much of the modern landscape was already recognisable: nearly all our villages and most hamlets existed then, and the proportions of farmland, woodland and moorland were not enormously different from what they are now... Our modern woods are the tattered and patched, but still unmistakeable, remains of a fabric that was woven in this remote age.

What about the assertion – still lingering in unenlightened places today – that whole woods were felled to build ships for the navy or to power the Industrial Revolution?

The proposition is nearly always stated as a vague gener-ality, unsupported by estimates of the acreage involved or by evidence of what exactly happened to specific woods. It is inherently implausible, for trees grow again, and a wood need no more be destroyed by felling than a meadow is destroyed by cutting a crop of hay.

In just 200 pages, Oliver had elevated the status of Britain's remaining old woods to precious, irreplaceable relics of social, cultural, historical and ecological significance, as important to every community, and as venerable as any church or stately home. He established that they were fundamental to our heritage and our identity, and he also left the reader in no doubt that they were in grave peril.

In some cases, as with the great woods of Bury St Edmunds Abbey, the destruction in the 1950s and 1960s equalled that in the whole of the previous 400 years... Casual observation suggests that a similar story could be told of nearly every sheet of the Ordnance Survey: of Dorset, the steep oak woods of Mid Wales, the Wye gorge, the Forest of Wyre, the hilltop woods of the Welsh border, and the romantic lichen-hung corkscrew oaks of the deep valleys of Dartmoor and Bodmin Moor. The long arm of destruction has reached from the Lizard Peninsula to remote Argyll.

The man who now found himself a minor celebrity cut an eccentric figure, invariably wearing an unruly shock of hair, red socks and sandals, deigning to don a dinner jacket for official functions. His eccentricity, of character as well as appearance, was not entirely deliberate. Most of those who knew him suspected he had a touch of Asperger's syndrome. He was socially awkward, inclined to lecture rather than discuss, and something of a loner. A friend who regularly welcomed him to carry out research in his own small wood said: 'His writing is very much like he was as a person. Very abrupt. You have to watch every word because he says such extreme things. He'll drop something in and then move straight on to the next point.'

Oliver ran many courses and gave many lectures. Undeniably, he was at his best in a wood, where he would become especially animated. Ted Collins, the former director of the Museum of English Rural Life, recalled that he fired everyone up: 'I walked with Rackham through woods and it was as if every other tree and every other mound had writing on it, but only he could read it.' And he could be quite charming to those who showed enthusiasm. John Barkham, the first ecologist at the University of East Anglia said of him: 'He always used to treat me as if I knew far more than I did. He had a way of somehow expecting everyone else to be as utterly dedicated as he was.'

Oliver followed up his initial success in 1980 with a heavyweight but still perfectly readable title that brought the depth of his learning to the fore. *Ancient Woodland: Its History, Vegetation and Use in England* expanded on its predecessor. Still largely focused on south-east England, it covered such subjects as pollen analysis and the woodland origins of place names, and it explored the different kinds of woodland and the history of their management. *Ancient Woodland* also bore the hallmark of all Oliver's work – characteristic hand-drawn maps with bold, quasi-medieval flourishes.

Nobody who was seriously interested in forestry and woodlands at that time could fail to be influenced by the weight of evidence in Oliver Rackham's writing. But words and compelling arguments are never enough. Oliver could be famously rude about foresters, and those with influence in the profession treated the views of this lofty Cambridge academic with some suspicion.

Tact and diplomacy were beyond him; a friend remarked that Oliver 'said what he thought and thought what he saw', and his forthright views were not always welcomed. Not only that, he showed an unworldly disregard for economics. Put simply, Oliver could not have effected a shift in attitudes and policies on his own. It needed a woodland conservation expert of equal gravitas, one who had what Oliver lacked, a shrewd grasp of human motivations. Woods cried out for a talented negotiator, a politically astute insider, someone who knew how to put theory into practice. Oliver found his foil in George Peterken.

* * *

Family lore has it that a Peterken ancestor fighting in the Jacobite uprisings of the early eighteenth century fled south. This Scot's descendants ended up in London, where George Peterken was born on an October day when fog called a temporary halt to the Blitz. George's interests gravitated towards his mother's roots, however. Her family home was in the New Forest and it was there, thanks to numerous family holidays and school camps, that he developed his love of woods in what old school friend and nature writer Roger Deakin called 'the wildwood of his youth'. A career in forestry had no appeal, though; the boy couldn't understand the attraction of a job where you would not live to see the fruit of your labours.

There is something deeply, fundamentally inquisitive about George Peterken. Like Rackham, he has a curiosity that does not seem to accept that things are just so; his mind is always asking why, reaching for the link between cause and effect and striving to understand it. It was while carrying out an ecology PhD at University College, London, that he found his metier.

Naturally, George chose the New Forest, his childhood playground, as the area for his research. He carried out a study of the factors determining holly growth there. Working with warden-naturalist Colin Tubbs, he began to discover riddles and sought solutions. By counting annual rings on the stumps of fallen trees, he learned that there was a period of nearly a hundred years when hardly any new trees grew, followed by a burst of regeneration after 1850.

But why? There was no evident 'natural' answer to this puzzle. Perhaps human history could help? The two men realised that a piece of legislation, the Deer Removal Act of 1851, which had led to the immediate culling of thousands of fallow deer to protect forest plantations, had resulted in a burgeoning of new hollies. It was a perfect correlation – an instant removal of the browsers and a tiny forest of liberated holly seedlings.

George had gained his first taste of making sense of the interplay between woods and human activity – and he loved it. 'The thing I liked about the ecology of woods was that time is an obvious element in a way that it isn't with, say, grasslands. You can read the history in the trees.'

George eventually found his way to a job in the woodland management unit of the Nature Conservancy at Monks Wood Experimental Station. His boss, Dick Steele, himself a forester, immediately advised him to join the Society of Foresters, a move that would stand George in good stead for the rest of his career. 'His view was that if you're prepared to spend a day standing around discussing Corsican pine plantations with foresters then you'll be accepted as an insider and they'll be prepared to discuss things with you, on the basis that you're a reasonable guy, even if you have odd views. If you come from outside, they'll simply reject you.' A case for conservation could thus be made from within.

George started the job in 1969 and was given licence to do pretty much what he liked. It was what he called 'a crazy, energetic time'. He was a man in his late twenties with drive and enthusiasm, working on woodlands during the week, and working *in* woodlands at the weekend, managing local nature reserves, gaining practical skills to inform his theoretical understanding. George was often volunteering alongside Oliver Rackham, the two men bonding on winter days over axes, saws and billhooks.

George became the Conservancy's roving woodland consultant, an itinerant peddler of expertise. He would be the significant other wheeled in by local staff to help tackle intractable problems. The wood owner would be impressed: if the Nature Conservancy was bringing someone 200 miles to pass judgement on their wood, he must have something worthwhile to say. George would always seek to understand and sympathise with the owner's viewpoint, finding constructive paths and compromises that would benefit the woods. He was the epitome of the very reasonable man. 'I'm more comfortable in trying to find common ground than having a row.'

Travelling anywhere from Cornwall to Caithness and all points between, mobile George was accumulating knowledge of woods throughout the country in a way that no one else ever had before. He began to realise that he could be dropped into any county in Britain and put it in context. 'I could go to a wood on the Black Isle, north of Inverness, and say "that wood's incredibly like the woods of west Herefordshire". And there was a good reason for it, because they were both on areas of Old Red Sandstone. No one in the two areas – 500 miles apart – was in a position to make that kind of connection.'

While he had gained knowledge in breadth, he also sought it in depth. In the late 1960s, George had got to know a number of woods in Lincolnshire, where the Forestry Commission had been cutting down lime trees, poisoning them and planting pines. During this wretched period of salvage, the Nature Conservancy was operating a policy adopted out of desperation. It would ask itself the question: which surviving woods were the best ones and could they negotiate to have these ones last in line for the bulldozers, just in case something came up to save them before it was their turn for destruction?

George had been tantalised by a comment made by natu-ralist Sir Hugh Beevor in the 1920s – that he could identify the surviving Domesday woodlands of Norfolk by the pres-ence of bluebells. George began to study the Lincolnshire woods in depth, using archives to identify which were ancient and which were recent. He was recording the plant species of both in an effort to discover which flowers were good indicators of ancient woodland.

He examined about 300 woods in detail and found around 50 flowers that were largely confined to older woods – these included wood anemone, herb paris, lily-of-the-valley and sweet woodruff. Then there were plants that were either exclusively in ancient woods, ancient hedge-rows or meadows that must once have been connected to ancient woods. When he stood among wild garlic, prim-roses, early purple orchids, moschatel and sanicle, he could make a compelling case for viewing them as key indicators of ancient woodland in that part of the country.

Understanding gained from elsewhere added to his

knowledge. George was one of a quartet of leading scientists who set up a historical ecology discussion group at the government's Monks Wood Experimental Station. In the course of dozens of meetings, they drew in talents from a whole range of fields: historians, historians of buildings, cartographers, geologists. Collectively, these specialists provided wider knowledge for a nucleus of people who were pushing boundaries. With Oliver often in the front row, these were exceptional gatherings, great melting pots of the arts and science.

And so George was able to research the woods of Lincolnshire, equipped with this wealth of information, and examine, not only the living plants, but also the banks, ditches and other earthworks, and trawl the Lincoln Record Office for historical records knowing exactly where to look.

One reason for choosing Lincolnshire was that it was out of range of Oliver Rackham. In his PhD days, Oliver had sought advice from George on woodland history. By 1973, the student had more than caught up. It was obvious to George that Oliver was making great strides in East Anglia and the East Midlands. It was George's home area, it was where he lived, but he had the wisdom to realise that if he went off to Lincolnshire, the two men wouldn't be treading on each other's toes.

George knew where Oliver was going in his work; he would often take him there:

> For a few years, if I was going east, I'd phone him up and ask him if he wanted to come along. I was his unofficial chauffeur. I would go round the wood mapping tree distribution or plant distribution, banks and ditches, but he'd be taking in and mapping so much more. I was always astounded at the number of things he could absorb simultaneously

and then produce a map afterwards. He was very quick to see patterns in anything. That was just one side of an outstanding intellect.

On many weekends, the two men would coppice together in their local woods. Though they followed their own research paths, there was a great deal of discussion and sharing and shaping of views. George was modest and generous-hearted towards Oliver, the man who, through his writing and lecturing, would become the better-known public figure, one who would often overshadow his own achievements:

> When you have a brilliant person whose interests completely overlap your own it does rather affect how you run your career. Anything I could do, he could do better. I actually had a contract for a book on woodland history before him, but stopped when I realised he was writing one too. I knew he would do his better than mine. Eventually we settled on a mode of operation; I was the conservationist and link to foresters, while he was the ecologist and source of most of the ideas. That was how we functioned.

George remembered the almost incidental nature of the decision to adopt a name for the woods they were talking about: 'I'd written an internal document for the Nature Conservancy and I was calling them "primary woodlands". I sent the paper to Oliver and said I'd be interested in any comments he had. His main comment was that you couldn't prove that "primary" woodlands dated back to the Neolithic period, but you could prove – with historical records, old maps for example – that a wood existed before a certain date. He suggested we call them ancient woodlands and I kinda said okay.'

That defining moment in the story of ancient woodland was seen at the time by its authors as neither original
nor particularly significant. Various contemporaries had
been studying what made certain woods different – Steven
and Carlisle had identified the unique character of native
pinewoods, for example. But neither George nor Oliver
were initially aware that 'ancient' woods had been recognised long before and forgotten. Professor Charles Watkins,
a rural historian at Nottingham University, discovered that
Board of Agriculture reports from the 1790s classified tree
cover in each country as either 'woodlands' or 'plantations',
the former representing the indigenous woods dating back
to who knows when. Such thinking had survived in the New
Forest Act of 1877 too, for it singled out 'ancient and orna-
mental woods'.

'Ancient woodland' was to be an inspired choice of
name, one that would help transform the fortunes of the
habitat it identified. In current phraseology, it was more than
a label; it was a brand. It had a currency that would chime
with Britain's growing appreciation in the early 1980s of
anything to do with heritage. Those two words became an
irresistible combination. They were strong and distinctive
enough to put on the cover of a book.

By the late 1970s, George and Oliver, together and
separately, were beginning to influence the rank and file
in forestry, the new breed less tainted by old school ortho-
doxy and blinkered thinking, as well as those longstanding
forester-naturalists who had been, for so long, in a tiny
minority. In places such as Flatford Mill in Suffolk, forestry
staff started to attend Oliver's courses on woodlands on a
personal basis. There was a build-up of people who were
looking for alternative ways of managing woods, and being

more realistic about what might be achieved.

One senior Forestry Commission scientist of the time talked of a 'vibrant, live debate' among staff, a challenging of the status quo. George remembered one of those, a Lincolnshire forester who joked with him about replacing the ancient woods with conifers, mimicking the way his bosses would look at replanting: 'If the ecology ain't right, we'll make it right'. Foresters would share these confidences with George, knowing him to be a man with a genuine interest in what they were doing: in short, someone who understood them.

A thoughtful forester summed up the thinking of the creative members of his profession: 'For the next 50 or 100 years, or longer, the forester's skill is displayed for all to observe, in much the same way buildings do for their architects. Unlike the farmer's harvest, giving an annual opportunity to reconsider, the forester, at best, has a once-in-a-lifetime opportunity.'

Too many foresters were programmed to fulfil only one objective, growing wood as economically as possible. George wondered why. This one-dimensional role seemed simply boring to him, compared with the multi-faceted jobs these foresters could have. Did they really want to spend their lives doing nothing but planting trees in rows like so many cabbages?

Owners

There is a place in the wood where no visitor ever goes. In 30 years, I have never set foot there. Today I have been invited in.

The broad ride through the northernmost part of Gransden Wood is like no other in the wood; it is green and grassy and there is none of the pounded, pulverised mud that surfaces every other path and ride. That's because nobody walks here, or rather almost nobody. It is the one part of the whole wood in private hands. Karl owns everything to the left, Ian everything to the right, and one of them is expecting me.

Halfway down the ride, I meet up with a chainsaw on a log. An orange safety helmet sits on the ground below, but its owner is nowhere to be seen. At last he emerges from the trees. Ian Robinson has a professional interest in the five-hectare plot he owns (the area of six football pitches). He's a greenwood worker; his raw materials are freshly cut green (i.e. unseasoned) timber from his own wood. I've seen photos of his handiwork – garden fences, arbour seats, benches and wood stores with shingle roofs, all made out of oak, Windsor chairs and stools from sycamore.

Ian is one of hundreds of woodsmen (and woodswomen) around the country who use a pole-lathe; in layman's terms, a lathe driven by a pole, powered by his own feet. To call his

work 'rustic', with the word's connotations of wonky, inde-
finable objects destined to break, would be an insult. Each
shapely piece celebrates the beauty of fine grain, dark bosses
and burrs, the unique markings of a single tree's growth; the
products are factory quality, hand-crafted. These things sell
in well-heeled Cambridge.

But not enough. Ian struggles to market himself. He finds
alternative, regular, steady income as a gardener, reminding
me of an old pianist-composer friend who drove the school
bus. Extraction is a big problem; you can cut a tree down,
but how do you get it out over soft ground? 'No way I want
to put a vehicle on the ride except when conditions are
right.' And that means summer, specifically a dry summer.
He carts some off over his shoulder, some in a wheelbarrow.
Some trees are left where they fall. He chops up others into
log piles, tower block homes for minibeasts.

We weave through thickets of trunks, saplings and seedlings. It is a wood without a path and I'm feeling a little
disorientated. Ian knows exactly where he's going; he's
owned this bit of wood for 20 years. 'There's a wild crab
apple somewhere round here.' He pauses and looks around.
'I don't exactly know where.'

There is a touch of the gardener in a person who carries
the story of every tree and bush in his head. Try this, try
that, see what grows. 'That's got away quite nicely,' he says
of a willow lately coppiced. 'I felled this the winter before
last,' he remarks, nodding at a fallen trunk that has left
space for stronger trees to spread and reach for the light.
Oak trees will respond with spreading crowns, ash less so,
he says.

On the other side of the ride is Karl Nightingale. He's a
biochemist working in Birmingham, who saw his purchase
as a new intellectual challenge, a place where he could both

potter and work hard. For him, the wood has fulfilled a lifelong ambition.

> I guess I have always thought about buying a wood as a retreat from the 'real world' since I was a kid. A combination of physical exercise, and seeing the fruit of your labour is something that appeals to me and my partner – it was very much a joint project. It also fitted in with how I imagined I might spend my retirement.
>
> I like the fact that it is an SSSI, so I can feel like a steward, and develop the wood as a long term project where I can see the effect of what we do. I also like the fact it is so obviously old – with its wood banks, hidden drainage ditches and old pollarded oaks.

Karl is an example of a new breed, a band of hobby 'woodies', who are becoming more important to the future of ancient woods as their numbers grow and the area of land they manage increases. Members of the Small Woods Association, for example, own as much woodland between them as the Woodland Trust, and they are an eclectic bunch: George Smith, for instance, owner of a nine-hectare wood in West Sussex, is a former detective chief inspector.

Today, there is a trend for whole woods to be bought, parcelled up and sold off in lots, with each woodland plot given a new name. They are advertised as if the would-be purchaser were buying a house without a building; a wood in Devon advertised online, is billed as 'A picturesque, ancient semi-natural woodland with a very attractive stream frontage.'

For many, their woods are weekend retreats, or holiday locations. Simon and Rachel Browne of Greater Manchester, for example, bought a piece of the North Wales they loved from holidays in their childhoods. In the commuter belt of southern England an 'ancient wood' label on a plot for sale carries a particular cache and a price to match, at just under £10,000 an acre. What would farmers of 1945 have said if they had been told that an acre of woodland was worth almost as much as an acre of prime arable land?

Professional opinion is divided on this new hobby wood phenomenon. Some doubt that a wood under multiple ownership can be properly looked after as a whole by people lacking expertise, each holding as little as two hectares, and using it for barbecues or camping. But many others take a relaxed view. The purchaser is often taking on an ancient wood that has suffered decades of neglect and most of these new 'wardens' have a strong desire to manage their woods for wildlife, and a willingness to learn. Can you love a wood to death?

The darkness before dawn

When the government's nature conservation body celebrated its 25th birthday in 1974, the influence of Rackham
and Peterken had yet to be felt. Oliver Rackham's first book
was a year away from publication and George Peterken was
still careering around the country, a paramedic of threatened woods, at the same time carrying out painstaking,
time-consuming research, as he built up a case for ancient
woodland.

The woodland unit of the NCC had little to cheer
about. Britain's entry to the European Common Market
in December 1972 had prompted the most devastating
period of woodland destruction by agriculture. There was a
wholesale grab to 'reclaim' more marginal land as farmers
buoyed by subsidies and improvement grants found it more
profitable than ever to convert trees to wheat and barley.
Stephen Mear at Waresley was just one of thousands who
took advantage when he grubbed out the second third of
his wood.

At the same time, the 1970s was the decade when a
well-fed nation forgot the years of hunger and deprivation,
forgot that it had nurtured and lauded its post-war food
providers. Fickle public opinion began to cast farmers in a
different light.

The first tremors were felt when research carried out

for the Countryside Commission and published in 1972 exposed 'fresh and deeply disturbing facts about the nature and scale of changes taking place' in Britain's countryside. We finally woke up to the reality of blighted landscapes, the drained marshes, the flowerless, featureless fields. One statistic in particular rattled public consciousness – 10,000 miles of hedgerow were being ripped out every year. 'Farmer bashing' was soon in vogue and a survey of 44 East Anglian farmers in 1978 found that more than three-quarters felt the public was hostile to them. Nobody was coming out to bless the crops any longer; not many farmers were being asked to open the summer fete.

The storm of opprobrium reached a peak in 1980 with the publication of a devastating book called *The Theft of the Countryside*. Its author, a gifted polemicist called Marion Shoard, a former CPRE employee who had spent four years professionally dissecting farming policies, was unsparing: 'Although few people realize it, the English landscape is under sentence of death... The executioner is not the industrialist or the property speculator... Instead it is the figure traditionally viewed as the custodian of the rural scene – the farmer.'

Farming supplied its own walking PR disaster to publicise woodland destruction. Hughie Batchelor came to farm in the beautiful winding Alkham Valley west of Dover, and acted like a madman let loose in an art gallery with a Stanley knife. Down came the hedges, out went the copses, his plough did for the flower-filled downland. Every time Batchelor saw green he saw red. Pathologically confrontational, all too willing to pose before a camera, he cast himself as a farming moderniser.

Locals feared for the fate of the wood on Batchelor's land. By far the best of a string of woods scattered along the valley slopes, Sladden Wood became the subject of 'discussions'. A week before a public meeting set up to safeguard the site took place, Batchelor sent his bulldozer in. Someone acted quickly to alert the council and a local official arrived double-quick at the farm, holding a Tree Preservation Order in his hand. Batchelor claimed he had lost his glasses, so he could not read the document. By the time he 'found' them, the wood had been flattened.

However, the wood that villagers dubbed 'the horizontal wood' was not lost. The following spring, technical assessor Colin Bashford judged that 'the remains were those of a poor coppicing operation and that the trees would regrow'. And so it proved. The TPO slapped on the horizontal wood prevented Batchelor from grubbing up the stumps. Today, Sladden Wood, its hornbeams, orchids and yellow archangels fall under the protection of the Kent Wildlife Trust.

The media pounced on Hughie Batchelor as its stereotype of the new farmer – greedy, philistine, anything but a custodian of the countryside. Yet public hostility and media scorn of this kind changed nothing fundamentally. In 1980, the bureaucratic wheels were still turning and a Forestry Commission official was still giving felling licences to farmers in Yorkshire's Vale of Pickering to convert their woods to agriculture.

Farm bulldozers never touched those woods in North Yorkshire. In the end, what stopped the agricultural blitz was simple economics. Europe was producing more food than it needed and the accumulation of so-called butter mountains and milk lakes had direct consequences for British farmers. Guaranteed prices fell and grants for 'improvements' disappeared. There was no longer enough of an incentive to make grubbing up a wood worthwhile. Within a decade, farmers were being paid to put hedges and woods back. It is tragic that so many farmers thought – and still do think – that woods are simply slow-growing crops. Plant a wood, take it out, plant another somewhere else.

How could the forestry industry be persuaded to change? The Forestry Commission had been hammered by a government policy paper in 1972 that questioned its role on financial grounds, as a previous paper had done fifteen years before. The Commission had countered with an increased emphasis on recreation – hundreds of way-marked trails and picnic sites, a third of a million campers in its forests every year, an enterprising individual bringing sculpture to Grizedale Forest in the Lake District. This was imaginative thinking.

It also started selling itself in terms of conservation. Desperate to win as many friends as possible, shaken by the public backlash against its treatment of the New Forest (see page 182), and embarrassed by incidents such as Powerstock Common (see page 185), where its failings were laid out in the media, it was beginning to soften its stance. Directors talked about placing greater emphasis on maintaining the woodland character of the countryside. Chairman Lord Taylor went so far as to state in 1973 that 'in certain of their woodlands, the maintenance of hardwoods, where silviculturally this is possible, is an essential part of the landscape'.

The impetus had gone out of the programme to coniferise broadleaved woodland. Through the 1970s, both the Commission and private forestry companies saw greater profits and less trouble in covering the cheap moors and bogs of upland Scotland and Wales with plantations.

Even so, the Commission continued to play a role in the destruction of ancient woods. Farmers had to obtain its permission to fell a wood. The legal position had not changed; woods in the lowlands continued to be cut down, sanctioned by the Commission. And, at the highest levels, it showed no inclination to stop this, take any steps to address the deterioration of the woods that were left, or promote their recovery. A new generation of ecologically aware staff was coming up through its ranks, readers of Rackham, followers of Peterken's published research. However, they were not yet in senior positions where they might wield some influence.

At the NCC, canny George Peterken knew the value of playing a very long game. Those government employees in conservation were like the pummelled underdog in a boxing ring, taking the punches, waiting for the chance to strike back. Opportune moments could be counted in years, or even decades.

George had a tendency to hold onto memorable phrases, especially spiky ones, mulling them over to see how problems could be resolved. A comment made by a senior land manager back in 1972 haunted him: 'If only owners and managers of woodland knew where such ancient woods were, they would do their best to protect them.'

Both George and Oliver Rackham were confident that they could identify the ancient woods that lay within the areas they had studied intensively. Could a way be found to locate them elsewhere? Ecologist Suzanne Goodfellow was given Norfolk as a guinea pig county. By studying old maps and dipping into archives, she was able to draw up a list of pre nineteenth century woods that would provide the basis for surveys in the field. It seemed to work.

The spark for action came in 1978, when, in response to a forestry paper produced by George Peterken, the Forestry Commission's director-general George Holmes snapped back, dismissing the concept of 'so-called ancient woodland'. It seemed clear that if the Forestry Commission hierarchy would not accept the existence of ancient wood-land without evidence, then George would have to give them evidence. 'The more knowledge you have, the more credibility you have,' he said. So began the creation of Britain's Ancient Woodland Inventory, with a team of NCC staff playing woodland detectives.

Ordnance Survey maps, tithe and estate maps, and the military survey maps laid out by General Roy in Scotland after the Jacobite rebellion, provided an objective basis for the surveyors, who then had the task of making creative judgements as to whether a wood was ancient or not. Names often helped provide clues: Oxpasture Wood in Sussex shouted of antiquity. Any wood with plantation in its name was almost certainly a non-starter. Appendix I: How to identify an ancient wood gives us a chance to imitate those detectives, to take on a practical role and look at the kinds of decisions and assumptions that the surveyors had to make.

A copy of *Who's Who* and dollops of charm equipped the youngest permanent member of the NCC team to act as a roving ambassador around Britain's stately homes. Jonathan Spencer was sent out to visit the big landowners and survey their woods. As a guest of Lieutenant Colonel Sir Arscott Molesworth-St Aubyn, he slept in a room that occupied a space bigger than the footprint of his house. The old soldier, the owner of Pencarrow House, near Bodmin, was thrilled to be told he was the possessor of huge woodlands with an ancient pedigree. Like so many other proud landowners, he had Jonathan's survey report bound in leather. Excited possessors of new-found heritage began writing to their surveyors, casually peppering their letters with references to 'semi-ancient natural woodland'.

Other great landowners were not so enthusiastic. The

managers of the Chatsworth Estate were all too eager to promote their Elizabethan origins in bricks and mortar, but less inclined to believe they possessed something almost twice as old in the shape of Scarcliffe Park. Jonathan Spencer remembers:

> They steadfastly refused to accept that this was an ancient woodland and yet it had all the characteristics of a deer park. It was a lovely wood with small-leaved lime and wild service trees. The officials were difficult, but they were also charming, so they let me roam around their archives in Chatsworth House. This was a big issue. It involved six or seven lunches.

Years before its surveyors had finished the Ancient Woodland Inventory (it has always been called 'provisional', since the information within is in a state of incompleteness), it was becoming clear that it was having a significant impact. George Peterken's deputy, Keith Kirby, was one of its main organisers. 'Its main value was that this wasn't an indefinite ask from the conservation bodies,' he says. 'We weren't asking for every bit of woodland to be protected; we were saying that this list and these particular sites are our bid for discussion.' Nobody, least of all another government body, could question the inventory's validity. Ancient woodlands had now been established as an undisputed scientific fact.

Pressure was brought to bear on the Forestry Commission from parliament itself. The NCC's woodland specialists fed evidence into a House of Lords select committee, which reported in late 1980 on 'Scientific Aspects of Forestry'. The committee's key recommendation for ancient woodland was perfectly clear:

The area of broadleaved woodland has already shrunk to an alarming extent and the Committee consider that it should not be allowed to decline further either by clearing for agriculture or conversion to conifers.

The government responded with little more than a belated 'thank you for your letter' type of reply. Their lordships were not standing for this; a group of noble glitterati, they included a physicist, a botanist, a zoologist, a barrister, a *Guardian* obituary writer and a Nobel prizewinner in chemistry. Led by Lord Sherfield, a former US ambassador, they retaliated after another fourteen months of government inaction by taking the near unprecedented step of producing another report, this time criticising the government's lackadaisical reply, and calling in the minister for an inquisition.

All through this period, the Forestry Commission had been spared scrutiny by the conservation movement. The Wildlife Trusts, CPRE, RSPB and active new groups called WWF, Friends of the Earth and Greenpeace had elected to throw their joint weight behind an enormous new piece of legislation that was grinding its way through parliament, designed to safeguard all species and habitats.

Some 2,300 amendments and 28 months of negotiation later, the Wildlife and Countryside Act 1981 became law. One of the key measures that had implications for ancient woodland was the extra protection it brought for SSSIs. Landowners still had to notify the Nature Conservancy Council before carrying out potentially damaging work on SSSIs. But now, the government was given a three-month period to agree to the proposals or work towards reaching some kind of agreement. Ninety-odd days to launch the lifeboat.

The three-month window for negotiation enshrined

in the Act certainly helped native pinewoods – more than three-quarters of them had been declared SSSIs by 1986. But only a tiny percentage of broadleaved woods would ever be afforded the protection of SSSI designation; what of the tens of thousands that had no official letters after their name?

By 1982, conservation groups were freed from the burden of pressing clause by tortuous clause of the Wildlife and Countryside Act into the statute book. They had also been boosted by influxes of new staff paid for by government job creation schemes. At last, they were in a position to lobby for ancient woodland. They stirred the hornets' nest, firing up journalists to raise awareness of woodland's plight and its profile in the public eye.

One of the most effective at this juncture was the CPRE, whose secret weapon was Robin Grove-White, a former scriptwriter of the BBC's *That Was the Week That Was*, a man who had the predator's habit of going for the jugular. Hailing from a landed background like many of the aristocracy he targeted, he looked the part with his suit and well-informed briefcase, and confronted ministers and civil servants over civilised lunches with a searingly sharp intellect.

Grove-White created a CPRE questionnaire, which was sent to English county councils, seeking their views on the losses and threats to small woodlands within their purview. The answers revealed some to be enlightened and others ill-informed. Some councils showed a keen appreciation of problems and were taking positive action to address them. Others were lamentably ignorant. Northamptonshire said 'there is no factual evidence that small woodland loss is a problem', though statistics would later show that, after 1930, the county lost more than 60 per cent of all its ancient woodland. Leicestershire appeared to be in a time warp, its county planning officer calling for Countryside Commission grants 'for clearance of derelict woodland'.

Something had to happen to shake things up, and something did. Not from the conservation movement, the NCC or the government. The catalyst was the Forestry Commission itself.

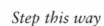

Step this way

At the tail end of winter, there is one last chance to put in running repairs, to move freely through the wood before the growing season turns tread into trample. The work done, we sit on a bench, flasks in hand, and watch to see the results.

A pair of feet is about to decide whether a primrose lives or dies. The feet are going down the path, skirting around the squishy mud in the middle, sliding out to the edges, seeking terra firma. The right foot lifts, moves to plant itself a little more to the right, then, in the space of less than half a second, and without conscious thought from the head above, draws itself back to step forward onto bare ground. We have been watching a live experiment, and it works.

We have spent the morning making crash barriers. When I first walked Waresley's paths 30 years ago, they were thready, single-file affairs with bluebells and primroses lining the verges. They are more like single-lane roads now and we are fighting the tendency towards dual carriageway. And the hard shoulder is taking a terrible hammering. 'Unsuitable footwear' persuades its wearer to take evasive action when confronted with mud, by landing on solid, virgin ground, crushing an emerging primrose under the tread of a trainer-clad heel. Then there are the short-cut fetishists, picking a pioneering path, carving a new route through the bluebells, over the bluebells, what bluebells?

In well-trodden London, one early solution to trampling was to put up a picket fence. Lesnes Wood keeps its visitors neatly corralled, and the spring flowers come up without a crushing imprint from city folk feet. Here in the country, Graham the Warden feels we need something that looks a little more natural, a rural buffer. Dutch elm-ridden logs, shedding bark over the path, provide a solid base. We stack and weave in freshly cut sycamore saplings and seedlings to give a brushwood natural hedge, forcing wandering feet in, not out. We're still taking out the progeny of progeny of non-native sycamores that were planted in Gransden Wood nearly 90 years ago. Me, I love sycamores, but they are inclined a little towards world domination.

After four hours of off-path walking and gathering of brushwood among the trees, I have a fair idea of the density of primroses growing here. All are showing their flat rosettes of leaves. Some are in flower already, though spring is still officially a few weeks ahead. These are the 'prima rosa', the first roses (they belong to a different family, but let not botanical accuracy spoil a good name). It feels to me as if there are not as many as there used to be.

That is not just a rosa-tinted view – photographs from the 1970s show path-side seas of yellow: primroses, oxlips and in-between hybrids, where there are occasional dots today. Some say the best shows were along the narrower path, and that millions of straying feet have kicked the life out of them. Others blame the muntjac deer that first found their way into the wood in the early 1990s. Nipped bluebell leaves are tangible evidence of their grazing.

There appears to be a bigger, invisible culprit. This one, isolated pocket of East Anglia is part of a phenomenon occurring throughout woodlands in Europe and North

America: the numbers of flowering plants are going down. Just as scientists struggled for decades to pinpoint the main reason for huge declines in house sparrows, they puzzled over the decrease in spring flowers. But many now believe there is a compelling explanation.

Nitrous oxide from vehicle exhausts is washed out of the air, falling within rain in the streets, on the fields and in the woods, increasing the concentrations of nitrogen in the soil. Enrichment may well be attracting greater numbers of particular animals from areas with lower nutrient levels which they cannot tolerate. Slugs and snails are sliding into the shady parts of the woods and eating a good share the plants. I will drive home today after spending hours trying to save primroses, and the car that takes me will be spewing out exhaust fumes full of nitrous oxide. Happy slugs.

A CHANGE OF HEART

Among the great battlefields of history, Loughborough University campus is not exactly up there with Bosworth Field, Leicestershire's other great place for a skirmish. But over three hot July days in 1982, it became the venue for a turning point in the ancient woodland story.

The gathering that was to bring about a transformation had its origins in a scientific backwater, where the Forestry Commission was finding new ways to revive old thinking. In the early 1980s, its research department – by definition always looking to the future – was starting to reassess oaks and other broadleaved trees. Could they be commercially viable after all? Commission scientists were used to being given free rein to experiment with new techniques. None did so with more startling results than Graham Tuley.

One of the biggest problems facing tree seedlings was that they were apt to be nibbled by animals or choked by weeds. Tuley invented a plastic sheath to shield them during their extra-vulnerable infancy. But when he dangled a thermometer inside on hot days he found it registered 48°C. Surely, he thought, the tiny seedlings couldn't survive in there? Yet he persisted with his experiment and, despite his misgivings, the trees thrived. Oak seedlings grown inside a plastic tube could grow three times as fast as those out in the open. Tuley's name is immortalised in the Tuley tubes we still find today, protecting millions of newly planted trees.

The Commission's research station at Alice Holt took on Julian Evans, a forester who had spent several years working in rainforests in New Guinea and pine plantations in Swaziland. He was employed to finish a job that had been started nearly half a century before, writing a manual on planting broadleaved woodland. The Blitz had incinerated the final proofs of the book that never saw the light of day (see page 47). Julian Evans started again from scratch and *Silviculture of Broadleaved Woodland* would be published to wide acclaim in 1984.

During the book's preparation, Evans pressed for a conference to be held as an opportunity for foresters and conservationists to share views on new ways of managing broadleaved woods. Having asked, he was given the responsibility of organising it. He set up a three-day meeting of minds to be run jointly by the Commission and the Institute of Chartered Foresters. The symposium, to be held at Loughborough University, was to be called 'Broadleaves in Britain'.

Those who have attended too many conferences for their own good are familiar with the dispiriting formula – a wearing procession of speeches of distinctly uneven quality, a lack of overall direction and an inconclusive finale. Some thought this would conform to type. A senior figure from the Commission's Edinburgh HQ turned up in his raincoat, still in Scottish summer weather mode, muttering: 'what's all this about broadleaved woodland?' It was the biggest ever meeting of its type. Nearly 250 delegates, including most of the Forestry Commission top brass, arrived at the futuristic venue. It even had roving mics. This was the 1980s.

The conference did not begin well for ancient woodlands. In his opening address, Commission director-general

George Holmes started on the defensive, suggesting that the Commission's latest census of woodlands indicated that, far from declining, broadleaved woods were actually increasing. Problem? What problem? Delegate Alan Mowle of NCC Edinburgh scribbled down: 'As a cynic, one was inclined to smell a rat.' But then, as speaker after speaker stood up, organiser Julian Evans noticed a change. 'There was an evolving mood through the conference. It was as if people were saying "There is a world that has been neglected and we should do something about it," he recalled.

The National Trust, guardian of 200,000 hectares, declared its policies transformed, with conifer planting distinctly a thing of the past. The Commission's own man in the Forest of Dean spoke positively of natural regeneration and replanting of deciduous trees. Forestry economists spoke encouragingly of potential opportunities to make broadleaves pay. George Peterken, viewed as a friend of foresters, hung out a bait in his presentation by offering an active role for forestry in revitalising ancient woodland. He gave a quantified national strategy for a whole habitat. Figures, targets... that all made sense.

George Holmes was no fool. 'He could sense the flavour of where this conference was going,' said Julian Evans. The boss and his directors huddled around a low table at coffee in earnest debate on the second day. Perhaps only George Peterken saw the significance of this moment. It was the critical point when the Forestry Commission decided, after decades of resistance, to change its philosophy.

A brilliant off-the-cuff speaker, George Holmes was mindful of internal politics and the need for face-saving. But once he had promised in an impromptu closing address that the Forestry Commission would take the lead, he was true to his word. George Peterken was secretly invited to a long lunch in a pub near Winchester with a senior Commission man and there the two government scientists began thrashing out the makings of an agreement for action.

* * *

Three long years later, a landowner started felling Little Linford Wood in Buckinghamshire. The local wildlife trust came to the rescue – reputedly with a donation from millionaire John Paul Getty. It was to be one of the last legitimate acts of destruction. On 24th July 1985, yet another George, the secretary of state for Scotland, George Younger, stood up in parliament:

> The Forestry Commission has now completed its review after wide consultations covering a period of some two and a half years, and my right honourable Friends the Secretary of State for Wales and the Minister of Agriculture, Fisheries and Food and I have agreed new policy initiatives designed to maintain and enhance the value of Britain's broadleaved woodlands for timber production, landscape, recreation and nature conservation.

> (HC Deb 24 July 1985 vol 83 cc559-63W)

The new measures were wide-ranging, recognising that there was more to the oaks, beeches, limes and hornbeams of broadleaved woodland than monetary value alone. A whole new grant scheme had, as one of its aims, the restoration of neglected woods. Firm measures were put in place to not only stem ancient woodland losses to farming and conifer forestry, but also to promote recovery. It was nothing short of a sea change.

One figure stood out during that period of negotiation and debate. The man who doubted the existence of 'so-called ancient woodland' was big enough to admit that he and the organisation he led had been mistaken. Not only did George Holmes have the strength of character to change the course of his ship, he had the authority and standing within to be obeyed by all his crew.

The secretary of state ended his speech that day with words that still resonate, even today: 'Now that our policy has been determined, we look to the many interests concerned – including the Forestry Commission, woodland owners, the Nature Conservancy Council, the Countryside Commissions and voluntary bodies – to work together in a spirit of co-operation to make it a success.'

Written in the wind

Along the main ride, spring is surging up from the roots, feeding the branches with nutrients, showing its power in swelling buds. The hazel bushes are waiting for the wind to shake their booty. I feel a cooling of my left cheek and an almost imperceptible waft jiggles the lamb's tail catkins, though only a little. Gently shaken, barely stirred, they come to rest; the wait goes on. The vital process of reproduction is left to a whim of a breeze.

Insect pollination makes sense to us, a parcel collection and delivery service, a payment in pollen, an almost guaranteed outcome. But wind pollination appears to have all the certainty of a message in a bottle. In the case of the hazel, a successful transfer from one bush to another, from one sex to the other, seems scarcely possible.

Male flowers dangle in profusion from every bush. Fat little catkins, light-coloured, densely packed, are, as yet, unripe. Fecundity comes in the looser, longer catkins, brightening with maturity. Peering closely at one gap-toothed catkin, I can see a spill of pollen, a smattering of grains half tumbling from the recesses, and spaces from which others have already dispersed. A single grain, waiting to become dislodged, must be just the right weight – light enough to be carried in the air, not so heavy that it will fall on barren ground.

The gust that lifts the pollen grain on its journey must carry it to another bush. The nearest neighbour lies through the stems of a coppiced ash and if it can be slalomed through the thicket, the grain must hit its target, a task akin to a dart hitting the board with only the bullseye on offer. The female flower resembles a sea anemone, thrusting out shocking red tentacle-like styles from its bud. But each lurid frond is only a couple of millimetres long.

A multiple miracle has occurred, for on one flower there are several specks. If the chances of fertilisation are a million to one, then there must be millions of millions drifting invisibly, coming in to land. On average, it takes 2.5 million pollen grains to ensure the fertilisation of a single hazel nut. So many to hit one little target.

We humans have manipulated chance to lengthen the odds against any of these hazelnuts ever growing into a tree. The grey squirrels we brought from North America will strip the bushes in August while the nuts are still green, before they are viable. And if any nuts on the trees do, by some miracle, escape the ravaging squirrels, fall to the ground and germinate, what is the likelihood of their tender first leaves being bitten off by the muntjac deer we introduced from China?

A Breakthrough for the pinewoods

If the immediate future of broadleaved woodland was decided over a civilised chat, the same could not be said for their conifer counterparts in the Scottish Highlands. In the spring of 1981, 400,000 breakfast tables shook at an editorial from RSPB director-general Ian Prestt in the charity's *Birds* magazine. Prestt opened up to the rest of Britain an issue which had been rumbling in the glens for a wee while. He announced that Thomson Scottish Forestry had purchased more than 1,400 acres of Abernethy Forest from the Seafield Estates and was planning to run it 'on wholly commercial lines, including ploughing and drainage and planting of lodgepole pine in part of the area'. The RSPB had, he said, 'made its disquiet clear'.

Prestt disclosed that the company had not only broken off discussions with the RSPB over its proposals, but had bypassed the NCC and liaised solely with the Forestry Commission on the understanding that its plans were kept secret. Why the secrecy? Prestt concluded indignantly: 'As a matter of principle, we consider it entirely wrong that plans which could damage or destroy a site of this nature can be kept from public debate. Abernethy Forest is part of Scotland's heritage and the public, which heavily subsidises what happens there through grants and tax relief, surely has a right to its say.'

Abernethy was a particularly sensitive place to tamper with. It was the RSPB's beating heart in Scotland, the home to Loch Garten's ospreys, a fairy tale story in its own right. For years, the charity had been buying up the coveted land, bit by bit.

A spokesman for Thomson Forestry said the company had offered the RSPB 70 acres (5 per cent of the disputed area) as a nature reserve, but had broken off negotiations because the charity had refused to compromise. Trade organisation Timber Growers Scotland voiced its support: 'Thomson have conducted negotiations in accordance with the law.' And that was a key, incontrovertible point. Whatever was discussed, agreed or disputed, the company was doing what was perfectly legal.

Just three years later, another storm blew up at Abernethy. A woman out walking her dog was aghast at what she saw. Earl Seafield had begun yet more felling of 'the largest surviving remnant of Britain's ancient Caledonian pine forest'. The largest, yes, but shrinking fast. Sixty hectares were removed and, once more, in a seemingly underhand way.

The estate had concluded a dedication scheme agreement with the Forestry Commission that included felling the old pines. However, even though the site was an SSSI, the Commission refused to show the plan to the NCC, since Earl Seafield's agent had instructed that it should be kept secret. Once again, the letter of the law was being followed, but what about the spirit? And what hope was there for privately owned pinewoods at Abernethy and elsewhere while legally sanctioned destruction continued?

In fact, this was to be the last big assault on pinewoods. In 1988, the RSPB pulled off what was then one of the biggest land purchases by a wildlife conservation organisation in Europe – 8,400 hectares comprising the entire Abernethy Forest Lodge Estate. English as well as Scottish purses opened to the tune of £1.8 million to help buy Scotland's great forest. In the same momentous year, the Forestry Commission launched a new woodland grant scheme to encourage native Scots pine planting, an initiative that flagged a significant shift in both policy and incentives.

When delegates met in Inverness for another pinewood conference in 1994, they had reason to down a good few whiskies in celebration. The National Trust for Scotland was on the verge of buying the enormous Mar Lodge Estate, and a new report confirmed that pinewood losses throughout the Highlands had been halted. And this time, the Commission was not only in attendance at the gathering; it was one of the three organisers.

A delighted Magnus Magnusson, presiding as chairman of Scottish Natural Heritage, gave a stirring oration: 'May I say how gratified I am that Scottish Natural Heritage should be jointly involved with the Forestry Commission and the RSPB in the organisation of this conference – a troika of bedfellows which would have been considered unlikely, even unseemly, only a few years ago.' A decade later, George Peterken claimed the salvation and ongoing restoration of the pinewoods was 'a massive, almost heroic, enterprise'.

REVIVAL

Oliver Rackham took hold of a brand-new axe and struck at a 70-foot tree. He was performing a ceremony that did not quite go to plan; it was as if he were launching a ship with an obdurate bottle that would not smash. The white-bearded sage in obligatory yellow hard hat had to stop twice for breath. At the age of 72, he was fighting a battle with a tree that refused to fall. Worried onlookers shuffled awkwardly. At last, he delivered the final blow, sending the huge tree down with a resounding crash. Everyone applauded. Someone began cutting the trunk into discs and handed them round as if they were giving out cake at a birthday party. And so it was that in 2011, Oliver felled the last conifer in Chalkney Wood.

Even in the darkest days when they clutched at every little positive, neither he nor George Peterken believed such things were possible. 'On the whole, destruction predominates in woods planted with conifers,' wrote Oliver in his seminal book of 1976. Over the course of the 20th century, nearly half of Britain's ancient woodland was converted to conifer plantations. The conifers had darkened hundreds of thousands of woods and smothered the ground in acid needles. Surely they were gutted and spoiled beyond redemption?

Chalkney Wood in Essex was where Oliver Rackham

dealt his symbolic blows to a Corsican pine on a day of calm after a storm. It marked the end of a story that had its origins in one man's gentle rebellion 25 years before.

Simon Leatherdale, an immensely likeable giant of a man who exudes enthusiasm and bonhomie, has been one of the Forestry Commission's most loyal servants. He joined the Commission straight out of school. Even now, five years into his retirement, he is still an eager advocate for his only employer.

At just eighteen years old, his first job was to cut down ancient woodland around his home territory of Christmas Common in Oxfordshire. Five years later, he was posted out to East Anglia, where he has stayed ever since.

There were places on his new beat where he could see the sense in growing conifers. They thrived in the sandy soils of Rendlesham and Tunstall Forests in Suffolk. But on wet, heavy clays, he could see all too well that they struggled against nature. He was taking out strong, healthy, vigorous ash seedlings and replacing them with Corsican pines. They grew so poorly that he had to support the weedy seedlings with stakes that cost more than the pines themselves. More and more, he began to question the economic argument for planting conifers there. Simon looked hard at me and beamed: 'My boss was a very nice philistine. When I asked him "why are we doing this?", the air turned blue. "Because the f#!@ing stock map says so!", he bawled.'

So there was Simon's answer: the reason they were planting conifers was because a piece of paper told them to.

Chalkney Wood fell under Simon's management, a lime wood on a cap of clay, with sandy, peaty sub-valleys peeling off, eroded by the meltwaters of Ice Age glaciers. The earliest occupying Romans drove a road straight through the middle on their way to Camulodunum, (present-day Colchester). The banks they threw up on either side of the road are perhaps the oldest Roman earthworks in Britain.

In the 1950s, the Forestry Commission bought two-thirds of the wood that had belonged historically to the earls of Oxford. While the county council continued to coppice the third it purchased, the Commission began to coniferise. Grand firs were put in. The world's fastest-growing conifers can race to the sky at three metres a year. But they do best in wet conditions and Essex has less rainfall than Jerusalem. The men who ordered the planting showed little appreciation or understanding of archaeology, setting Lawson's cypresses into the Roman banks and across the road itself. Even after 40 years, they were still spindly saplings, each a mere 4cm in diameter.

In the mid-1980s, the blighted Chalkney Wood was stripped of its status as an SSSI by English Nature, the successor in name to the NCC. Simon Leatherdale began a secret rebellion. At first, he did it when no one was looking. He started thinning the conifers, removing the odd tree or three where he could see potential in a surviving but cramped deciduous tree. Small-leaved lime stumps began unfurling leaves the size of saucers. Broadleaved trees broadened their crowns, and shed copious amounts of seed.

As Commission staff throughout the region were distracted by clearing up after the Great Storm of 1987, Simon became emboldened to do more felling. It nearly got him the sack.

When management caught up with him, he could point to profits – the Commission was making money from the immature conifers he was removing. And he was doing a nice little line in selling hardwood coppice for firewood. A higher tier of management entered the fray, demanding that Simon fill the gaps he had created by planting yet more Corsican pines. Stubbornly persistent, Simon ignored the order and carried on with his broadleaved mission.

The man with a pittance of a salary and two children to support might have lost his job, but for support from an unexpected quarter. English Nature moved to reinstate the wood's SSSI designation and now bestowed awards for good management on Simon, a timely intervention that showed great political acumen on its part. Oliver Rackham appeared on the scene to praise the Forestry Commission for its enlightened work. The Commission could hardly sack a man for being successful.

Years later, the same senior manager who had insisted Simon Leatherdale replant with Corsican pine wrote him a personal letter in which he said 'you were right all along'. And in this wood at least, Oliver was right too, for he had made an exception here to his general opinion:

> the coniferized part of Chalkney Wood, Essex, is, for the moment, by no means a write-off; the plantation is patchy and much of the underwood survives.

We can be grateful that the Commission didn't do a very thorough planting job all those years ago. Among the coppiced hornbeams, you can see knobs in the ground if you look hard enough, the slowly rotting stumps of red cedar. Elsewhere, you might tilt your head back and forth, and, with practice, spot straight gaps through trees where lines of conifers once stood. But if there is nobody to draw your attention, you might walk through Chalkney Wood today, and have no idea of its shady past.

All over Britain, we began to rediscover, in the last years of the 20th century, the vestiges of ancient woods in written-off conifer plantations. We found them in ditches, gullies and ravines, where no conifers would grow – little oases of broadleaved trees, with wood anemones, orchids and primroses still growing under their canopies, as they had before the axe and chainsaw laid waste to all around.

Scraps held on among rocky outcrops, on wood banks and in damp hollows where long ago foresters with bags full of spruce seedlings and not much time said 'no, not there'. They endured as 'picture frames', the bands of ancient woodland around boundaries that had been left alone for reasons of appearance. They lasted in plantations that failed, or those, like Chalkney Wood, that were patchy. Woodland flowers clung on in glades and rides, and fritillaries still flitted up and down them seeking nectar.

Even some veteran trees in wood pasture survived the axe. Ranger Jason Wood took me up the hill at the National Trust's Croft Castle Estate in Herefordshire to meet some very old characters. Under an Iron Age hillfort, we came to the dead hulk of an oak that was maybe 500 years old.

People have cut down trees and done it quickly ever since we wore deerskins and painted on cave walls. Archaeologist of *Time Team* fame Phil Harding told me a Neolithic tree feller could easily bring down an oak with a simple stone axe in a day. But the man who took his axe to this particular tree had no intention of felling it. The blows he struck almost a century ago are still visible – great slashes and gouges that had split the bark and penetrated the trunk all the way round. Here was the pity and waste of ring-barking – that a forester should be paid to kill a tree he knew to be of a great age, without even felling it and making use of its wood. All this so that it would not compete with a sackful of spruce seedlings for light, water and nutrients.

There was not a shred of bark left on this oak. It did not survive the blows, but others did. In other trees within Croft Castle, a wonderful estate full of characterful Treebeards, ring-barking maimed but did not kill. Miraculously, there was still enough connective tissue linking the roots and crown, producing a lesser harvest of leaves every year, but a harvest nevertheless. The National Trust is rightly proud of its wounded veterans.

All over Britain, other delights began to appear as the conifers came down. When mammal experts Pat Morris and Paul Bright were commissioned to carry out a nation-wide survey of dormice, they were specifically barred from searching in conifer plantations within 'former' ancient woods – on English Nature's assessment that these were not conservation sites and therefore should not be considered. Perhaps they could not believe that these rare mammals could hang on in habitats that had been so trashed. But sometimes, they did. Forester Rex Cartwright was paid to clear larches from one such location, Hope Valley in Shropshire.

Someone had said there were dormice in the area – everything was there for them; there was quite a bit of bramble, honeysuckle and hazel bushes. So I started putting up dormice nestboxes. One day – it must have been August or September – I took the top off a nestbox and a dormouse popped up. I'd never seen a dormouse before in my life but I knew immediately what it was, a furry little golden critter. I opened another box and about six shot up the tree. There was quite a little colony there. Hope indeed.

In those early years after policies changed, and in the rush to turn things around, foresters did what foresters did: they felled whole plantations without any fuss. Conservationists couldn't wait to purge their woods of conifers and did likewise. The result in both cases was disastrous. Like someone taken out of a dark dungeon into the light, or fed chocolate cake after months of starvation, the trees found it all too much. Deciduous trees that had grown for years in shelter were suddenly exposed in open ground, and were physically unprepared. High winds blew over mature trees and saplings alike. Plain-speaking foresters call it windthrow.

Areas the size of football pitches, all of a sudden bathed in full sunlight, were colonised, but not by the specialist woodland flowers that were hoped for, the anemones, bluebells and wild garlic that could spread by stealth in the brief spring light before shade. Instead, coarse pioneers – brambles, nettles and bracken – filled and choked the void. Old trees, their mosses and fungi adapted to humid conditions, found themselves prone to dessication in open clearings. Better a damp forest than a dry desert.

Conservationists and foresters thought again and looked for a gentler approach to restoration. Fittingly, it was the organisation that had driven so much conifer planting that would be in the vanguard. The owner of one-third of what would become known as Plantations on Ancient Woodland Sites (PAWS), the Forestry Commission led efforts to find the best ways to restore them. Most woodland owners today have followed its lead, plumping for an approach that Simon Leatherdale found by accident at Chalkney Wood. A gradual removal of conifers over decades preserves shade, humidity and shelter for the precious remnants of the ancient woods they are trying to nurse back into condition.

The scale of restoration has been staggering, and it is still going on today. The Woodland Trust has taken a lead, targeting about 10,000 woods through much of Britain. Whole private estates have turned policies on their heads. The conifer plantations put in by the duchy of Cornwall's head forester are being taken out by his successor. The Cranborne Estate of Dorset and the Gascoyne Cecil Estate of Hertfordshire now strip out conifers in favour of broadleaves. But how does an individual estate owner undo the lifetime's work of his own father?

* * *

A generation ago, the 7th Baronet Askew of the Planche, Suffolk (who answers to George) wasn't just crossing the parish boundary; he was walking around someone else's woods, and coming back with some very odd ideas.

George Askew is the son of a very important figure in the Royal Forestry Society, a man who spoke at every meeting. Major Agnew, the 5th baronet, had dallied with broadleaved planting on the Rougham Estate in his youth, but the results had been disappointing, and he was quickly persuaded to become a conifer man. His son George had grown up watching the family's ancient woods gradually converted year after year to conifers. 'My father and his forester would work on it and there would be me grumbling in the background.'

George had returned to work on the estate in 1979, and was soon infected with new thinking. It was to neighbouring Bradfield Woods (see page 65) that he absconded to attend evening guided walks. He saw a future, and it was coppice. Disapproving of his son's ideas, the major was nevertheless a kind man, who allowed him a little bit of room to do what he wanted. He wouldn't totally quash his son's plans; however, he would do nothing to progress a kind of forestry that was pure anathema to him.

Meanwhile, maintaining discretion was essential for the young man at a particular venue. 'I used to go to Royal Forestry Society meetings and they were promoting my father's style of management,' he recalled. 'If anyone mentioned the word "coppice" they would be treated as an absolute eccentric, a lunatic.'

Five years after inheriting the estate, George became that lunatic, except that his ideas are no longer thought eccentric. He turned, as so many landowners do, to professional forestry consultants to show him the way, men with vast experience and a portfolio of estates all trying to do the same thing. They coloured in maps of his woods, with each band of yellow, blue, orange and green representing a stage in a five-year plan – thinning here, felling there, coppicing in this corner, letting natural growth come up in another section. 'I'm under no delusion that it is ever going to make any money,' he tells me.

On a winter's day when it poured and poured, I walked around the woods with forestry consultant Rod Pass, to see George Askew's woods in transition. We paused under a tall, straight Douglas fir next to the path. We stood for a while to admire this great tower block. I looked up and up and thought of coal tits and goldcrests nesting in its rafters and teasing seeds from its cones.

'The major was a very fine forester,' said Rod. 'I think I'd be inclined to leave that one as it is.' A strong current of respect rushed through in his words – respect for the father, respect for the son, respect for each doing what they thought was right at the time. And perhaps I truly understood at that exact moment, as the rain ran under my collar, into my pockets, turning the folded paper map in my fingers into pulp, and we stood paying homage to that giant, that you can only turn the clock back so far. There are times to accept the present and build for the future with what we've got.

ASH TO ASHES

In times of plague, society would do what it felt was necessary to reduce the spread of contagion. Sometimes action could be brutal – when plague ran through the city of Venice in 1576, the afflicted were simply bundled into boats and rowed out to an island to die. No one was spared, not even the great painter Titian, who was no longer a celebrated artist, but a man with septic boils. Frightened citizens in affected areas held bags of sweet-smelling herbs to their noses – nosegays to ward off evil in the air.

A plague of sorts seems destined to run through Britain's woods. We could stop the contagion if we could still the breeze, but, at the time of writing, we have only metaphorical nosegays. Ash dieback, a fungal infection from the Far East carried on the wind in invisible spores, is but the latest in a procession of unwanted and unintended imports to strike at our trees. It has precedents, stretching back at least as far as 1908, when the white powdering of oak mildew, a native of the tropics, was first spotted on leaves that should have been green and healthy.

Ash dieback, and a potentially greater hazard, the emerald ash borer beetle (also from the Far East), which was last tracked advancing west into Poland, could between them wipe out all of Britain's 26 million ash trees. Consider just one characteristic of this exceptional tree: at both ends of the growing season, the ash is unwittingly generous. Oak and beech trees draw all the goodness out of their leaves in autumn and cast off brown, acidic husks, barely palatable, slow to rot. The ash does things differently. It sheds whole leaflets still green, still full of minerals, quickly recycled, providing ready nutrients for the flowers of spring. Almost a thousand species of wildlife depend on the ash. Disease could not happen to a nicer tree.

Nearly all of our elms, predominantly trees of the hedgerow, died a generation ago, an event that had a devastating effect on the landscape and a profound impact on millions of tree lovers. Just about the same number of ash trees are imperilled and this is a tree of both hedgerow *and* woodland. At this point, we could get very depressed. But should we?

Barely an hour ago, I was walking out of Waresley Wood's sick neighbour. Ash dieback was first spotted in Oliver Rackham's beloved Hayley Wood some four years ago, and while the great man saw it manifest itself, he is no longer around to chart its course. And a slow course it is too, for a visitor might walk down the main thoroughfare as I did, yet not see any sign of it at all.

But it is there all right. I found a few sad saplings, bare sticks stained in sickly shades of winered and brown. Saddest of all, a young tree with a wilted head, its new leaves green but limp. This is the dieback. It only arrives once summer is underway, and the fruiting spores of the fungus time their release to perfection, filling the air in their billions, falling on leaf stalks, the narrowest of landing pads. The young trees are most susceptible.

It is the oddest thing, coming into Waresley Wood now to look for something you hope not to find. On the cusp of midsummer, every tree that is going to do so has broken into leaf. There is thunder in the air. A jigging mosquito worries little about the first spatter of rain – it has eyes only for my bare calf.

The very first patch of open ground is flagging up defiance. Ash seedlings have exploded into leaf along the margins of the ride, as if registering a shoulder-to-green-shoulder show of solidarity. 'Sick? Not me, boss.' There is ash, ash, and yet more ash. Overlooking this multitude of robust children are their parents, just as healthy, leaflets fanned out like half-opened venetian blinds. Graham the Warden tells me he has seen no ash dieback in the wood. All is well then?

Halfway down the ride, I find them. The same leafless, sickly stems, tanned with blight. There are just a few, but that is more than enough to launch a plague. And what is so pathetic is that each stem bears dark buds, swollen with the potential that will never be realised.

Last winter, when news broke about the advance of the emerald ash borer beetle (at that time thought to have reached Sweden – mistakenly, as it turned out), I wanted to get a sense of what it could mean for this wood. I picked one of the side paths and walked at glacial speed, keeping a tally of the trees. I counted 246 and 193 of those were ash. On the basis of that random sample, about four-fifths of all of the wood's mature trees might be expected to die.

The two diseases combined would be a tragedy for the ash, but it would not mean the end of the wood and so many others like it. Relentlessly positive foresters with a lifetime in trees keep setting me back on the path, dragging me out of despondency. A wood is a living thing; when one tree falls, another will take its place. And though 955 species of wildlife rely on ash, leading ash dieback scientist Ruth Mitchell tells me that most of those could switch their dependency to other trees. There are other reasons to think there might be some hope too, not least the species' extraordinary genetic diversity. Could this tree evolve its way out of trouble?

One thing is certain, ash disease will be a big thing in our lifetimes. It may only be a blip in the life of a wood.

WHAT NEXT?

It would be a rash thing to predict the future of our ancient woodlands with any confidence. Natural history is littered with bold prophecies and pronouncements that are held up afterwards for ridicule or met with incredulity at such preposterousness. Hindsight is an unkind tool. What do we make of the pre-war worldly-wise forester who found 'a line of red squirrel tails hung on a fence' in Suffolk and declared confidently in *Country Life* that red squirrels 'are *not* disappearing', or the poor editor who worried in the RSPB magazine that the biggest post-war threat to the countryside would come from... wait for it... aerodromes? He fretted: 'One often hears the comment, "The whole of the country will be full of them eventually".'

Even as little as a decade ago, we could not have foretold all that has now come to pass. We could not have anticipated the tree diseases that have crossed continents, more often than not locked in the hold of an aircraft. We could not have guessed accurately (and we still can't) the likely impacts of accelerating climate change. We have yet to plan for the threats that a rapidly expanding human population and a consequent growth in housing, industry, roads and rail will pose for woods. As Norman Starks, the director of conservation at the Woodland Trust says: 'We thought the pressure on woods was getting less. It's getting more.'

Rather than wallowing in gloom, we can take heart from the experts. I turn to Jonathan Spencer, senior ecologist with the Forestry Commission, a man who has explored more of Britain's ancient woods than most, and whose 33-year career has spanned both the Commission and government conservation bodies. If anyone is able to tap into trends, catch prevailing opinions and follow research based on a foundation of knowledge, it is Jonathan. He is unashamedly upbeat: 'Ancient woods have a long, long history of being used and that could be their salvation. It should be possible for us to use them to generate the conditions that supported their interesting wildlife in the first place.'

The word 'use' has been a running thread through this story. The Oxford English Dictionary defines 'useful' as 'having the qualities to bring about good or advantage; helpful in effecting a purpose'. Our ancestors discovered that woods were useful to them. They used them, and then found they were no longer useful. The conservationists of the late 20th century won a victory in that they prevented more 'useless' woods from disappearing. That is a cause for celebration, but we are not – in a manner of speaking – out of the woods yet, simply because the question of 'use' has still not been properly addressed.

A single statistic keeps coming up in my head. How much of the woodland that was being coppiced in the past is being coppiced today? The answer is just under 2 per cent. So many woods are simply neglected. Spindly trees grow tall, crowded together, the canopy closes over, the bluebells and butterflies shaded out, year after year, until they are gone. Beneath the crowns of such woods there is only darkness.

Conservationists and foresters are united in railing against what they call 'a return to the Dark Ages'. Rod Leslie is one of the most experienced and knowledgeable conservationist foresters. He identifies the necessary dynamic: 'Management is a defining characteristic of ancient woodland – the interaction between man and nature.' Human intervention shaped the woods we value today; how do we bring them back to life?

It is time to separate the practical from the romantic. The past can inform the future, but it cannot replace it. If we have any doubts over that, we need only to look at what has changed.

Neither the medieval or even the early 20th-century woodsmen had to contend with deer. Yes, there were a few, but not the numbers that there are today of red, roe, muntjac and fallow deer. I encountered herds of fallow deer dozens strong in a Hertfordshire wood last winter. Others see herds numbering more than a hundred. All those deer, all those mouths, are nipping plants and tree seedlings in the bud, eating away the future.

Members of the Deer Initiative did a back-of-the-envelope calculation that showed we would need to cull 300,000 deer every year in England alone *just to stand still*. Oliver Rackham said deer were the biggest threat to ancient woodland. Two years after his death, they still are, and a few thousand marksmen perched in platforms bagging small numbers for the pot will not tackle the epidemic. Conservation groups need no longer hide behind 'our members wouldn't like it' when it comes to controlling deer. There is agreement and acceptance, even among a sentimental public, that it has to be done.

We also have grey squirrels, one of our less successful imports. Woodsmen of yore could grow trees for timber, knowing that they would be suitable for buildings and furniture. Not any more. During the spring and summer, young grey squirrels strip bark in territorial acts of vandalism, stunting and deforming the trees. We are forced to import oak from parts of Europe that grow straight trees in the absence of grey squirrels. Ours are all but unuseable.

Better ways of controlling squirrels are appearing. One is the use of a natural predator. Pine martens once lived throughout Britain, at a time when the grey squirrel was confined to an area of eastern North America that was devoid of tree-hunting predators. The discovery that pine martens are keeping grey squirrel numbers down in parts of Ireland and Scotland has stimulated reintroduction initiatives in the Forest of Dean and the Borders. There may be more to come, though some of those who breed and release 55 million pheasants and red-legged partridges into the countryside every year may have opinions on that.

People are beginning to graze animals in wood pasture under veteran trees again, just as our ancestors did. But they are also parking their cars in the shade of great old trees, or rolling lorries over the invisible roots to erect stages for outdoor performances. Thousands of feet tramping the grounds of popular stately homes are compacting the soil, reducing the ability of trees to take in water and nutrients from the crushed earth. We need to reduce the pressure.

Tree diseases and climate change both present challenges. If an ash wood is stripped out by disease, should we be more accepting of the continuing presence of non-native sycamores and conifers in the wood for the sake of maintaining the structure? Are any trees better than none at all? And if – in climatic terms – Scotland starts to behave like Kent, and Kent takes on the characteristics of the Mediterranean, how will our woods cope?

We can take a positive, proactive approach. Ancient woods can, and should, present us with opportunities to alleviate the effects of climate change. There must be an economic case for firewood in a low-carbon economy, a biofuel that doesn't result in tropical rainforests disappearing. In an age when flooding has become an ever-present threat, forests in the uplands slow the flow of water, forests in the lowlands store it. Oak trees, good for wildlife, drought-resistant, resilient in the face of climate change, are also wonderful at carbon sequestration. It is time to plant more?

Let us not forget the magic, delight, solace and physicality of ancient woods. They are good for us, good for our health and well-being. Woods exercise us and make us happy. They offer largely untapped opportunities to unite communities, they can help us educate children through initiatives such as the outdoor classrooms of Forest Schools, in ways that no other habitat offers. The volunteers who go out coppicing get exercise to ward off heart disease and diabetes, the trees get much-needed light to grow next year's flowers. Greenwood crafts are flourishing; how much satisfaction can one person get from making a spoon? Can that be multiplied a million times over?

Fundamentally, value must go back into the woods. How many of the people who benefit from walking their dogs in Waresley Wood contribute to its upkeep? In one sense, perhaps we should return to a medieval model in which the services and products of a wood are paid for. The next generation of professional coppice workers will need to earn a living wage, and that can't be made by flogging a few beanpoles. As one conservationist says: 'Making money matters, because no one is going to pay for work on the scale big woods need.'

We need new thinking and radical solutions. Perhaps some of Jonathan Spencer's positivity comes from meeting people with vision, who are inspired by the past to lead us on paths into the future. They are woodland entrepreneurs who offer us a tingling taste of what is possible.

One of the most radical and least likely developments originates from the deeply conservative heartland of south-east England. It is a revolt that may yet help to revolutionise our thinking, not just about ancient woodland, but in the whole way we treat our landscapes.

It is taking place in a pocket of Sussex that is rapidly becoming like nowhere else in the British Isles. An island of astonishment, it is not immediately obvious as you approach; it lies unobtrusively within a countryside where one farm looks very much like the next. Even some of the residents only a few miles away don't know about it.

Yet on a May morning before the insects are up, you could be forgiven for thinking you were standing in the African savannah. A grassy field, a veldt raked, furrowed and dung-dropped by giant herbivores, has a scatter of thorn bushes. The big beasts are roaming out there, somewhere. Slip into a patch of woodland, where an animal has left cloven-hooved tracks like those of a giant deer, and climb a stepladder onto a canopy tree platform, to see a long-horned beast in the distance giving birth. There are half-glimpsed birds just in from Africa everywhere, a tumult of birdsong, louder and more varied than those we have come to accept as our meagre lot elsewhere. From the tallest tree, a cuckoo calls.

At the start of the millennium, such a scenario was inconceivable. The owner of Knepp Castle was – on the face of it – just another barley baronet, growing corn to the very edges of every field, dousing them in chemicals, flailing every hedge. There was one big snag. Charlie Burrell was farming at a loss. For every year his crops made a profit, there were nine in the red. He diversified into ice cream and yoghurt. It made no difference.

Charlie's estate sits on a 320-metre thick cap of Wealden clay, a claggy soil with the appearance and consistency of French mustard. There was a sound reason why Saxon farmers left vast tracts of woodland over this part of Sussex. It was, and still is, rubbish land for farming.

An ancient oak in need of first aid changed everything. When experts from the Ancient Tree Forum came to advise Charlie on a veteran tree that had a big crack in its trunk, they took a long appraising look around. They saw the last gasps of a twelfth-century deer park that had been ploughed in wartime and every year since. The ancient trees were islets in seas of wheat, their roots had been cut by tractors and were unable to absorb water and nutrients because heavy combine harvesters had compacted the soil around them. These trees were starved and suffocating. You could do things differently, they said.

They took Charlie to the Netherlands to see another way of managing land. He was shown a vast wilderness of polder only fifteen miles from Amsterdam, a simulation of a landscape that might well have existed throughout Europe before humans, when wild boar, wild horses, deer and super-sized cattle-like beasts called aurochs traversed the land. A Dutch forester-ecologist called Frans Vera was leading the Oostvaardersplassen (literally: wetlands to the east) project, letting modern-day equivalent animals manage it, as their near ancestors would have done in prehistoric times. In the plane on the way home, Charlie declared himself a convert to what is now known as rewilding.

Within a decade, 250 miles of internal fences came down and Knepp Castle had its full complement of four-footed land managers. Free-ranging Tamworth pigs played the role of wild boar, rooting in the soil, tilling and furrowing to turn over the seed bank and open up opportunities for new plants, making bare patches for mining bees and wasps. Exmoor ponies filled in for wild horses, spreading seeds in their dung, on their fur, between their hooves. Longhorn cattle were Sussex's aurochs, giving birth and raising their young out in the open. These were nature's coppicers, lumbering around, snapping off tree stems at the base, replicating what human tools might have done otherwise. Herds of fallow and red deer were brought in to browse. Charlie now recast himself as a rancher.

Is it a farm? Is it a game park? Jurassic Park without a roar? A monster three times my weight comes out of the hedge. It's a giant sow, a truly free-range pig that has no sty, no trough, no root vegetables dumped in a quagmire of mud. It swings its hips in a 230kg shimmy towards me but pays me no attention, its snout working the grass. This animal can fish for swan mussels and open them with its trotters. Some pig.

I walk close enough to the cows in the middle of the field to take their picture. They have created a matriarchal society for themselves, with year-old bull calves still suckling from their smaller mothers. Is it going too far to suggest these domesticated animals are inching back towards wild behaviour?

Charlie's version of rewilding has produced some startling results for the estate's ancient woodland. Most strikingly, the boundaries are no longer as clearly defined: bushy growth of sallow, rose, hawthorn and blackthorn has spilled out from hitherto sharp woodland edges. It stirs memories in the very old residents of the neighbouring village of the less manicured, less regimented countryside of their childhoods. Oak saplings rise out of the middle of brambles and bushes, whose thorns protect them from inquisitive tongues and teeth. Will these slender pioneers be the veterans of the 23rd century?

Certain types of wildlife have proliferated: there are more purple emperor butterflies at Knepp than in any other place in Britain, more nesting turtle doves than in the whole of the National Trust's quarter of a million hectares combined, one fiftieth of Britain's nightingales making their oak leaf nests in Knepp's bushes, 13 species of bat, 23 species of beetle feasting in every organic cowpat.

Inevitably, other wildlife has done less well. The rootling pigs have trashed the bluebells in a copse like nothing else since the Middle Ages, when wild boar were the hairy vandals. But is the threadbare carpet that survives a truer record of what Britain's bluebell woods were like in a time when they were full of the pig's ancestors? Are we learning something out of trial and error?

Not everyone is happy. Some visitors come to the estate to say: 'I think what you're doing is disgusting. It's immoral.' They say Charlie should be growing crops instead of wild-life. But meat from the animals is sold, the dairy barns are industrial units, campers fill the fields to go on wild safaris and the whole enterprise is making money. There are more people working on the estate today than when the family bought it in 1787.

Butterfly expert Matthew Oates is halfway up an oak tree searching for adult purple emperors. He is one of a dozen or so professional naturalists lured to the experi-mental honeypot that is Knepp Castle. He enthuses about this place as 'new-age wood pasture'. This is a modern approach to an ancient habitat; dynamic, evolving, ever-changing. It is one kind of future.

About 500 miles north of Knepp Castle, in a place where autumn follows hard on the heels of spring, one forest is shrinking, while another is emerging out of hardened hillsides. Around Aberfoyle, the self-styled 'Gateway to the Trossachs' above Glasgow and Edinburgh, the trees of the Queen Elizabeth Forest Park were planted with a 20th-century definition of forests – a giant plantation of trees – in mind.

Times change. The Forestry Commission is felling those conifer plantations, opening up wide clearings, letting the broadleaved trees of the ancient burn-side woodlands breathe and spread out, weaving paths and cycle tracks through the forest. The promise is that more than a third of the land will *not* be planted up. It's a measure of how far the Commission has come that it should not just contemplate, but actively pursue, a policy of leaving behind a world of uniformly straight trunks, darkness and shade. Forester Dave Anderson tells me, with a knowing grin, that they are even ring-barking some of the conifers to kill them *in situ*. The broadleaved trees' revenge?

A glen's hop to the north of Aberfoyle, the reformed Commission has turned a problem into an enormous opportunity. And it has friends to help.

Loch Katrine was one big worry for Scottish Water when it found that sheep on the surrounding bare hills were giving Glasgow a tummy bug. For 150 years, piped water from the zigzag loch had supplied the city with all its daily needs, but, earlier this century, the pooing, piddling animals were found to be contaminating the loch with harmful bacteria. The sheep had to go. What to do with the overgrazed slopes, pounded by generations of cloven hooves?

New thinkers in the Commission produced a new vision, and made a bid to lease the water authority's land. It's theirs for the next 150 years. Out of the Commission's inspired thinking, the Great Trossachs Forest has appeared.

It is Britain's biggest National Nature Reserve and makes up a sizeable part of the Loch Lomond and the Trossachs National Park.

Way back, the whole area was part of a royal hunting forest, used by kings and nobles between the thirteenth and seventeenth centuries. It was, and will be again, a forest in the medieval sense of the word, a quilt of meadows and moors, with ancient and restored ancient woodland binding the whole and, crucially, given space and the means to expand.

The Commission drew in its neighbours as partners. The Woodland Trust's Glen Finglas Estate abuts its eastern edge and RSPB Scotland's Inversnaid laps the shores of Loch Lomond to the west. All three signed a sponsorship deal with BP that commits each partner to the objectives of a 200-year project. The staff talk of coming back with their children, their grandchildren, returning at the age of 90 to lean on a fence and see the legacy of their work. I see them turn to the hills when they speak, their faces scrunched up against the sleeting snow. They all do it – cast their eyes towards hope and promise.

Less than a decade into the project, there are already inklings of a 22nd-century future. These Highland forests were suppressed and retarded by excess. Victorian estate owners planted rhododendrons as evergreen cover for the birds they wanted to shoot. More than a century on, there is still an acidic undergrowth of bushes that smother all other life, and an annual bill of £10 million to keep them in check.

The Woodland Trust bought part of the biggest sheep farm in Europe at Glen Finglas, and reduced a flock that was stripping the land of its natural assets from 3,000 to 300. People had lived in the glen before the sheep came, and had been careless of the forest, grazing too many cattle, chopping down too many trees and lopping off too many branches. In the 1950s, officialdom decreed there should be a reservoir in Glen Finglas, to act as a feeder lake for Loch Katrine. It persuaded the people out of the glen, and drowned their settlements.

Today, deer are the bane of highland forest regeneration. There are 200,000 more red deer in Scotland than there were in the 1980s, an accumulation of failures on the part of landowners to control their numbers. Red deer make for the sun-kissed west-facing slope of Finglas in winter. The leafy growth from giant pollards that have stood since the time of King James VI is out of browsing reach, but there seems little chance of a new generation of trees rising from under their gnarled trunks.

The contrast could not be greater in swathes of the forest where red deer are excluded. High fences are cleverly positioned to be largely invisible to us, concealed in dips and below contours over the hillsides. All three partners want, as much as possible, for the trees to decide where they will grow for themselves. Birch and rowan are sprouting from bare mountain slopes. Alders are beginning to fill the boggy burn-sides.

Decisions were made to plant in the upper glens where no seeds would carry from far, far below, where ribbons of ancient woodland cling to lochsides. A million trees have gone into the soil on this higher ground and, already, willows, juniper, oak and hazel are becoming visible from the loch shores as dark flecks on the tussocky hills. A gifted Commission forester with a passion for broadleaves, a profound understanding of soils and a keen eye for long-term aesthetics, plants as if sowing a bag of mixed seeds broadcast, simulating natural growth so that dense clumps will alternate with thinner patches of trees. Once, conservationists rejected the idea of planting trees to restore woodland as an admission of failure. In certain places today, such as these barren hills above the loch, it has become an act of pragmatic necessity.

People are this project's lifeblood and its legacy, and money has to grow on these trees. Holidaymakers are being lured from the twin giants of Glasgow and Edinburgh to walk or cycle the new Great Trossachs path and the West Highland Way, and to spend in restaurants, hotels and tearooms, to pay the wages of the wardens, foresters and administrators who will manage this land. A 'visitor gateway' at the foot of the Woodland Trust's Lendrick Hill epitomises the thinking, an unmanned centre with touch screens, children's activities, books laid out that are never stolen, comfy cushions on benches and underfloor heating. There is a simple looped walk here around a small ancient woodland. Some may think it nature-lite, but this is a like-it-or-not reality that may ensure the forest's development and guarantee its survival long after the grants run out.

Last words

It's bluebell time again, an email has come in from Graham the Warden and I'm holding a trowel.

I'm heading into a middling ancient wood in middle Britain, a footpath-cum-ride there-and-back walk with the landowner's permission; 'Private Keep Out' signs block every offshoot track, every opening with the potential for exploration barred.

The ride divides two sides of the same wood, but it is not so much a division as a gulf. On one side, it is quite apparent that foresters were here last winter. The last conifers – no more than a handful among the oaks – have been felled and bluebells circle the prostrate trunks. I almost leap with delight at such tangible evidence of active, positive work. Making the wood a better place.

A long time ago, there must have been bluebells on the other side of the path too. I carry my trowel across, creep under the trees of a maturing spruce plantation and find myself crouching in deep, deep shade. My trowel digs down one centimetre, two centimetres, three, four, five. At eight centimetres, it finally slides into soil. There are a whole lot of needles in between, their acidic tannins and phenols long since oozed into the earth.

The seeds of ancient woodland flowers can stay dormant in the soil for no more than 30 years. Someone might fell these trees and rake away the needles, but in densely planted places like this, time has run out and there will be no reawakening. It is time to turn back to the bluebell side of the wood, away from the ancient wood that is gone, to the reviving wood of the present and the future.

I read Graham the Warden's email. He has signed a petition to parliament that has a straightforward demand: 'Give all ancient woodland statutory legal protection.' Surely that's not beyond the bounds of possibility since there are so few of them?

He has sent me the reply he received, a standard, formal response from the Department for Environment, Food and Rural Affairs that begins: 'Woodland cover in England is at its highest level since the 14th century.'

Perhaps that may be true, but, given such a specific question, would you give equal weight to the trees on either side of the path – the bluebell wood on one side, a spruce plantation on the other? If the paintings of the National Gallery were at risk, would we be happy with a response that said Britain has lots of paintings?

The same response offers with one hand, acknowledging that 'ancient woodlands are an irreplaceable habitat', and then takes away with the other: 'a range of mitigation and compensation measures... may be offered by developers to offset loss or damage, where developments affecting ancient woodland and veteran trees may receive planning permission'.

There we have it; woods are vital unless it is deemed otherwise. Cut down a wood, plant trees somewhere else, job done. It is thanks to the heroes of this story that we can truly understand what 'irreplaceable habitat' means. And that's exactly why we must carry on battling to save them.

Our generation can enjoy ancient woods like none before,

because the Woodland Trust, Wildlife Trusts, National Trust, RSPB, Forestry Commission and numerous others allow, invite and welcome us into thousands. National treasures, every unique one of them. Go into an ancient wood as soon as you can, and feel your spirits lift.

Appendix I: How to identify an ancient wood

How do you tell if you are in an ancient wood? If a mystery tour deposited you in the middle of a clump of trees, how would you know whether you were looking at something dating back hundreds of years, or a more recent creation? Those in the know tell me – and it has been said so many times that it has become a mantra – 'there are only four or five people in the country who can be reasonably confident they have found an ancient wood'.

The few people who dedicated much of their working lives to studying and carrying out ancient woodland surveys went to thousands of woods, and gained expertise that an amateur would find very difficult to acquire. But don't give up right now. It is possible for all of us, with a smattering of knowledge, a questing spirit and a great deal of enthusiasm, to play woodland detective.

Our guide for this rough and ready section is Peter Quelch, a forest detective with impeccable credentials. He spent nearly 40 years working for the Forestry Commission in locations as diverse as Cumbria, Shropshire, Cambridgeshire, and all over Scotland. The advice here comes with Peter's approval. Of course, it is in no way comprehensive – how could it be when woodland historians spend years perfecting their skills and there is so much to learn? But it gives us an introduction to the evidence we are looking for, and the kinds of questions we should be asking.

The first question we might ask is, why? Why bother? For one answer, it's great fun. We can all get a whole lot of pleasure from trying to read a wood. For another, we can travel to the heart of a city to find a practical illustration of how it can enrich our lives.

In a north London park called Cherry Tree Wood, city ecologist David Goode would often sit at a table in the open-air café, see the grass lawns in front of him, the tennis court, the children's playground, and overhear snatches of conversation from latte drinkers at the next table. Many times, he heard people exclaim proudly that 'this is an ancient wood!' They knew that because the sign at the gate had told them so.

He would watch them stroll along the tarmac paths through the trees, but, as far as he could see, to the dog walkers and the amblers, they were just trees. They could have been any trees, in any location, a mere backdrop to a pleasant walk. And that is fine. But they were missing something that might have deepened and added value to their experience, just as surely as a knowledgeable cathedral-goer knows to lift the seat of a choir stall and see beneath a carved monk blowing a raspberry on an old misericord.

A little knowledge is a marvellous, illuminating thing. If you strolled around Cherry Tree Wood after reading this, you'd see history at the base of its big hornbeam trees. You would see that those huge trunks rise from the gnarled remnants of coppice stools, last cut at a time when women made more money out of selling firewood from this wood than their husbands could earn from a day toiling in the nearby fields. You could search for wood anemones, and realise that you're in a wonderful place of rare beauties, the flowering emblems of antiquity.

You could easily play detective at home too, clicking on Victorian maps online to find that 'Cherry Tree Wood' is marked as Dirthouse Wood. Search further to discover that it earned its former unsavoury name because it was next to the pub where horse manure and human, er, 'night soil' was delivered as farm fertiliser. And you could even drink to horseshit at the White Lion itself! It's still there on the old Great North Road. For those local people who walk through Cherry Tree Wood in ignorance, it would surely add to a sense of place, a sense of community, a sense of connectedness. Imagine parents telling their children that the park they played in was once named after poo.

You can unearth meaning for yourself and truly begin to understand what makes ancient woods special. You could do it with the woods near you, or you could do it on holiday, with a whole new set of clues. Here's how.

Your first visit

Let's start by imagining a likely scenario. You've stumbled on a wood, either on a walk or out on a drive. There are no information boards, not even a sign to tell you the name of the wood, and you have no map. What evidence can you find for yourself on the ground?

First of all, where does this wood sit in the surrounding landscape? Is it in a steep valley, on a slope or a ridge? Is it in a boggy spot where you wish that your trainers could magic themselves into wellies? Is it well away from the nearest village? Old woods tended to hang on in the places that were hardest to cultivate and on the boundaries of parishes.

Do the edges of the wood tell you anything? A plain ditch around part or even all of the perimeter may be a recent addition – dug by a farmer to drain adjoining fields. However, a ditch with a raised bank in front of it suggests a barrier to keep grazing animals out. The bank might be less than a metre high today – not even enough to keep out an athletic mouse – but once it would have been much higher to stop pigs, sheep or cattle from getting into the wood. This hints at medieval origins. In hilly parts of Britain where there is plenty of stone, you might find a moss-covered drystone wall serving the same purpose.

Strange banks, dips and hollows within the wood will set you thinking. A low earth bank running through the heart of the wood could mark a parish boundary or an old division of ownership. Shallow pits could be ponds dug for drovers' cattle, diggings of clay to make bricks, sawpits for old woodsmen (the 'topdog' pulled on the saw from above, the 'underdog' standing in the pit, drew on the saw from below), or the depression left by a charcoal worker's kiln. All of this is – at least for the moment – glorious, groundless (as it were) speculation, but it sure stokes the imagination.

Study the living evidence. Remember the Cambridge lecturer's advice: 'When entering a wood, first look up at what is above you'. The species of broadleaved trees may give some pointers. A single species growing in rows will be a plantation; a scattered range of trees, for example oak, ash, field maple, hawthorn and hazel, is far more likely to mean natural growth. If you discover small-leaved lime (a tree not to be confused with common lime), then you are probably in an ancient wood. If you find a wild service tree – each leaf a distinctive miracle of complex symmetry – then an ancient wood is all but guaranteed.

In many woods, the ancient component will not have survived intact. Since a third of woods were – to a greater or lesser extent – cleared and planted with conifers (or sometimes broadleaved beech or poplars, for example), you may find a patchwork effect.

You may need a book to help with tree identification, especially if you are trying to identify a tree without leaves. Large, comprehensive flower guides will include trees, but you might prefer one dedicated to trees and shrubs as a rounded, more informative guide.

There may be evidence surviving in the handiwork of long-dead woodsmen. This is much easier to seek out in the winter months when the trees and their stumps aren't obscured by leaves and plants. You may find a thick-trunked old pollard, or a line of them marking the wood-land boundary. Or you may find clear signs of coppicing.

There is a coppiced hazel at the end of my garden and I know how old it is – I planted it. A seriously old coppiced tree will have a broad stool that is one, two or even three metres across, and multiple stems shooting out of its base. Tellingly, there will be at least some evidence of decay in the stool. My juvenile garden-fresh hazel shows a clean bill of health. There may be a rot hole looking like the eye socket in a skull, where one stem was cut long ago, and nothing sprouted in its place. And there will probably be a number of trees that are, or have been, coppiced. All of this builds up a picture of how the wood was used. If coppicing or pollarding was carried out, the chances are they took place over a long period of time.

You have a two-month window when most woods will reveal some of the strongest clues of all. If you visit between April and June (the exact period varies depending on geographic location and weather), you'll be there when most of the flowers are in bloom. It's before the trees in leaf have closed the canopy and dimmed the interior, and the plants have gone to seed.

Botanists have long recognised that there are 'key

woodland indicators', plants that are more or less restricted to old woods because they are slow or ineffective colonisers of other habitats. At the same time, these plants are supremely adapted to living in a spot that is under shade for a significant part of the year.

There are certain strong indicators of ancient woodland that are reasonably easy to see because they grow in profusion, and are fairly easy to identify too. These are: wild garlic (also called ramsons), wood anemone, bluebell, wood sorrel and primrose. Others, trickier to identify (or even find!) include: sweet woodruff, hairy woodrush, common cow-wheat, herb paris and sanicle.

It's a persuasive but not infallible list: bluebells can spill out of ancient woodland into planted woods, or, in some parts of the country, they may grow elsewhere (on open ground on Dartmoor, for example). They may even be relics of a long-lost wood. And not all of these species are found absolutely everywhere – wild garlic is far rarer in the east.

An expert botanist with a fair amount of time might be looking for 100 woodland indicators in any single wood, the list varying from country to country, region to region. These few plants will give you an indication, though.

Giving it a name

So far, we have looked at what you might find purely by visiting an unknown wood, possessing no other knowledge whatsoever. In all probability, you'll want to see where you've been or where you're planning to go, by looking at a map. Knowing the name and shape of the wood opens up more possibilities.

There may be hints to the nature and age of your wood in its name. Woods named after the nearby parish or settlement are often very old. For example Waresley Wood was called after the village; it 'belonged' to a village of Saxon origin. Over the brook, Gransden Wood is effectively (geographically and geologically) the same wood, except that it lies in a different parish and would have had different owner(s). One sizeable wood may have different names, often originating from different ownerships.

An old wood may have been given its name at a time when the person who named it spoke a different language, or at least a different version of English. Numerous woods have their origins in pre-Conquest Old English, although that might not be immediately apparent because the words have been modernised. Grove, hurst, shaw and hanger are all mutations of Saxon names for wood. Carr (a wooded marsh), -land and -storth all derive from Old Norse. Copse came from Norman French (meaning 'to coppice'). Woods with 'coppice' in their name are usually ancient. Some will indicate usage – a hazel wood outside Bath may once have had its hazel rods cut to make chimney brushes, hence Sweeps Coppice. Jackson's Coppice in Staffordshire was surely named after Jackson, whoever he may have been. 'Copse' is less reliable, since it has been given to plenty of small, modern woods too – a charming faux-medieval appellation.

Woods may be named for their function, character or owner. Spring Wood comes from the medieval use of the word 'spring', which in this case meant spring growth – i.e. coppice. Hillcombe Coppice is one of thousands of ancient woods that tell it like it was – a coppiced wood on the side of a hill. Burnham Beeches, Burnt Oak Wood and Ashmore Wood all describe the trees predominant in those woods at naming time.

Lady Wood, Bishop's Wood, King's Wood, Queen's Wood and Earlstrees all link back to their one-time ecclesiastical or noble owners. Lozenge-shaped woods with the word 'park' in their name are likely to have been enclosed parks for keeping deer, dating back to the thirteenth century or earlier.

There are names that nearly always rule out the possibility of a wood being ancient. The first written record of the word 'spinney' only appeared in 1597. The word means 'wood of thorns', so this suggests a thicket of hawthorn or blackthorn sprouting from a field. 'Covert' was used to denote a small, planted wood harbouring foxes or pheasants. 'Plantation' is, well, a plantation.

Don't rely too heavily on names, though: as we saw earlier, today's Cherry Tree Wood is Victorian Dirthouse Wood with a makeover. Current maps will take you so far – you need, as in so many cases, to draw on more than one source of information.

Shaping up

It's very hard to work out the shape of a wood when you're walking around it. Paths are dead straight, or wind around, doing their best to disorientate the visitor. But an Ordnance Survey map is irrefutable, and helpful too. Amoeba-or tadpole-shaped woods are more likely to be ancient than straight-edged ones. They preserve the quirks that develop over centuries – evidence of piecemeal nibbling-away by agriculture at the edges, ownership along irregular zigzag or sinuous boundaries, fixed by the earth bank or stone wall that delineated them centuries ago, or natural geological boundaries.

In contrast, plantations may sit within rectangular fields enclosed from the eighteenth century onwards, or the trees may be simply planted in straight lines. Modern woodland clearance might result in irregularly shaped woods ending up with a straightened edge or two, but the general rule still holds.

Doing your homework

Praise be to the internet. No exploration of a potentially ancient wood can be complete without a trawl through the archives to make sense of what you have found. Thanks to an incredible ballooning of digitisation over the last decade, there's less need to go to a library, a records office or a national archive; much of what will help you is down-loadable on your computer. You can even bring up an aerial view of the wood you are studying, snapped by a Luftwaffe cameraman.

The best starting point is the most reliable mapping system in the world: the Ordnance Survey. At a click of a few buttons, you can access maps for every square mile of Britain stretching back to the 1840s. Here you have a fixed point of certainty. At the very least, you can find out whether the wood you're exploring existed 150+ years ago, whether it had the same shape in Victorian times, whether main tracks ran along the same paths as they do today, and even, in the six inch to a mile scale, the type of woodland – broadleaves or conifers.

The maps are, to some extent, impressionistic. Mapmakers were instructed in 1906 that 'trees in a large wood should be artistically grouped and not crowded together'. Even so, the level of detail is astonishing. You might find the odd Christmas tree conifer symbol in a sea of deciduous clouds. It won't be an error, but a graphic representation of what was on the ground – a Victorian owner's enthusiasm for growing the occasional exotic tree in their otherwise broadleaved wood, or evidence of a trend at that time for planting conifers to 'nurse' the seedlings of broadleaved trees such as oaks.

Such is the rapidity of change that it would be pointless to give specific web addresses here to help you – simply type in keywords, for example 'old ordnance survey maps of Scotland', and see what comes up in your search engine.

Other maps may take you further back in time. Scotland has the military survey maps of General Roy from around 1750, as well as a remarkable series produced by a man called Timothy Pont, who stepped out of St Andrews University in 1583 and began mapping his country. Plenty more cartographers turned out maps of variable quality. Use these maps with caution, for they may not be as reliable. The cartographer could – at times – depict what he imagined to be there.

England and Wales have a plethora of maps, too, such as tithe maps, old estate maps and enclosure maps. These were often private maps commissioned for specific purposes, so they will show the information the commissioner of the map wanted to find out about. The owner of a large estate might want to record the number and position of timber trees in their woods, for example, since they were worth money. Generally, larger landowners kept better records. If you are following this line, it is important to ascertain the owners of your wood at different points in time.

Not everything you seek is online. You can trawl the National Archives to see what is available and pick over clues in the Domesday Book, Britain's oldest survey. But if you want to dig deeper, and find privately produced maps and other historical documentation (such as estate accounts and manorial and monastic records), you may want to seek advice from an archivist – try your local council or library for advice. You may find a local historian has done some of the work for you already and written all about the wood you're exploring.

Go, and go again

Once you've been fired up by written evidence, you'll want to go back to your wood to confirm what you've learned and even look for more clues. It's best to go at different times of the year too, for each season will throw up new evidence. In winter you can see the bumps and dips that are not as apparent in summer. Snow is best of all for showing them up, though a good, sharp frost can also work. You might see corrugations on the ground – traces of ridge and furrow farming from a time when that part of the wood was a farm field. Or you might find what you think is the flattened remains of a charcoal hearth.

A return to the library or the internet may help you find out if your wood is tied to wider economic uses. Is it in an area where there was smelting for lead, iron or tin? Could that hole in the ground be the result of a brick-maker's diggings? Or is it something else altogether?

You can seek out people who can tell you more, the oral evidence route. As a Boy Scout in the early 1960s, Peter Quelch was advised to 'ask the oldest local inhabitant' for information about the past. Thousands of teenage boys must have played 'spot the walking stick'. At that time, there were still some old boys alive who had actually been woodsmen. But their sons, daughters and grandchildren may still be living locally. Ask around.

Only take your detective work as far as enjoyment carries it. If it's your mission, make it a happy one.*

And the result is...

Finally, if you really want to know the (almost definitive) answer... Conclusions from the Ancient Woodland Inventory are published online, the findings superimposed on present-day Ordnance Survey maps. So you can click on your wood and see if the experts decided whether it was ancient or not. Of course, you could do that before you start your quest, but I find it's more rewarding to discover afterwards whether your conclusion matches that of those who know best.

Why stop there? You'll find other ancient woods around the one you're studying, and want to explore them too. Good luck!

---

* A good source of information for further research is *The Woodland Heritage Manual*, edited by Rotherham, Jones, Smith and Handley. At the time of writing, a new, updated edition was in preparation.

Field checklist for how to identify an ancient wood

An easy reference list to be copied/captured on a
phone and taken into the wood.

Key things to look for:

Name – What is the name/names of the wood?

Shape – Is the wood irregularly shaped or rectangular?

Physical location – Is the wood on a hill, slope or wetter
ground outside a town or village?

Features – Is there evidence of banks, old walls, ditches,
pits, ponds and inexplicable bumps and dips?

Tree species – What is the mix of trees? Are they all deciduous? Are there conifers?

Plants – Are there ancient woodland indicators (e.g. wood
anemones, ramsons, bluebells, wood sorrel, primroses
(March–June only)?

Management – Are there signs of old coppice stools and
pollarded trees?

Oral evidence – Are there local people who can tell you
anything?

Appendix II: Wood words

All of the technical terms that appear in the book are included in this list, but you'll also find other wood words here that might be helpful, together with succinct definitions for all.

Afforestation/ afforest
: To plant trees on land that's not been wooded for some time. Historically it also meant to place an area under FOREST LAWS.

Ancient tree
: A very old tree, often of great girth, in the latter stages of its life. Also used to mean one that is of particular interest (e.g. the historic Major Oak in Sherwood Forest). See also VETERAN TREE.

Ancient woodland
: Woodland that has been under *continuous* tree cover since 1600 (or 1750 in Scotland). If it's been extensively harvested by coppicing or felling but not replanted, it's ancient semi-natural woodland. Only 'semi-natural' because it's been shaped by humans. If it's been replanted, it's ancient replanted woodland.

Ancient woodland indicators
: Species (mainly flowering plants and ferns) that tend to be found in old established woodlands. For more information see page 269.

Ash dieback
: A fungal disease of ash trees. It was detected in Britain for the first time in 2012, in imported trees. Ash dieback causes leaf loss, CROWN dieback, and, in most cases, the death of the tree.

Assart	An archaic term, meaning an area of land cleared of trees, usually to establish a homestead and a small farm.
Besom	A broom made from birch twigs – the classic broom used by witches (and Hogwarts students).
Billhook	The COPPICER'S main tool – a curved, hand-held blade used for cutting through smaller woody material.
Bole	The main part of a trunk, before it separates into branches.
Brash	The small and usually low-value branches trimmed from trees up to about head height. In forestry, this task is part of the routine care of timber trees and is called brashing.
Broadleaved woodland	Woodland where the CANOPY contains less than 10% CONIFERS: broadleaved trees are those that are not CONIFERS. They are usually DECIDUOUS but holly and yew are broadleaved trees, despite being evergreen.
Browsing	Browsing animals eat leaves, tender shoots or other soft vegetation above ground level, including the leaves and shoots of trees. Compare with GRAZING.
Bryophyte	A huge group of plants which includes mosses and liverworts.
Canopy	The top layer of a wood – the uppermost branches and the leaves of the taller trees. The canopy is said to 'close' when the leaves come out and, umbrella-like, shade the ground below.

Carr	Woodland on wet and boggy areas, mainly willow or alder in most cases.
Chase	A private hunting area, which may have been forested or open (also called a FIRTH).
Clough	A narrow wooded valley in northern England. See also GILL, DINGLE.
Common	Land over which people exercised traditional rights, such as to graze animals, or gather firewood.
Conifer	Strictly, a tree on which the seeds are borne in a cone (e.g. a pine cone). Usually evergreen (compare with BROADLEAVED, DECIDUOUS).
Coppice	A broadleaved tree whose trunk has been cut close to the ground, to encourage the growth of shoots which can then be harvested (as POLES). CONIFERS will die if cut like this.
Coppice with standards	An area of woodland where most of the trees are COPPICED, but a few (usually a different species) are allowed to grow into full-sized trees. Thus we may have hazel coppice with oak standards.
Copse	A small, broadleaved woodland. Originally it would be a COPPICED woodland but now the term is applied more widely.
Cordwood	One of many traditional woodland products, cordwood is small or split wood, cut into short lengths and sold by the cord for firewood, charcoal-making etc (for a definition of cord see page 149).

Crown	The top of a tree – the branches and the upper part of the trunk.
Deciduous	A tree that sheds all its leaves in winter – the opposite of evergreen.
Dutch elm disease	A fungal disease of elm trees, introduced from North America and spread by a species of bark beetle. In the 1960s and '70s, it killed the majority of Britain's elms.
Dingle	Wooded valley. See also CLOUGH, GILL.
Enclosure	Land that was once held in common was often 'converted' to single ownership and marked with banks, ditches, walls or hedges. Enclosure often leaves features of historical significance within a wood.
Epicormic growth	Small twigs that sprout directly out of the trunk, sometimes at the site of damage or following an increase in light availability (perhaps when surrounding trees are removed). These can form substantial, bushy clumps.
Estovers	The historic right of tenants to take wood from their landlord's woodlands for repairing buildings and so on.
Even-aged stand	An area of woodland where the trees are all about the same age, often an indication that the area has previously been felled and replanted.
Exotic	Species that are not naturally found growing in this country and therefore are not considered NATIVE. Also called non-native.

Faggot	A bundle of thin wood tied with twisted bands and used for fuel, or to strengthen ditch or wood banks. Traditionally the bands, called withies, were made of thin, flexible ash, birch, hazel or willow.
Field layer	The second-lowest layer of vegetation in a woodland, including flowers and ferns. See also GROUND LAYER.
Firth	See CHASE.
Forest	Can be used today to mean a large (usually conifer) woodland, but historically it meant land to which forest laws applied.
Forest laws	Introduced by the Normans to protect wild animals for the nobility to hunt. Robin Hood (if he actually existed) would have broken forest laws when he hunted the deer in Sherwood Forest!
Gill/ghyll	Narrow ravine. See also CLOUGH, DINGLE.
Glade	An open area in a wood. Relatively sheltered and open to the sun, glades can provide a variety of habitats for butterflies, bees and flowers.
Grazing	Grazing animals eat vegetation, usually grass, which is growing on the ground. Compare with BROWSING.
Ground layer	The 'bottom' layer of vegetation in a wood. This will include mosses, lichens, flowering plants and seedlings. See also FIELD LAYER.
Hanger	Medieval word for a wood on the side of a steep slope or bank.

Hardwood	A general term for broadleaved, non-coniferous trees and their timber. Conifers are *SOFTWOODS*.
Hectare	A metric measure of area. One hectare equals 2.471 acres, or 10,000 square metres. To help you visualise it, one hectare is between 1.2 and 1.6 football pitches.
High forest	A forestry term referring to tall, straight trees suitable for timber.
Humic layer/ humus	Mainly, partially decomposed vegetation. Soil is complex and contains inorganic parts (such as sand) and humus, the organic part. This can also contain broken-down animal remains, which are recycled into food and minerals for plant growth.
Hurdle	A small gate made of woven wood (e.g. hazel or willow), used for temporary animal shelters. Also much appreciated by gardeners for rustic fencing.
Leaf litter	The layer of undecayed plant material on the woodland floor. In time it will become *HUMUS*. Leaf litter can be full of insects and other organisms feeding on the leaves and on the moulds they support; because it excludes light, it can also suppress seed growth.
Lop and top	The cut smaller branches and twigs that have no commercial value.
Maiden	A tree that has never been cut (i.e. not *COPPICED* or *POLLARDED*) and thus has a single main stem.

Mast	The seeds of beech, but also sometimes of other trees. Cunningly, these trees produce abundant mast in occasional years, referred to as 'mast years', and much less in others. Creatures that eat the mast can't rely on it to support increases in their populations, and, in a mast year, so much is produced that they cannot eat it all. This guarantees good amounts of the tree's seed will survive to grow.
Mycorrhizal fungi	Fungi that live within the soil, often as long filaments. They grow in a symbiotic relationship with plant roots, the partnership providing both with better access to food.
Native	Species that have arrived in an area naturally, without the assistance of people, since the last Ice Age. Compare with EXOTIC.
Old growth	A tree that has not been managed (e.g. COPPICED) for over 200 years.
Pannage	Traditionally, autumn feed for pigs in woodland, e.g. beech mast or acorns). It could also be a payment for letting pigs graze in woodland.
Park	This word traditionally referred to land containing widely spaced trees that was enclosed for domestic or wild animals. You can sometimes see a 'park' in its former sense around stately homes.
Plantation	A wood where the trees have been planted by people, normally for timber production. Plantations often contain CONIFERS but they can also be of BROADLEAVED trees.

Pole	A slender young tree or branch from a COPPICE or POLLARD, of the right size to use as poles (e.g. for fencing or thatching).
Pollard	In a sense, this is a COPPICE in the air! A tree whose trunk has been cut two to four metres above the ground, then allowed to regrow to provide a crop of young branches. The advantage of pollarding is that the fresh young growth is out of reach of BROWSING animals.
Primary woodland	Land which has never been anything other than woodland since the end of the last Ice Age.
Ride	A wide, usually unsurfaced path or track, used for access, extraction of cut timber and shooting.
Sapling	A young tree between one and two metres high.
Saproxylic	A tongue-twister of a word (pronounced *sapro-silic*), meaning relating to dead or decaying wood. Hence saproxylic beetles and fungi feed on dead or decaying wood. They play a vital role in breaking down the wood and releasing nutrients for the growth of new plants.
Secondary woodland	Woodland that now grows on land that, at some time in the past, was cleared of trees and had a different use (e.g. as pasture or arable). EVEN-AGED tree growth can be a giveaway.

Seed bank	Many seeds in a woodland will fall to the ground and remain dormant in the soil or the LEAF LITTER layer, sometimes for many years. If light gets to them because trees fall or the surface is disturbed there can be a sudden flush of growth. However, very few woodland plant seeds will be viable after 30 years.
Shaw	Small wood or copse (from the Saxon word *sceaga*).
Softwood	A general term for CONIFERS and their timber. BROADLEAVED, non-coniferous trees are HARDWOODS.
Spring	A word that in medieval times was used to describe a COPPICED woodland.
Standard	A tree with a straight trunk of at least 1.8 metres, which is suitable for timber. Sometimes these are grown together with COPPICE – see COPPICE WITH STANDARDS.
Standing timber	A crop of timber trees that are still growing. They may be sold for timber while still standing, the volume and quality of the timber being estimated.
Stool	The permanent base of a COPPICED tree, usually at ground level. Regrowth occurs from buds around the edges. Stools can be metres across, and have often rotted away in the centre.
Succession	The gradual change in the vegetation over time, as some species decline and new ones arrive.

Understorey	The plants growing under the main CANOPY of a woodland.
Veteran tree	Usually (but not necessarily) a very old tree, it has significant cultural, biological or aesthetic value (sometimes all three). See also ANCIENT TREE.
Wildwood	The original forest that grew at the end of the last Ice Age. The oldest woodland of all, surviving only as fragments, if at all.
Wood pasture	A very open type of woodland, a cross between grassland and woodland.

ACKNOWLEDGEMENTS

Although he is no longer able to read nor understand what I write, I wish to record my thanks to my dad, Rudi Niemann, for trying to teach me the names of trees on many fondly-remembered walks together. He planted something in me, even if what I thought was an acorn turned out to be a hazelnut. The late Rod Blanco of the Cheshire Wildlife Trust furthered my education by handing me a tree nursery to manage, for which I am also grateful.

A conductor on the podium at the end of a concert will wave his baton to acknowledge the special performances of soloists. Since the research for this book involved interviews with no fewer than 102 people, I have a whole orchestra to single out and a full choir behind them. I owe a special debt to the generous people who took me out to various woods and forests. Their enthusiasm was contagious, and I hope I have conveyed some of the magic they imparted to this enraptured listener.

Particular thanks is also due to those who commented on particular chapters, those who ferreted out remarkable pieces of history, and those who had the courage to be frank about what they did and believed at a time when people held different values. I have tried to simply lay out a story before the reader. If I have offended anyone, I apologise. It was never my intention.

At the core of the story is Waresley Wood, and so I am grateful to Charles, John and Liz Mear of Wood End Farm for their openness in telling a difficult story. Graham Moorby (the eponymous 'Graham the Warden') was ever-present and always helpful, with back-up from Mark Ricketts at the Beds, Cambs and Northants Wildlife Trust HQ. Former staff Nancy Dawson, Nicholas Hammond, and Peter Walker had rich memories for me to plunder.

Locally, and in the wider wildlife trust movement, Tim Sands, Alec Bull, Tony Whitbread, David Streeter, Harry Green, Rex Cartwright, Ioan Thomas, John Comont, Brian Eversham, Pete Fordham, Geoff Hearnden all gave freely of their time. Support came from Adam Cormack, Anna Guthrie, Rob Parry, Jo Atkins, Nigel Ajax-Lewis, Liz Tregenza, Sarah Gibson, Maria Jonsson,

Rob Brunt, Annette Traverse-Healy, Jo Dickson, Caroline Flitton, Sheila Wells, Angela Bucknall and Siân Williams. Among former staff at the various government conservation bodies, George Peterken was outstanding in giving of his unrivalled expertise. Keith Kirby, Eric Roberts, James Archibald, Martin Ball, Peter Marren, Brian Davis, Ray Woods, and Alan Mowle, all shared with me their considerable knowledge. I'm grateful to Martin Tither for his skill at finding vital interviewees.

Exceptional individuals from the Forestry Commission helped me understand this enormously impressive organisation and its 'Road to Damascus' story. Peter Quelch, Jonathan Spencer, Simon Leatherdale, Rod Leslie, Paul Tabbush, and Julian Evans were unstinting with their expertise and wonderful stories. Graham Tuley, John Voysey, and Elspeth Macdonald added yet more colour. Academics Charles Watkins, Mike Martin, Brian Wood, John Barkham, and Jeremy Burchardt steered me at various points on the journey. Ian Rotherham was a delightful and knowledgeable companion in his home city of Sheffield. The late Oliver Rackham left us all wisdom in his books.

The Woodland Trust's first director John James was enormously encouraging throughout – the highlight was a memorable day in Aversley Wood. Sue Morris was a great compere in the Trossachs, ably assisted by Rob Coleman of the RSPB and Dave Anderson of the Forestry Commission. The RSPB's Fraser Lamont and Yvonne Boles added still more on a snow-flurried day. Liz Hamilton taught me a great deal as we splashed around Wormley Woods. The Woodland Trust's Norman Starks, Karl Mitchell, Julian Purvis, Nigel Douglas all gave time to be interviewed. Margaret James, Ruth Hyde, Alison Kirkman, Dean Kirkland, and Paul Wright added support. Gwyn Williams of the RSPB and I toured Waresley Wood in a trip down memory lane. The RSPB's Nick Phillips, Clifton Bain, Ian Bainbridge, Des Duggan, Tony Pickup, Simon Marsh delved deep into current thinking and former lives. David Anning, Richard Winspear, Stewart Taylor, Gareth Morgan, Rob Hume, John Underhill-Day, Kelly Thomas, and librarians Lisa Hutchins and Elizabeth George also helped out.

Jason Wood of the National Trust gave me a flying tour of Croft Castle. Matthew Oates and Ray Hawes were marvellous storytellers. Thanks also to Madeleine Gower and Tom Seaward. Oliver Hilliam and David Conder drew on archives and memories to give the CPRE perspective. Fellow Guardian Country Diarist Phil Gates was a wonderful help throughout. Other diarists – Ray Collier, Jim Perrin, Graham Long, Susie White, Mark Cocker and Paul Evans – brought insights and lyricism.

Andy Byfield, Trevor Dines and Dave Lamacraft of Plantlife provided expertise in an area that certainly cried out for it. Jill Butler and Vikki Bengtsson of the Ancient Tree Forum did likewise with the much misunderstood veteran trees of wood pasture. Chris Skinner of High Ash Farm was a compelling orator, Penny Green, a super guide with big wheels at Knepp Castle, Ian Robinson, equally fine in Gransden Wood, John Fowler generously gave permission for me to use his interview with the late Jock Carlisle. Londoner John Burton cast his mind back to the 1940s, and staff at the Museum of Rural English Life showed friendliness and marvellous efficiency. Mike Parry proved that a mathematician can also be a perceptive editor and a willing guinea pig.

Foresters Rod Pass, Harry Barnett, and Arran Dennis showed passion and a love of their profession on a tour of the woods of Rougham Estate. Owner George Agnew followed up with his modest recollections, full of wisdom.

A big thanks to the many others interviewed, as individuals or belonging to organisations many and various: Brian Williamson, Debbie Bartlett, Nigel Petter, Penny Condry, Ted Collins, Simon Humphreys, Ruth Mitchell, Peter Clegg, Peter Friend, Peter Roberts, Piers Voysey, Donald Pigott, Rob Fuller, Simon Browne, David Goode, Gavin Fauvel, Pat Morris, Peter Walker of Gransden, Louise Bacon, Mairi Stewart, Micky Astor, Ruary Mackenzie, Jenni Tubbs. New Networks for Nature ambassador Katrina Porteous provided a lyrical evocation of the past, and fellow steering group member Jeremy Mynott offered encouragement. Fellow author Midge Gillies gave moral support in the latter stages.

A whole host of people also helped in diverse ways, including: Karl Nightingale, Patrick Brown, Richard Pollitt, Charlie and Issy

Burrell, Nick Owens, Kate Blincoe, Sarah Rhodes, Mark Boyd, Mike Unwin, Tom Wall, Jan Rodgers, Mark Telfer, Rod Stallard, Tim Kellett, David Lovelace, John Edmondson, Catharine Sadler, Cathy Farnworth, Jan Haseler, Austin Weldon, Rob Lambert, Stephen Coleman, Jim Froud, Val Smith, David Broughton, Chris Donnelly, Andrew Warrington, David Howdon, Peter Jarvis, Linda Smith, Mary Sheridan, Roger Parsons, Rosemary Marshall, John Griffin, Chris Preston, Julian Vallance, Hilary While, Shaun Hurrell, Elisabeth Dunn, Kate Smith, Phil Harding, Stephen Ward, Ian Froggatt, Dan and Liz Watson, Iain Duncan, Ian Baker, Phil Tidey, Richard Thomason, Andy Banthorpe, Chris Manning, John Knight, Sonia Starbuck, Alan Birkett, Jean Lumb, Jayne Heathcock, John Presland, Alan Rayner, John Barker, Amanda Allsop, Dick Greenaway, Richard Fortey, Judith Tsouvalis and Anthony Burton.

Aurea Carpenter, Rebecca Nicolson, Paul Bougourd, Klara Zak, Catherine Gibbs at Short Books proved to be a winning team, for the third book in succession. Emma Craigie gave direction at an important time.

Finally, I owe the greatest thanks of all to my partner and wife Sarah, who not only edited, photographed, researched and accompanied me on numerous visits, but also had to put up with far more than she deserved.

INDEX

POWERSTOCK
COMMON

HIGHGATE
WOOD

BRADFIELD
WOODS

FOXLEY
WOOD

APPIN
FOREST

SELSDON
WOOD

GAIT BARROWS

HOLLYBANK
WOOD

CHAPEL
WOOD

NORRIDGE
WOOD

GLEN MORE

ECCLESALL
WOODS

SOUTH
WOOD

PENNSYLVANIA

COED PEGGY
GILES

GLEN
AFFRIC

WERN
GOCH

SPRING
WOOD

WELL
WOOD

HOWE
WOOD

COED
CAEGWYDDAU

LOWER
WOODS

MARKS
HILL

HELL
COPPICE

HARRY'S
WOOD

GLEN
FINGLAS

LEIGH
WOODS

FOXLYDIATE
WOOD

BOGGART
HOLE CLOUGH

INVERSNAID

MAR

GREYSTONE
WOOD

ELMSTEAD
WOOD

GREAT
FRITHSDEN
COPSE

GLEDHOW

WALTON
WOOD

CHERRY TREE
WOOD

BISHOP'S
WOOD

SCARCLIFFE
PARK

DEVICHOYS
WOOD

EARLSTREES

NEW FOREST

NORMAN'S
SHAW

CASTOR
HANGLANDS

WATNALL
COPPICE

QUEEN'S
WOOD

BLACK WOOD
OF RANNOCH

LONG LEAKE
COPPICE

PETTS WOOD